MW00534056

Immigrants on Grindr

Andrew DJ Shield

Immigrants on Grindr

Race, Sexuality and Belonging Online

palgrave
macmillan

Andrew DJ Shield
Leiden University
Leiden, The Netherlands

ISBN 978-3-030-30393-8   ISBN 978-3-030-30394-5   (eBook)
https://doi.org/10.1007/978-3-030-30394-5

Cover image: Igor' Gerbovnik/EyeEm
Cover design by eStudio Calamar

This Palgrave Macmillan imprint is published by the registered company Springer Nature Switzerland AG
The registered company address is: Gewerbestrasse 11, 6330 Cham, Switzerland

To Ib: Livet er ikke det værste man har

Acknowledgements

I am grateful that the Danish Council for Independent Research continues to fund truly unfettered research, such as *Immigrants on Grindr*. This gratitude extends also from the other participants of the "New Media, New Intimacies" team, all of whom provided helpful suggestions about my work over the years: Rikke Andreassen, Maria Christensen-Strynø, Katherine Harrison, Michael Nebeling Petersen, and Tobias Raun.

I am endlessly indebted to three professors who forever changed the ways I think: Dagmar Herzog, who taught me how to contextualize and historicize words, images, and ideas; Jan Willem Duyvendak, who engages with the curious around the world as if they are his closest colleagues; and Mari Jo Buhle, who taught me to look for archives everywhere.

At Roskilde University's Department of Communications and Arts, where much of this book was written, I thank those who provided thoughtful feedback: Sine Just, Susana Tosca, Kim Schrøder, Randi Marselis, Jakob Feldt, Garbi Schmidt, Marie Brobeck, Julie Uldam, and Mostafa Shehata.

A number of supremely sharp and generous scholars across the globe also took time to read and discuss parts of this book: Nicholas Boston, Sharif Mowlabocus, Sara Louise Muhr, Florence Villesèche, Alexander Dhoest, Lukasz Szulc, Marlou Schrover, Nancy Baym, Tarleton Gillespie, Stefanie Duguay, Kaarina Nikunen, Debra Ferreday, Gavan Titley, Annette Markham, Sarah Hackett and Kate O'Riordan: I am honored to have met and worked with you throughout this process. I'm also grateful for the ongoing conversations with Ann Wilson, Jens Rydström, Peter Edelberg, Gert Hekma, Mattias Duyves, and Fahad Saeed.

To my high-school guidance counselor, Mel Butarro, who ran our Gay-Straight Alliance: did you know you were effectively my first teacher of queer studies?

To my mother, sister, and grandmother—Diane Juster, Emily AJ Shield and Judith Jaffe Juster—who amaze me with their energy, involvement and curiosity; to other loving family throughout the world: Chris, Henry, Maya, Nora; Britt, Aage; Jay, Dani, Rowan; cousins near and far; Madeleine, Michelle, Henning, Andrews, Veninderne, and so many other lovelies: thank you! And of course, to Ib, *du er det beste jeg vet...*

CONTENTS

ABOUT THE AUTHOR

Andrew DJ Shield is Assistant Professor at Leiden University, where he specializes in sexuality, migration, and diversity studies. He is the author of *Immigrants in the Sexual Revolution*, and co-founder of the Leiden Queer History Network. He lives and bikes in Amsterdam and Copenhagen.

LIST OF FIGURES

LIST OF TABLES

"We all have a responsibility… to save them": Immigrants, Gays, and Those Caught in Between

In order to contextualize that an Arab immigrant in a European metropolis in 2015 might sign onto his favorite gay hook-up app and receive a message accusing him of links to ISIS, or that a young Danish man with Pakistani parents might glance down at a Grindr pop-up notification telling him to "go back to your country," we must first understand the complex politics of immigration and sexuality—and however they overlap—in northwest Europe in the early twenty-first century. Then we can explore how these politics play out in a sexually charged online platform for primarily gay men, such as Grindr, and ascertain the consequences for LGBTQ immigrants attempting to build social connections in Europe today.

For decades, LGBTQ rights have grown increasingly intertwined with political and journalistic discussions of immigrant cultures and integration, particularly in Scandinavia but also notably in the Netherlands. A peculiar strand of "pro-gay, anti-immigrant" rhetoric grabbed Dutch national attention around 2000, when an emerging populist party (List Pim Fortuyn) argued that immigrants from particularly Muslim-majority countries were homophobic and sexually conservative, and that their cultural attitudes were enough to justify not only new policies on integration, but also restrictions on immigration. Since 2006, this pro-gay, anti-immigrant rhetoric has been a cornerstone of the Dutch politician Geert Wilders' populist Party For Freedom; further, Wilders (a heterosexual) has attempted to export this political framework to Denmark and Sweden, among other countries,

© The Author(s) 2019
A. DJ Shield, *Immigrants on Grindr*,
https://doi.org/10.1007/978-3-030-30394-5_1

by pronouncing to politicians and journalists that "violence against homosexuals…ha[s] become part of daily life" in the Netherlands (due to Muslims), and thus politicians and journalists must "express [their] opinion[s] about Islam," since imams expressed their disapproval "about our freedoms and… about gay men and women."[1] While elsewhere in Europe and the United States, this pro-gay, anti-immigrant rhetoric has not taken hold within the political Right—which still tends to ignore or reject LGBTQ issues—Wilders' rhetoric has become strategically effective in Scandinavia.

With the dramatic increase in especially Syrian asylum applications in 2014–2015—also known as the European refugee "crisis"—the porous border between Copenhagen (Denmark) and Malmö (Sweden) closed for the first time in over five decades, and immigration laws tightened (especially in Denmark, which attracted international condemnation for passing a "jewelry law" allowing authorities to confiscate asylum seekers' valuables, including wedding rings). Denmark elected a right-wing government (led by Venstre from 2015 to 2019) that pledged to introduce an "emergency brake" to stop the alleged "uncontrolled flow" of refugees and migrants, while "setting higher demands on refugees and immigrants' ability and will to integrate into Danish society."[2]

At the same time, and for the first time, a Danish right-wing government acknowledged that sexual orientation, gender identity, and the right to choose one's partner were "fundamental" rights; and they pledged to protect equality "regardless of sexual orientation and gender identity."[3] It is within this context that a right-wing Minister responded to a report on homosexuality and immigration in Denmark—a report that actually showed that over 70% of immigrants felt homosexuality "must be accepted in society"—by proclaiming that there were still "pockets of Danish society where you cannot take your freedom and equality as givens," and that "we" must "say very clearly to these groups" that Danes "do not take religion

---

[1] Andrew DJ Shield, *Immigrants in the Sexual Revolution: Perceptions and Participation in Northwest Europe* (Cham, Switzerland: Palgrave Macmillan, 2017), 1–3, 7fn7–9. Wilders delivered the first quotation to the Danish People's Party in July 2008, and the latter to the Free Press Society in Sweden in October 2012.

[2] All translations (e.g. of Danish government platforms, newspaper articles, academic publications) in this book are by the author. Government platforms are all available online; this 2016 platform was entitled, "For et friere, rigere og mere trygt danmark" [For a Freer, Richer, and More Safe Denmark]. See also Andrew Shield, "When Pro-Gay Means Anti-Muslim," *The Murmur* (21 March 2017): 44–45.

[3] Ibid.

into consideration when it comes to freedom and rights."[4] This problematic religion was clearly Islam; indeed, the Minister altered her statement when speaking to a Christian newspaper, but still emphasized that "certain ethnic minority" groups needed to learn Danish (sexual) freedoms.[5] It is also within this context that one can establish the motive of a non-LGBTQ member of the populist and anti-immigrant Swedish Democrats who attempted to host an LGBTQ Pride event in an immigrant-heavy Swedish suburb, and who insisted coyly that the event was certainly not an attempt "to provoke a Muslim aggression."[6] Gradually over the past decade, pro-gay, anti-immigrant politics became an undisputable facet of the Scandinavian Right.

The liminal figure of the LGBTQ immigrant—if mentioned at all in these political and media discussions—seems to do little to destabilize the dominant understanding of immigrants as sexually conservative and homophobic. When a politician or journalist *does* acknowledge LGBTQ people with immigration background, there is usually the assumption that their largest obstacle in Europe is overcoming the homophobic oppression of their families and diasporic communities. A 2015 survey of young LGBTQ Danes did indeed find that those with migration backgrounds were less likely to "come out" (that is, to declare an LGBTQ identity) to both parents, and more likely to have received threats of physical violence.[7] However, the report also showed that 71% of these queer migrants were open about their sexuality "most of the time" (compared to 83% of "overall" LGBTQ Danes); indeed, 87% of these respondents were open about being LGBTQ to (at least some) friends (comparable to the 91% of "overall"

---

[4]Milla Mølgaard, "Hver tredje nydanske homoseksuelle har overvejet selvmord" [One in Three New Danish Homosexuals Has Contemplated Suicide"], *Politiken*, 30 September 2015, https://politiken.dk/forbrugogliv/sundhedogmotion/art5591593/Hver-tredje-nydanske-homoseksuelle-har-overvejet-selvmord.

[5]Britta Søndergaard, "Hver tredje homoseksuelle nydansker har overvejet selvmord" [One in Three Homosexual New Danes Has Contemplated Suicide], *Kristeligt Dagblad*, 30 September 2015, https://www.kristeligt-dagblad.dk/danmark/hver-tredje-homoseksuelle-nydansker-har-overvejet-selvmord.

[6]Jan Sjunesson, quoted in Daniel Sallegren [in Swedish], "Arrangören bakom Järva Pride vill se fler förortsparader" [Organizers of Järva Pride Want to See More Suburban Parades], Gaybladet.se (30 July 2015), last accessed Autumn 2019 via http://gaybladet.se/arrangoren-bakom-jarva-pride-vill-se-fler-forortsparader-234987/.

[7]Bjarke Følner et al., *Nydanske LGBT-personers levevilkår* [New-Danish LGBT People's Living Conditions] (Copenhagen: Als Research, 2015).

LGBTQ Danes). Nevertheless, media outlets across the spectrum fixated on findings that underscored differences between these groups—such as that respondents with immigration background were more likely to report violent threats from family than "overall Danes" (19% vs. 1%)—and this brief media moment helped solidify public opinion that LGBTQ people with immigration background faced fierce oppression and had "mental problems," in contrast to the adjusted population of tolerant, white Danes.[8]

Fahad Saeed, the foreperson of the Danish organization for LGBTQ ethnic minorities "Sabaah," addressed this 2015 survey to the media: "This investigation is really, really important. It would be a shame if this was merely used to established facts that confirm prejudices about ethnic minority groups, and then nothing more is done."[9] Despite Saeed's urging, the report did little to disrupt the pervasive idea that "we" Danes were tolerant to LGBTQ issues, in contrast to "them," those Muslims who need saving.[10]

On the eve of Copenhagen's city elections in 2017, a mayor of Copenhagen took the microphone at Oscar Café, a cozy LGBTQ bistro on Copenhagen's newly Christened "Rainbow Square," and steered the debate toward a topic close to his heart, immigration:

> I think that if we look at [LGBTQ] people with a foreign background—especially with Muslim background—there are homosexuals who could use an extra hand. That's something that we all have a responsibility for—to try to save them from it. Because that's not an easy environment to be a homosexual in. So that's an extra task we have.[11]

---

[8] E.g. Mølgaard; Søndergaard; Mads Bonde Broberg and Simon Roliggaard Andersen, "Undersøgelse: Hver ottende indvandrerhomo er blevet udsat for vold" [Every Eighth Immigrant Homo (or Gay/Lesbian) Has Been Exposed to Violence], *Jyllands-Posten*, 1 October 2015, https://jyllands-posten.dk/indland/ECE8072616/Unders%C3%B8gelse-Hver-ottende-indvandrerhomo-er-blevet-udsat-for-vold/.

[9] Mølgaard.

[10] Lila Abu-Lughod, "Do Muslim Women Really Need Saving? Anthropological Reflections on Cultural Relativism and Its Others," *American Anthropologist* 104, no. 3 (September 2002): 785; Lila Abu-Lughod, *Do Muslim Women Need Saving?* (Cambridge, MA: Harvard University Press, 2013).

[11] Carl Christian Ebbesen at Oscar Bar & Café (10 November 2017). Recorded and translated by self. "Save them from it" (or "Save them out of it") translated from *"red dem ud af det."*

The (heterosexual) politician was Copenhagen's first mayor from the notoriously anti-immigrant Danish People's Party (DF).[12] DF's attendance at Oscar that night was not obvious: for years, the party had been on the forefront of political campaigns *against* LGBTQ issues like marriage and adoption rights (until that stance became less advantageous around 2013)[13]; DF shied away from LGBTQ-hosted debates in Copenhagen during the 2015 federal elections[14]; and DF's platform did not mention LGBTQ-related issues. But following the success of pro-gay, anti-immigrant politics from Venstre's coalition, the DF mayor decided to address the living conditions of LGBTQ people with immigration backgrounds. In doing so, he used rhetorical tools popularized by Wilders: he elided immigrants with Muslims, and contrasted immigrant attitudes toward homosexuality with the assumed progressiveness of Europeans; further, he argued that "we" had a responsibility to save "them" from their culture. "We"—those in the room, presumed to be non-Muslim, non-immigrants—had a responsibility to save "them," those oppressed, invisible, disenfranchised immigrant LGBTQs.

LGBTQ people with immigration background in Europe, and organizations like Sabaah, face obstacles that extend beyond homophobia in their diasporic communities: many experience racism within white-majority spaces, including LGBTQ spaces.[15] This racism frequently has a sexual

<hr/>

[12] At the time of writing this, DF's most recent Facebook posts called for constituents to reject the following: halal meat, special religious considerations for Muslims, and financial support for refugees in the municipalities: Dansk Folkparti on Facebook; accessed November 2017 via https://www.facebook.com/danskfolkeparti/.

[13] DF wanted to pass a "Rights of the Child" bill that would have insisted on a child's right to a father and a mother: [in Danish] "The Danish People's Party says *no* to homosexuals' right to adopt children – a *no* that we stick firmly to. And we say a resounding no to church weddings for homosexuals. And we do this out of respect for children, for marriage, for the law, for tradition and for the church."

Pia Kjærsgaard, "Pia Kjærsgaards ugebrev: Homoseksuelle kirke-vielser er ikke en kamp for værdier men en kamp imod ægteskabet" [Pia Kjærsgaard's Weekly Letter: Homosexual Church-Weddings Are Not a Struggle for Rights, but a Struggle Against Marriage], Press Release of the Danish People's Party, 22 March 2010, https://danskfolkeparti.dk/pia-kjaersgaards-ugebrev-homoseksuelle-kirke-vielser-er-ikke-en-kamp-for-vaerdier-men-en-kamp-imod-aegteskabet/.

[14] E.g. the political debate at VerdensKulturCentret in June 2015.

[15] Anti-Muslim and anti-immigrant rhetoric in LGBTQ spaces relates to the theory of "homonationalism," a term coined by Jasbir Puar in 2009 (using mainly U.S.-American examples). Whereas studies of homonationalism tend to focus on how LGBTQ people use xenophobic and Islamophobic rhetoric to win acceptance for LGBTQ rights, the pro-gay, anti-immigrant rhetoric outlined in this book focuses more on how mainstream politicians

component, such as when white LGBTQs express sexual exclusions or fetishes in racial and ethnic terms. Related, this racism also has an online media component, as LGBTQs broadcast their racial-sexual attitudes on dating and hook-up platforms.[16]

A key moment for debates on (online) racism in the Copenhagen LGBTQ community occurred already in 2013, when Sabaah organized a panel addressing an infamous message board on the popular Danish dating website Boyfriend.dk called (in Danish) "I'm not turned on by Asians." At a packed event, Sabaah drew widespread attention to this online space, and to problematic racial discourses within the LGBTQ community more generally.[17] Racial exclusions in sexually charged spaces persisted, nonetheless; thus at a 2017 Copenhagen Pride panel about Grindr cultures (foreperson) Saeed attested that Grindr users were still "perpetuating a lot of sexual racism within our community... being marked as okay because 'This is just my preference.'"[18] Thus, the concept of "sexual racism" (Chapter 5) is not alien to the Danish LGBTQ community; nevertheless, few tackle this topic outside of Sabaah.

The concerns of LGBTQ people with immigration background—in tandem with scholarly literature by and about LGBTQ racial minorities—extend far beyond issues of familial oppression. Many feel disconnected from white-majority LGBTQ spaces due in part to unrecognized racism and xenophobia. As LGBTQ immigrants in Europe increasingly use social media to find positive information and representations of homosexuality,[19] *Immigrants on Grindr* asks how belonging and exclusion can be felt in online spaces.

---

strategically nod to LGBTQ rights in order to justify anti-immigrant policies. Jasbir Puar, *Terrorist Assemblages: Homonationalism in Queer Times* (Durham, NC: Duke University Press, 2007).

[16] See also: Jesus G. Smith, "'No Fats, Fems, or Blacks': The Role of Sexual Racism in Online Stratification and Sexual Health for Gay Men" (PhD diss., Texas A&M University, 2017).

[17] Sabaah Debat, "Tænder ikke på asiater" [I'm Not Turned on by Asians], 19 February 2013, https://www.youtube.com/watch?v=qvSuHQPFWGw.

[18] "Grindr and Sex Culture," Panel at Copenhagen Pride with Kristian Møller, Fahad Saeed, Niels Jansen, and Andrew Shield, 16 August 2017, http://kanal-1.dk/14-grindr-sexkultur-lystfulde-politiske-hadefulde-perspektiver/.

[19] Alexander Dhoest, "Media, Visibility and Sexual Identity Among Gay Men with a Migration Background," *Sexualities* 19, no. 4 (2016): 412–431; Alexander Dhoest, and Lukasz Szulc, "Navigating Online Selves: Social, Cultural and Material Contexts of Social Media Use by Diasporic Gay Men," *Social Media + Society* 2, no. 4 (2016): 1–10.

About This Book

This book disrupts the pro-gay, anti-immigrant rhetoric in much of northwest Europe by honing in on gay and trans immigrants' experiences in white-majority LGBTQ spaces, online or offline, and the complicated ways that immigration status, race, sexuality, and transgender identity intersect in these subcultures. How do smartphone technologies enable gay and queer immigrants to connect to local LGBTQs? What types of relationships do these immigrants hope to build? How can these technologies assist in finding friends, housing, or local information in a new country? What factors contribute to immigrants' feelings of inclusion in, or exclusion from, a host country's LGBTQ communities? What role does race and/or country of origin play in an immigrant's ability to connect with locals? How might "mainstream" preconceptions about foreign ethnicities, races, or religions—such as those outlined thus far—surface online?

Immigrants on Grindr tackles these questions in the context of the greater Copenhagen area. More specifically, the book sheds light on one specific "community": the online world of "hook-up" platforms aimed primarily at gay men, such as Grindr, the most widely recognized and utilized platform during the period of research (2015–2019). The concepts "gay," "Grindr," "the greater Copenhagen area," "immigrant," and "race" are clarified at the end of this chapter.

Empirically, the book's data and analysis draws from the following: (1) semi-structured interviews with Grindr users who immigrated to Copenhagen or Malmö since 2010 mainly from countries that Scandinavian authorities categorize as "non-Western"; (2) selections from the profile texts of an estimated 6000 Grindr users who logged on from within the greater Copenhagen area; (3) several events by and/or for LGBTQs in Europe with immigration background, in which I participated or led discussion (e.g. WelcomeOUT for LGBTQ asylum seekers and refugees in Uppsala, Sweden in 2016 and 2017; the International Conference on Religion and Acceptance at University of Amsterdam in 2017, organized by Maruf, the Dutch organization for queer Muslims; a Sabaah discussion group about Grindr and race); and (4) informal conversations I had with Grindr users, online and offline.

Chapter 2, "'The Glittering Future of a New Innovation': Historicizing Grindr Culture," introduces the reader to the scholarly field of "Grindr studies," a term that could be applied to much of the research on gay men's digital cultures since 2010 or so, when dating and networking platforms largely moved to mobile phones and utilized geo-locative technologies to connect (mainly) men to other men within their immediate proximity. These works build largely from research on digital cultures since the 1990s, and thus Chapter 2 also contextualizes Grindr studies historiographically. Yet the literature review takes an unorthodox approach: I overview scholarly literature on gay men's digital cultures and race online since the 1990s in tandem with my own personal experiences within gay chat rooms, websites, and smartphone apps since the 1990s.

Chapter 3, "'Remember that if you choose to include information in your public profile… that information will also become public': Methods and Ethics for Online, Socio-Sexual Fieldwork" is geared at scholars collecting (and presenting) quantitative or qualitative data via Grindr, and/or recruiting interviewees via Grindr (or related platforms). How can an app like Grindr assist scholars with research? How can one collect and present "archives" of Grindr data ethically? What should one consider before connecting with Grindr users for face-to-face interviews? This chapter reviews many of the ethical challenges unique to scholars conducting ethnographic research in sexually charged online environments, and includes self-reflections on my own position as a gay immigrant in Copenhagen who studies other gay immigrants in Copenhagen.

Having situated this research in various debates inside and outside academia, and having laid out the methods for conducting research on and with immigrants on Grindr, the following three chapters analyze the empirical material gathered from 2015 to 2019 in the greater Copenhagen area.

Chapter 4, "'I was staying at the camp, and I met this guy on Grindr and he asked me to move in with him': Tourists, Immigrants, and Logistical Uses of Socio-Sexual Media," builds the foundations for understanding the "socio-sexual" character—that is, the blurring of sexual, platonic and logistical networking—within the communications and networks of Grindr and related platforms; in doing so, it explores why socio-sexual platforms might be enticing to those who are new in town. What is unique about the ways "newcomers"— tourists, immigrants, refugees—use platforms aimed primarily at gay men?[20] What are their experiences connecting with locals,

---

[20]Andrew DJ Shield, "New in Town: Gay Immigrants and Geosocial Dating Apps," in *LGBTQs, Media, and Culture in Europe*, ed. Alexander Dhoest, Lukasz Szulc, and Bart Eeckhout (London: Routledge, 2017), 244–261.

and when are these social connections enduring? Newcomers attract attention in sexually charged online spaces; but how does this allure compare for tourists and refugees? Ultimately, Chapter 4 underscores that newcomers' experiences on Grindr can differ based on country of origin, reason for migration, and race.

Thus Chapter 5, "'Tend to prefer sane, masculine, caucasian (no offense to other flavours though)': Racial-Sexual Preferences, Entitlement, and Everyday Racism" hones in on how a Grindr user's subject position relates to experiences of racism, xenophobia and Islamophobia online. How do migrant, racial, sexual, and gender identities intersect on Grindr? The chapter overviews sexual-racial fetishes and exclusions on Grindr, and also examines issues from everyday Othering to derogatory insults.[21] Thinking broadly about the concept of racism, this chapter identifies at least five dominant patterns of racist speech that people of color (both Scandinavian-born and immigrant) are likely to face on Grindr.

Having established that race- and ethnicity-related discourses circulate on Grindr, Chapter 6, "'White is a color, Middle Eastern is not a color': Drop-Down Menus, Racial Identification, and the Weight of Labels," scrutinizes the technology of Grindr—such as its interface and advanced search features—for the platform's role in encouraging discourses about race. Grindr's interface highlights "ethnicity" (or rather, race) as a primary drop-down menu through which users should define themselves (alongside height, weight, age); the menu provides a limited set of options, from which a user can choose only one selection. Consequently, users can "filter" their potential connections by this "ethnicity" menu, which effectively means that the technology enables race-selective browsing. Chapter 6 overviews the cultural and historical biases embedded in the "ethnicity" labels of Grindr and related platforms, and interrogates how immigrants in the greater Copenhagen area interpret, identify with, or reject these labels. How do users who potentially identify as both "Middle Eastern" and another label—such as "Black" or "White"—negotiate this drop-down menu? How do users assign "value" to different labels? Where do alternative discourses about race and ethnicity circulate?

---

[21] See also Andrew DJ Shield, "'Looking for North Europeans Only': Identifying Five Racist Patterns in an Online Subculture," *Kult* (the Journal of Nordic Postcolonial Studies), no. 15 (2018).

The concluding chapter, "'*Vi hygger os!*': Challenging Socio-Sexual Online Cultures" highlights the themes connecting each chapter. The culture of a socio-sexual platform, including the way that discourses about race circulate, is context-specific: discussions of race on Grindr reflect (aspects of) dominant conversations about race and migration in the greater Copenhagen area. Further, the technology and its creators also shape an online culture. Those seeking to build more inclusive online cultures must address both wider cultural issues as well as specific technological facets of an online platform.

The interviewees for *Immigrants on Grindr* all moved to the greater Copenhagen area since 2009, when Grindr was released on the second-generation iPhone (see Table 1.1). Most responded to my Grindr researcher profile (detailed in Chapter 3) in which I identified myself as a gay academic looking to speak to those who were "new in town" about their experiences on Grindr and related platforms. After the first five interviews (which included two gay men from within the European Union), I refocused the research to emphasize the experiences of immigrants from countries categorized as "non-Western" by Scandinavian authorities, partly because dominant discourses tend to fault these immigrants (especially from Muslim-majority countries) for their lack of cultural assimilation, and partly because "non-Western" immigrants are more likely to experience racialization on account of visible difference (see keyword "race" at the end of this chapter). Perhaps also due to the fact that the researcher profile included some Arabic text, fifty-percent of interviewees had origins in Muslim-majority countries. East Asian immigrants frequently contacted the researcher profile, resulting in 4–5 interviews with immigrants from this part of the world, including one transgender woman. Only two interviewees from sub-Saharan Africa contacted the researcher profile, though one did not appear for his interview. During a later phase of research, I followed through with two white-identified (and non-Muslim) asylum seekers from Russia, partly because their narratives nuanced the book's intersectional discussions on xenophobia. The "snowball" method was not employed, partly to ensure a more diverse representation of social circles, and partly to maintain anonymity between informants.

Chapter 3 argues in favor of interviewee recruitment via Grindr, rather than through more traditional methods like posting bulletins in LGBTQ establishments in Copenhagen and Malmö. For my previous book, *Immigrants in the Sexual Revolution*, I located interviewees via chat rooms and websites geared primarily at gay men (to speak about life and activism,

Table 1.1 Overview of the interviewees whose narratives contributed to this book

Pseudonym	Country of origin	Approx. year of migration to Scand	Schema	Month of interview
Angelo	Greece	2013	EU Citizen	October 2015
Asen	Bulgaria	2015	EU Citizen	October 2015
Caleb	China	2013	University, then work contract	October 2015
Şenol	Turkey	2010	University, then work contract	October 2015
Yusuf	Egypt	2013	(Political) asylum	October 2015
Sami	Israel	2015	Marriage	October 2015
Pejman	Iran	2013	Green card	December 2015
[not referred to by name]	China	2015	Work contract	December 2015
[not referred to by name]	France (of Arab descent)	2013	EU Citizen	December 2015
Parvin	Iran	2015	Green card	February 2016
Ali	Iraq	2014	Asylum	February 2016
Nir	Indonesia	2014	University	July 2016
Abdul	"Arab country" of the Gulf Cooperation Council	2014	University	August 2016
Azim	Egypt	2014	(Political) asylum	November 2016
Christina	"Asia"	2010	Marriage	March 2017
Daniel	Nigeria	2016	Asylum (seeker)	May 2017
Matthew	China	2015	University	June 2018
Stepan	Russia	2017	Asylum (seeker)	June 2018
Pavel	Russia	2017	Asylum (seeker)	June 2018
Mehmet	Turkey	2017	Asylum (seeker)	June 2018

and immigration and race, in the 1960s–1980s). These digital platforms allowed me to contact informants from geographically diverse areas, despite my location in a capital; and my respondents were not limited to those who patronized LGBTQ drop-in centers and bars, but also included those who were relatively isolated from LGBTQ offline spaces.

There are some additional demographic details that are not included in Table 1.1, so as to avoid providing too much personally identifiable information for each interviewee. Of the nineteen cisgender (i.e. non-transgender) males, all identified as gay at one point during our interview. Three also used other labels: one tended to use the word "queer"; another said he had identified as "situationally gay" before moving to Scandinavia, but that he now identified with the label gay; and one was married to a woman and had children (who still lived in his country of origin), but said that he had come to identify as gay in Scandinavia, and struggled with if and how he would tell his family.

Half of the interviewees were based in Denmark, and half were based in Sweden (i.e. the greater Malmö area). Many mentioned their ages in their online profiles or during interviews; a rough breakdown by age: four were in their forties, thirteen in their thirties, and three in their twenties.

I did not ask interviewees to state their racial or ethnic identifications, but race-related topics came up in all conversations, and most shared their own labels of identification and/or the labels that Scandinavians attributed to them. Some of these labels corresponded to Grindr's "ethnicity" menu (scrutinized in Chapter 6). Table 1.2 illustrates a tally of racial and ethnic designations used by interviewees; note that when interviewees provided several identifications during the interview (e.g. Middle Eastern, Arab, black, Nubian), all labels received a tally. Additionally, all interviewees identified at some point with the nationality of their country of origin (e.g. Chinese, Egyptian).

All interviewees had some form of legal residency, but this was not a requirement. Of those who arrived as asylum seekers, two had their cases

Table 1.2 Labels related to interviewees' (self-reported) racial and ethnic identities		
	9	Middle Eastern
	6	Arab
	6	Asian
	5	White
	3	Prefer not to identify with a label
	2	Black
	2	Did not mention racial/ethnic labels
	2	Mediterranean
	1	Han
	1	Igbo
	1	Latino
	1	Nubian
	1	Sephardic

accepted before the interview, and five had pending cases during the interview; of those five, one contacted me after our interview to share that his case had been accepted.

No aspect of interviewees' narratives was falsified except for their names; and in some cases, the year of migration was changed by one year.[22] Of those most concerned with anonymity, two interviewees asked me to obscure their country of origin and suggested a region; hence one interviewee is from "an Arab country in the Gulf Cooperation Council" and another is from "an Asian country."

All interviews were conducted in English. This is a limitation, as no interviewee had English as a first language. However, all interviewees preferred English to Danish or Swedish, despite that most were studying Danish or Swedish.[23] Additional details about the process of planning for, conducting, transcribing, and analyzing semi-structured interviews can be found in Chapter 3.

KEYWORDS

Gay vs. LGBTQ

Since its inception in 2009, Grindr has been an app primarily used by gay men; but there is a notable presence of trans women as well bi men (e.g. in the greater Copenhagen area), followed by those who identify as something else, including as trans men, non-binary, and straight men. Hence, this book refers to Grindr and related platforms as "geared primarily at gay

---

[22] All interviewees provided informed consent about their participation in a research project that would be disseminated in international publications and presentations. Interviewees were told that pseudonyms would be used, and most agreed. In two cases, interviewees enthusiastically offered their real names; but I chose to pseudonymize them, partly so that I would not seek their approval before publication. Having completed ethnographic research in the United States, I have undergone training in research ethics by the Institutional Review Board (IRB). The interviews involved no risk to the interviewees with one exception: the possible sharing of sensitive information including "outing" an informant. Some constellations of information are more personally identifiable than others; thus, I redacted neighborhoods of residence, occupations, areas of study, and references to extended families in Scandinavia. Chapter 3 discusses my avoidance of "personally identifiable information" and other considerations about anonymity; see also Sven Brinkmann and Steinar Kvale, *InterViews. Learning the Craft of Qualitative Research Interviewing* (London: Sage, 2015), 68–69.

[23] Scandinavian words or phrases scattered the conversation, such as technical terms related to immigration. Arabic was not used beyond rapport-building.

men," but avoids referring to a typical user of these platforms with male pronouns (he/him/his).

Grindr changed its outward communications about its user base in 2018. From 2009 through 2017, Grindr advertised itself as an app for "gay men."[24] Its 2017 press kit still boasted that Grindr was "the world's largest all-male mobile social network" that connected "**men with other men** in their area who want to chat or meet up," and thus linked "**gay men** to the world around."[25] Christina's interview that year challenged the conception of Grindr as a "gay male" space.

In 2018, however, Grindr added two new drop-down menus—"Gender identity" and "Pronouns"—and provided a gamut of options for transgender women, transgender men, and non-binary people, alongside information about trans-related terms, identities, and pronoun use (e.g. they/them/theirs as a singular pronoun). At this time, Grindr updated its description (such as in Apple's app store and on its website) to reflect this diversity of users: it promoted itself as "the world's largest social-networking app for **gay, bi, trans, and queer people**."[26] Thus, it is possible to refer to Grindr as a "GBTQ" space, even though this not a common acronym.

Since Grindr has no presence of lesbian cis-women, it is misleading to describe the online space as LGBTQ. However, some findings in this book relate to the LGBTQ community more broadly, as users also discuss their experiences in mixed organizations, bars, social circles, and other LGBTQ spaces. Future research on dating platforms aimed at lesbians (e.g. Brenda, HER) could expand on this book's analysis of online GBTQ subcultures.

"Grindr Culture" and Other "Socio-Sexual" Platforms

Grindr (detailed more in Chapter 2) emerged as the first app that utilized a smartphone's geo-locative feature to connect primarily gay men; over

---

[24] This phrasing is consistent with their 2015 Press Kit, which proclaimed that Grindr was a "lifestyle brand" that "connect[ed] **gay men** to the world that brings them happiness," and which had "supplanted **the gay bar** and online dating sites as the best way for **gay men** to meet the right person." "Fact Sheet [2015]," Press and News, Grindr; downloaded Summer 2015 via Grindr.com.

[25] "Fact Sheet [2017]," Press and News, Grindr; downloaded March 2017 via Grindr.com. Emphasis added.

[26] Grindr, "About," last accessed Fall 2017 via https://www.grindr.com/. Emphasis added.

the past decade, Grindr became the most ubiquitously known app among gay men in Denmark. "Grindr culture" refers to the social codes, patterns and behaviors online that comprise the culture of the app. The term is a direct reference to Sharif Mowlabocus' 2010 book *Gaydar Culture* (also detailed in Chapter 2), and extends his ethnographic analysis of gay website culture taking into consideration two major developments since 2010: the first is technological, namely the development and increased availability of smartphone technologies; the second is social, and points to the popularization—or rather, the omnipresence—of social-networking platforms.[27] Chapters 2 emphasizes that Grindr cultures build directly from earlier socio-sexual online platforms.

But the titular and methodological focus on "Grindr" is not meant to overemphasize the app's centrality in (L)GBTQ subcultures. Many Grindr users have similar profiles and experiences on other platforms, such as other geo-locative apps geared primarily at gay men (e.g. Scruff, Hornet, Growler, Jack'd, Blued, Chappy, or the app versions of Gaydar, PlanetRomeo, Recon, or Qruiser, a Scandinavian platform) and "mainstream" dating platforms (e.g. Tinder, Happn, Bumble, OkCupid).

Grindr describes itself as a "social network," but in common parlance, it is spoken of as a "hook-up" app, meaning an app where people primarily seek sex, often with no "strings" (commitments) attached. Many users seek a variety of non-sexual relationships alongside dating and sex in Grindr profiles, such as for friends, gym buddies, tour guides, roommates, and clients (Chapter 4). Thus Grindr might best be described as a platform for "socio-sexual" networking, as this term emphasizes the processes of interpersonal communication among those open to forming erotic, platonic, and practical connections, sometimes simultaneously.

Socio-sexual platforms potentially include any social media with flirtatious components to their online cultures, including Instagram, Facebook (especially private groups), Snapchat, Kik, YouTube, Tumblr, Skype, and so forth. The term "socio-sexual" could also apply to defunct platforms (e.g. gay.com chat rooms, Craigslist personal ads).

[27] Robert V. Kozinets, *Netnography: Redefined* (Los Angeles: Sage, 2015). When Kozinets wrote the 2009 edition of *Netnography*, he estimated that there were "at least 100 million," though perhaps more, who participated in online communities as part of their regular social experience (22fn1). In the 2015 edition, he noted that there were 1.3 billion active monthly users of Facebook, as well as 6.9 billion mobile-phone subscriptions (including individuals with multiple phone subscriptions) (2 and 22fn1).

"Immigrants" and "Race" in Scandinavia

I use the word "immigrant" in its literal sense to refer to someone who migrated from one country to another. Too often in Europe, the word "immigrant" is used in relation to the children and grandchildren of immigrants, which is a usage I wholeheartedly reject. This usage of "*x*-generation immigrant" sticks mainly to racial minorities (i.e. non-white people) and sometimes to white religious minorities (e.g. some Muslims). I similarly reject using the term "Dane" (or "ethnic Dane") to refer to people with no (known) background outside of Denmark, since Dane refers to citizenship. Thus, I refer to "white Danes" in this book, even though this is a surprisingly uncommon term in Denmark.[28]

In especially Chapters 4 and 5, I focus on "people of color," but this is not precisely the same as my group of interviewees. Three of my interviewees—two Russians, and one Bulgarian—identified only as white, and should not be included in this group. The term "people of color" is a useful way to speak of the experiences shared by "non-white" people in white-majority societies; in Scandinavia, the group "people of color" includes most people with immigration background from Asia, Africa and the indigenous Americas, debatably most from the Middle East and North Africa, and more controversially, possibly even immigrants from other Mediterranean areas such as southeast Europe. Those who practice Islam or who are perceived to be Muslim face additional racialization, which intersects with their positions in terms of race and migration status. The group "people of color" includes Scandinavian-born people of color.

"Out of curiosity, how many of you were asked to define your race when you applied to college?"

This is a question I ask to two different groups of students I've taught in Denmark: to U.S. American students studying abroad in Copenhagen; and to Danish and European students based at a Danish institution. When I ask the U.S. American students, every hand in the class shoots up. To them, it is obvious that a university would ask about an applicant's race in the

---

[28] Lene Myong, "Adopteret: Fortællinger om transnational og racialiseret tilblivelse" [Adopted: Tales of Transnational and Racialised Origins] (PhD diss., Aarhus University, Copenhagen, 2009); Rikke Andreassen and Uzma Ahmed-Andresen, "I Can Never Be Normal: A Conversation About Race, Daily Life Practices, Food and Power," *European Journal of Women's Studies* 21, no. 1 (2014): 27–28.

Note: This section is one of several about race in Denmark; see also Chapters 2 (race online, literature), 3 (self-reflections on race), 5 (racism), and 6 (racial drop-down menus).

name of diversity (regardless of whether or not the applicant answered the optional question). But to my Danish and European students, the response is usually a look of confusion. Inevitably a Danish student chimes in to tell me that official Danish documents are not allowed to ask about race. An Italian student, or a Belgian, raises her hand to ask, "But what do you *mean* by race?"

Denmark does not ask inhabitants to identify by "race" on official forms, nor do most European countries (except notably the UK).[29] In many countries formerly occupied by Germany during World War II, the term "race" is still associated with Nazism[30]; this partially explains why official documents in Denmark only keep track of residents' countries of birth, and the countries of birth of their parents. Consequently, Denmark can only provide data about—for example—the number of Danish residents who "have at least one parent born in a non-Western country," and this longwinded term is sometimes employed when providing data about racial minorities. Thus, the dominant Danish conception of a racial minority is someone who is a non-Western immigrant and not part of the Danish "ethnic" culture. Journalists and politicians tend to route around the terms "person of color" or "racial minority" with labels about migration status (e.g. "immigrant," "second-generation immigrant"), religion ("Muslim"), and foreign ethnicity ("of ethnic origin," "bilingual").[31]

There are obvious flaws in collapsing the categories of racial minority and non-Western ethnic minority: an African-American from the United States is a "Western" immigrant, a white South African is a "non-Western" immigrant, and a grandchild of Pakistani immigrants is no longer marked as a Dane with immigration background. Lene Myong, who is a Nordic gender and race scholar and an expert on transnational adoption, has shown how Korean adoptees also disrupt the "ethnic Dane" versus "racial minority" distinction: most are raised by (white) Danish parents and socialized entirely with the Danish language and dominant culture. But as racial minorities,

---

[29]The former Soviet Union also had a unique history of race reporting on censuses.

[30]E.g. Andreassen and Uzma Ahmed-Andresen, 27. See also Rikke Andreassen and Kathrine Vitus, eds., *Affectivity and Race: Studies from Nordic Contexts* (Farnham: Ashgate, 2015).

[31]Andreassen and Ahmed-Andresen, 28. Rikke Andreassen noted in 2014, "Despite the different etymological meanings of these terms, they are often used interchangeably" in Denmark.

they are also excluded from the group of "ethnic Danes," similar to children and grandchildren of immigrants.[32]

Feminist activist Uzma Ahmed, who was born and raised in Denmark and has Pakistani ethnic background, reflected on this misuse of "ethnicity" in Denmark:

> I am always labeled as 'ethnic', but it would be more useful for me to talk about race and racial appearances... I feel that I cannot get away from my ethnicity. Even though I am born and bred here and hold Danish citizenship, I can never escape my ethnicity – because of my racial appearance.[33]

Also in a Swedish context, race scholar Anna Adeniji (among others[34]) has acknowledged that racial minority Swedes navigate the world simultaneously as Swedes and "not really Swedes," among other racial-identity paradoxes.[35]

But also among Nordic academics, the terms "people of color" and "racial minorities" are becoming more widely used to underscore the visible differences inhabiting the position of many migrants and their descendants.[36] In their introduction to *Media in Motion*—about immigration and media use in the Nordic countries—the editors Elisabeth Eide and Kaarina Nikunen included a sub-heading entitled "Nordic whiteness and hybridity," where they acknowledged some of the difficulties scholars face when discussing race in a Nordic context. For example, many immigration studies homed in on specific ethno-national groups (e.g. Turks in Denmark, Somalis in Sweden), so scholars sought to avoid "essentializing immigrants into

---

[32] Myong.

[33] Andreassen and Uzma Ahmed-Andresen, 28.

[34] Ylva Habel, "Whiteness Swedish Style," *Slut* 2 (2008): 41–51.

[35] Anna Adeniji, "Searching for Words: Becoming *Mixed Race*, Black and Swedish," in *Afro-Nordic Landscapes: Equality and Race in Northern Europe*, ed. Michael McEachrane (London: Routledge, 2014), 156.

[36] Nordic scholarship increasingly examines racialized (and postcolonial) positions, including critical reflections on whiteness, inspired by theorists such as Stuart Hall, Edward Said, Gayatri Spivak, and Homi Bhabha. See Suvi Keskinen and Rikke Andreassen, "Developing Theoretical Perspectives on Racialisation and Migration," *The Journal of Nordic Migration Research* 7, no. 2 (June 2017): 64–69 (Special issue: "Developing Theoretical Perspectives on Racialisation and Migration."). On whiteness and the myth of "colorblindness" in a Danish context, see discussion of Myong in Chapter 6.

one homogeneous group."[37] But the editors argued that there was merit in doing research "from a multi-ethnic perspective," and one way of doing so was to highlight studies that foreground race. By doing so, scholars can better address topics like systemic inequality and structural racism.[38]

There is much more to say about the specifics of race and racism in Scandinavia.[39] For example, Myong has criticized a culture in which Danes brush off racist comments as "just a joke," and has underscored that speech or actions can be racist despite the "intent" of the offender (see Chapter 5). Others have pointed to Denmark's historical "amnesia" about its role in the trade of enslaved Africans, about its colonization and exploitation of the Caribbean and West Africa (among other places), about Sweden's role in advanced eugenic "science,"[40] and about the imprisonment and deportation of Roma and other "foreign" groups. Each chapter in this book continues the discussion of race in Denmark from a different angle: on my own racial position in Denmark, and in relation to my interviewees (Chapter 3); on the racial politics of the "gay cosmopolitan tourist" versus the queer migrant (Chapter 4); on the applicability of Philomena Essed's notions of "everyday racism" and "entitlement racism" to Denmark and Sweden (Chapter 5); and on the burden of racial labels (Chapter 6).

---

[37] Elisabeth Eide and Kaarina Nikunen, "Introduction: Change of Climate," in *Media in Motion: Cultural Complexity and Migration in the Nordic Region*, ed. Elisabeth Eide et al. (Surrey, UK: Routledge, 2011), 14–15.

[38] Rikke Andreassen and Lene Myong, "Race, Gender, and Researcher Positionality Analysed Through Memory Work," *Nordic Journal of Migration Research* 7, no. 2 (2017): 97.

[39] See, for example, the following selection in English: Peter Hervik, "Limits of Tolerance and Limited Tolerance: How Tolerant Are the Danes?" in *Racism in Metropolitan Areas*, ed. Rik Pinxten and Ellen Preckler (New York and Oxford: Berghahn Books, 2005); Peter Hervik, *The Annoying Difference: The Emergence of Danish Neonationalism, Neoracism and Populism in the Post-1989 World* (New York and Oxford: Berghahn Books, 2011); Susi Meret and Birte Siim, "Gender, Populism and Politics of Belonging: Discourses of Right-Wing Populist Parties in Denmark, Norway and Austria," in *Negotiating Gender and Diversity in an Emergent European Public Sphere*, ed. Birte Siim and Monika Mokre (New York: Palgrave Macmillan, 2013); Adeniji.

[40] Bolette Blaagaard and Rikke Andreassen, "The Disappearing Act: The Forgotten History of Colonialism, Eugenics and Gendered Othering in Denmark," in *Teaching 'Race' with a Gendered Edge*, ed. Brigitte Hipfl and Kristín Loftsdóttir (Utrecht: ATGENDER, 2012), 91–103.

"The Greater Copenhagen Area"

This book refers to "the greater Copenhagen area" and sometimes more simply to "Copenhagen," which is imprecise. The empirical data for this research come from both the area traditionally described as the metropolitan Copenhagen area, as well as from Malmö, the third largest city in Sweden. I considered using the local term "Øresund Region," but this term is not commonly understood outside of Scandinavia (and is also larger than the area of focus).[41]

There are important differences between the socio-political contexts in Copenhagen and Malmö. Sweden had a much higher volume of accepted refugees during this period of research, most notably in 2016. In 2015, Denmark had a record 21,316 asylum seekers, more than half of whom came from Syria, Iran, and Afghanistan; but anti-immigrant Danish politicians took harsh measures to deter asylum seekers. Consequently, Denmark only saw 6235 applications in 2016, and even fewer thereafter. In 2018, Denmark saw an historic low: only 2600 asylum seekers opened cases that year (mostly from Syria and Eritrea) and the majority of them already had residence through family reunification.[42]

Sweden, on the other hand, handled over 100,000 asylum applicants *in 2016 alone*, of whom 67,258 were accepted. Syrians, Afghanis, and Iraqis topped the list of applicants. The previous year (2015), Sweden accepted 32,531 of its 58,802 applicants. But Sweden too implemented efforts to curtail applications—in tandem with greater EU policies—so the number of asylum seekers also dropped dramatically.[43] Swedish anti-immigrant sentiment was quite visible during these years, especially among those affiliated

---

[41]The 36-kilometer radius used in quantitative data collection (see Chapter 3) includes a bit of Roskilde (Denmark), but stops short of other cities in the region, such as Helsingør (Denmark), Lund (Sweden), and Helsingborg (Sweden). The radius does *not* include the parts of northern and eastern Sealand that are sometimes included in the greater metropolitan area of Copenhagen.

[42]The acceptance rate dropped from 85% in 2015, to 72% in 2016. Denmark had 3479 applications in 2017 (with Syrians as the largest group), of whom 36% were accepted. Michala Clante Bendixen, "How Many Are Coming, and from Where?" *Refugees.dk* (information on refugees in Denmark), last accessed Fall 2019 via http://refugees.dk/en/facts/numbers-and-statistics/how-many-are-coming-and-from-where/. Note: this website has been updated consistently for several years.

[43]Though the number of applicants dropped in Sweden since 2016, the number of people granted asylum still remained (disproportionately) higher in Sweden than Denmark: 27,205 applications were accepted in 2017, and 11,217 in 2018. Swedish Migration Agency, "Asylum

with the populist Swedish Democrats, which is a strong parallel with the Danish socio-political context.

Copenhagen and Malmö are connected via their LGBTQ communities. The Pride committees on both sides of the Øresund (the waterway between the cities) coordinate festivities annually in August. Throughout the year it is common for especially gay men from Malmö to travel to Copenhagen to attend gay bars and parties. As one interviewee (originally from the Middle East) explained:

> There are some options here [in Malmö], but more options, more nightlife, and it's cheaper in Copenhagen. And you can meet friends. I was even dating a Danish guy for a while last year, so I was often in Copenhagen.

Copenhagen has a dozen predominantly gay and/or LGBTQ bars—one of which is primarily female—that are open daily, ranging from cafés with restaurants, to smoky dance bars, to sex clubs. Malmö is also known for a vibrant LGBTQ community—one in which women, queer-identified people, and sober people are perhaps more visible—and attracts some LGBTQ Copenhageners. Because of LGBTQ travel between the two cities, I considered it valid and necessarily to study experiences on both sides of the Øresund. But during the first year conducting this research, Sweden reintroduced border control for the first time since the 1950s, which meant that those traveling from Copenhagen to Malmö had to present a passport for entry into Sweden; this hindered the ability of some to travel freely, such as asylum seekers with pending applications.

This chapter overviewed the overlapping areas of immigration and sexual politics in northwest Europe, and justified new research about gay, bi, trans, and queer immigrants' experiences with racism and exclusion in (L)GBTQ environments. New ethnographic research about migrant and/or queer subcultures will increasingly have an online component. Thus in Chapter 2, we turn to a review of scholarly research about online cultures—especially gay men's sexuality and race in online communities—in order to contextualize the historic and cultural significance of apps like Grindr for fostering networks and subcultures.

Decisions [Year]", last accessed Fall 2019 via https://www.migrationsverket.se/English/About-the-Migration-Agency/Statistics.html.

Works Cited

Abu-Lughod, Lila. *Do Muslim Women Need Saving?* Cambridge, MA: Harvard University Press, 2013.

Abu-Lughod, Lila. "Do Muslim Women Really Need Saving? Anthropological Reflections on Cultural Relativism and Its Others." *American Anthropologist* 104, no. 3 (September 2002): 783–790.

Adeniji, Anna. "Searching for Words: Becoming *Mixed Race,* Black and Swedish." In *Afro-Nordic Landscapes: Equality and Race in Northern Europe*, edited by Michael McEachrane, 149–162. London: Routledge, 2014.

Als Research [Press Release]. "Nydanske LGBT-personers levevilkår" [New-Danish LGBT-Peoples' Living Conditions]. Als Research, 1 October 2015. http://www.alsresearch.dk/news/174/61/01-10-15-Nydanske-LGBT-personers-levevilkar.

Andreassen, Rikke, and Lene Myong. "Race, Gender, and Researcher Positionality Analysed Through Memory Work." *Nordic Journal of Migration Research* 7, no. 2 (2017): 97–104.

Andreassen, Rikke, and Uzma Ahmed-Andresen. "I Can Never Be Normal: A Conversation About Race, Daily Life Practices, Food and Power." *European Journal of Women's Studies* 21, no. 1 (2014): 25–42.

Bendixen, Michala Clante. "How Many Are Coming, and from Where?" *Refugees.dk* (information on refugees in Denmark). Last accessed Fall 2017 via http://refugees.dk/en/facts/numbers-and-statistics/how-many-are-coming-and-from-where/.

Blaagaard, Bolette, and Rikke Andreassen. "The Disappearing Act: The Forgotten History of Colonialism, Eugenics and Gendered Othering in Denmark.' In *Teaching 'Race' with a Gendered Edge*, edited by Brigitte Hipfl and Kristín Loftsdóttir, 91–103. Utrecht: ATGENDER, 2012.

Brinkmann, Sven, and Steinar Kvale. *InterViews: Learning the Craft of Qualitative Research Interviewing.* London: Sage, 2015.

Broberg, Mads Bonde, and Simon Roliggaard Andersen. "Undersøgelse: Hver ottende indvandrerhomo er blevet udsat for vold" [Every Eighth Immigrant Gay Has Been Exposed to Violence]. *Jyllands-Posten,* 1 October 2015. https://jyllands-posten.dk/indland/ECE8072616/Unders%C3%B8gelse-Hver-ottende-indvandrerhomo-er-blevet-udsat-for-vold/.

Dhoest, Alexander. "Media, Visibility and Sexual Identity Among Gay Men with a Migration Background." *Sexualities* 19, no. 4 (2016): 412–431.

Dhoest, Alexander, and Lukasz Szulc. "Navigating Online Selves: Social, Cultural and Material Contexts of Social Media Use by Diasporic Gay Men." *Social Media + Society* 2, no. 4 (2016): 1–10.

Eide, Elisabeth, and Kaarina Nikunen, eds. *Media in Motion: Cultural Complexity and Migration in the Nordic Region.* Surrey, UK: Routledge, 2011.

Følner, Bjarke, Mikkel Dehlholm, and Jasmin Maria Christiansen, *Nydanske LGBT-personers levevilkår* [New-Danish LGBT People's Living Conditions]. Copenhagen: Als Research, 2015.

Graversen, Mathilde. "Hver tredje LGBT-nydansker har overvejet selvmord" [One in Three LGBT New Danes Has Contemplated Suicide]. *Berlingske*, 1 October 2015. https://www.b.dk/nationalt/hver-tredje-lgbt-nydansker-har-overvejet-selvmord.

Grindr. "About." Accessed Fall 2017 via https://www.grindr.com/.

Grindr. "Fact Sheet [2015]." Press and News. Downloaded Summer 2015 via Grindr.com.

Grindr. "Fact Sheet [2017]." Press and News. Downloaded March 2017 via Grindr.com.

"Grindr and Sex Culture." Panel at Copenhagen Pride with Kristian Møller, Fahad Saeed, Niels Jansen, and Andrew Shield, 16 August 2017. Archived and last accessed Autumn 2017 via http://kanal-1.dk/14-grindr-sexkultur-lystfulde-politiske-hadefulde-perspektiver/.

Habel, Ylva. "Whiteness Swedish Style." *Slut* 2 (2008): 41–51.

Hervik, Peter. *The Annoying Difference: The Emergence of Danish Neonationalism, Neoracism and Populism in the Post-1989 World*. New York and Oxford: Berghahn Books, 2011.

Hervik, Peter. "Limits of Tolerance and Limited Tolerance: How Tolerant Are the Danes?" In *Racism in Metropolitan Areas*, edited by Rik Pinxten and Ellen Preckler. New York and Oxford: Berghahn Books, 2005.

Jensen, Emilie Rask. "Hver tredje homoseksuelle nydansker har overvejet selvmord" [One in Three Homosexual New Danes Has Contemplated Suicide]. *DR*, 1 October 2015. https://www.dr.dk/ligetil/indland/hver-tredje-homoseksuelle-nydansker-har-overvejet-selvmord.

Keskinen, Suvi, and Rikke Andreassen. "Developing Theoretical Perspectives on Racialisation and Migration." *The Journal of Nordic Migration Research* 7, no. 2 (June 2017): 64–69 (Special issue: "Developing Theoretical Perspectives on Racialisation and Migration.").

Kjærsgaard, Pia. "Pia Kjærsgaards ugebrev: Homoseksuelle kirke-vielser er ikke en kamp for værdier men en kamp imod ægteskabet" [Pia Kjærsgaard's Weekly Letter: Homosexual Church-Weddings Are Not a Struggle for Rights, but a Struggle Against Marriage]. Press Release of the Danish People's Party, 22 March 2010. https://danskfolkeparti.dk/pia-kjaersgaards-ugebrev-homoseksuelle-kirke-vielser-er-ikke-en-kamp-for-vaerdier-men-en-kamp-imod-aegteskabet/.

Kozinets, Robert V. *Netnography: Redefined*. Los Angeles: Sage, 2015.

Meret, Susi, and Birte Siim. "Gender, Populism and Politics of Belonging: Discourses of Right-Wing Populist Parties in Denmark, Norway and Austria." In *Negotiating Gender and Diversity in an Emergent European Public Sphere*, edited by Birte Siim and Monika Mokre. New York: Palgrave Macmillan, 2013.

Mølgaard, Milla. "Hver tredje nydanske homoseksuelle har overvejet selvmord" [One in Three New Danish Homosexuals Has Contemplated Suicide]. *Politiken*, 30 September 2015. politiken.dk/forbrugogliv/sundhedogmotion/art5591593/Hver-tredje-nydanske-homoseksuelle-har-overvejet-selvmord.

Myong, Lene. "Adopteret: Fortællinger om transnational og racialiseret tilblivelse" [Adopted: Tales of Transnational and Racialised Origins]. PhD diss., Aarhus University, Copenhagen, 2009.

Puar, Jasbir. *Terrorist Assemblages: Homonationalism in Queer Times.* Durham, NC: Duke University Press, 2007.

Rychla, Lucie. "Every Third Homosexual of Non-Western Ethnic Descent Living in Denmark Has Considered Suicide." *CPH Post*, 1 October 2015. http://cphpost.dk/news/every-third-homosexual-of-non-western-ethnic-descent-living-in-denmark-has-considered-suicide.html.

Sabaah. "[Debat:] Tænder ikke på asiater" [Debate: I'm Not Turned on by Asians], 19 February 2013, https://www.youtube.com/watch?v=qvSuHQPFWGw.

Shield, Andrew DJ. *Immigrants in the Sexual Revolution: Perceptions and Participation in Northwest Europe.* Cham, Switzerland: Palgrave Macmillan, 2017.

Shield, Andrew DJ. "'Looking for North Europeans Only': Identifying Five Racist Patterns in an Online Subculture." *Kult* 15 (June 2018): 87–106.

Shield, Andrew DJ. "New in Town: Gay Immigrants and Geosocial Dating Apps." In *LGBTQs, Media, and Culture in Europe*, edited by Alexander Dhoest, Lukasz Szulc and Bart Eeckhout, 244–261. London: Routledge, 2017.

Shield, Andrew DJ. "When Pro-Gay Means Anti-Muslim." *The Murmur*, 21 March 2017, 44–45, last accessed Autumn 2019 via murmur.dk/when-pro-gay-means-anti-muslim/.

Smith, Jesus G. "'No Fats, Fems, or Blacks': The Role of Sexual Racism in Online Stratification and Sexual Health for Gay Men." PhD diss., Texas A&M University, 2017.

Søndergaard, Britta. "Hver tredje homoseksuelle nydansker har overvejet selvmord" [One in Three Homosexual New Danes Has Contemplated Suicide]. *Kristeligt Dagblad*, 30 September 2015. https://www.kristeligt-dagblad.dk/danmark/hver-tredje-homoseksuelle-nydansker-har-overvejet-selvmord.

Swedish Migration Agency, "Asylum Decisions [Year]", last accessed Fall 2019 via https://www.migrationsverket.se/English/About-the-Migration-Agency/Statistics.html.

FURTHER READINGS

Further readings on immigration and sexual politics in northwest Europe, aside from those cited elsewhere in this book

Akin, Deniz. "Queer Asylum Seekers: Translating Sexuality in Norway." *Journal of Ethnic and Migration Studies* 42 (2016): 15.

Andersson, Magnus. "Multi-contextual Lives: Transnational Identifications Under Mediatised Conditions." *European Journal of Cultural Studies* 16, no. 4 (2013): 1–18.

Andreassen, Rikke. "Gender as a Tool in Danish Debates About Muslims." In *Islam in Denmark: The Challenge of Diversity*, edited by Jørgen S. Nielsen, 143–160. Lanham, UK: Lexington Books, 2012.

Bang Svendsen, Stine H. "Learning Racism in the Absence of 'Race'." *The European Journal of Women's Studies* 21, no. 1 (2014): 9–24.

Bracke, Sarah. "From 'Saving Women' to 'Saving Gays': Rescue Narratives and Their Dis/continuities." *European Journal of Women's Studies* 19, no. 2 (2012): 237–252.

Buhl, Frederik Kristensen. "Det, vi så i Köln, har vi aldrig tidligere set i Europa" [What We Saw in Cologne, We Never Saw Before in Europe]. *Politiken*, 16 January 2016. https://politiken.dk/udland/int_europa/art5607045/%C2% BBDet-vi-s%C3%A5-i-K%C3%B6ln-har-vi-aldrig-tidligere-set-i-Europa%C2% AB.

Cava, Mica. *Visceral Cosmopolitanism: Gender, Culture and the Normalisation of Difference*. London: Bloomsbury, 2007.

Dhoest, Alexander, Lukasz Szulc, and Bart Eeckhout, eds. *LGBTQs, Media, and Culture in Europe*. London: Routledge, 2017.

Drud-Jensen, Mads Ted, and Sune Prahl Knudsen. *Ondt i Røven* [Pain in the Ass]. Copenhagen: Høst, 2005.

El-Tayeb, Fatima. *European Others: Queering Ethnicity in Postnational Europe*. Minneapolis, MN: University of Minnesota Press, 2011.

Farris, Sara. *In the Name of Women's Rights: The Rise of Femonationalism*. Durham: Duke University Press, 2017.

Fauser, Margit. *Migrants and Cities: The Accommodation of Migrant Organizations in Europe*. Farnham, UK and Burlington, VT: Ashgate, 2012.

Gajjala, Radhika. *Cyber Selves: Feminist Ethnographies of South Asian Women*. Walnut Creek, CA: AltaMira Press, 2004.

Horsti, Karina. "Overview of Nordic Media Research on Immigration and Ethnic Relations: From Text Analysis to the Study of Production, Use and Reception." *Nordicom Review* 29, no. 2 (2008): 275–293.

Hübinette, Tobias, and Carina Tigervall. "To Be Non-white in a Colorblind Society: Conversations with Adoptees and Adoptive Parents in Sweden on Everyday Racism." *Journal of Intercultural Studies* 30, no. 4 (2009): 335–353.

Hvilsom, Frank. "'Efter Köln stiger jeg ikke ind i en elevator alene med en dansk kvinde'" [After Cologne, I'm Not Getting into an Elevator with a Danish Woman]. *Politikeni*, 16 January 2015. https://politiken.dk/indland/ art5612834/%C2%BBEfter-K%C3%B6ln-stiger-jeg-ikke-ind-i-en-elevator-alene-med-en-dansk-kvinde%C2%AB.

Jivraj, Suhraiya, and Anisa de Jong. "The Dutch Homo-Emancipation Policy and Its Silencing Effects on Queer Muslims." *Feminist Legal Studies* 19, no. 2 (August 2011): 143–158 (Special Issue: Liabilities of queer antiracist critique).

26   A. DJ SHIELD

Kallenbach, Christian. "Parti uddelte asylspray på gågaden: - Det er svinsk" [Party Gives Out Asylum Spray on the Streets: 'This Is Disgusting']. *TV2*, 25 September 2015. http://nyheder.tv2.dk/lokalt/2016-09-25-parti-uddelte-asylspray-paa-gaagaden-det-er-svinsk.

Klausen, Jytte. *The Cartoons that Shook the World*. New Haven, CT: Yale University Press, 2009.

Kristiansen, Cecilie Lund. "Flygtning: Man snakker ikke rigtig med pigerne i toget i Danmark" [Refugee: You Don't Really Chat with the Girls on the Train in Denmark]. *Politikeni*, 30 January 2016. https://politiken. dk/indland/art5609347/Flygtning-Man-snakker-ikke-rigtig-med-pigerne-i-toget-i-Danmark.

Liljeström, Marianne, and Susanna Paasonen, eds. *Working with Affect in Feminist Readings—Disturbing Differences*. London: Routledge, 2010.

Mainsah, Henry. "'I Could Well Have Said I Was Norwegian but Nobody Would Believe Me': Ethnic Minority Youths' Self-Representation on Social Network Sites." *European Journal of Cultural Studies* 14, no. 2 (2011): 179–193.

Mainsah, Henry. "Transcending the National Imagery: Digital Online Media and the Transnational Networks of Ethnic Minority Youth in Norway." In *Media in Motion: Cultural Complexity and Migration in the Nordic Region*, edited by Elisabeth Eide and Kaarina Nikunen, 201–218. Surrey, UK: Routledge, 2011.

Mepschen, Paul, Jan Willem Duyvendak, and Evelien H. Tonkens. "Sexual Politics, Orientalism and Multicultural Citizenship in the Netherlands." *Sociology* 44 (2010): 962–979.

Nebeling Petersen, Michael. "'… Med et regnbueflag i hånden': Fortællinger om homoseksuelle inklusioner og homonationalisme" [...With a Rainbow Flag in Hand'": Stories About Gay Inclusions and Homonationalism]. *Lambda Nordica* 16, no. 1 (2011): 41–68.

Nebeling Petersen, Michael, Katherine Harrison, Tobias Raun, and Rikke Andreassen. "Introduction: Mediated Intimacies." In *Mediated Intimacies: Connectivities, Relationalities and Proximities*, edited by Rikke Andreassen, Michael Nebeling Petersen, Katherine Harrison, Tobias Raun, 1–16. London: Routledge, 2017.

Østergård, Emil. "Livet i et walk-in-closet – om etniske minoritetshomoseksuelles håndtering af deres seksualitet" [Life in a Walk-in Closet: On Ethnic Minority Homosexuals' Handling of Their Sexuality]. Masters thesis, Copenhagen University, 2015.

Tonkens, Evelien, M. Hurenkamp, and Jan Willem Duyvendak. *Culturalization of Citizenship in the Netherlands*. Amsterdam: Amsterdam School for Social Sciences Research, 2008.

Wekker, Gloria. *White Innocence: Paradoxes of Colonialism and Race*. Durham, NC: Duke University Press, 2016.

CHAPTER 2

"The glittering future of a new invention": Historicizing Grindr Culture

I have had to explain Grindr to hundreds of (often heterosexual) people who are unaware of the app. Fortunately, most of them had heard of Tinder, the smartphone-only app that enables users to make basic dating profiles, view the profiles of potential matches within a bounded geography (determined by the geo-locative positioning of one's smartphone), and chat—textually and with photos—in anticipation of eventually meeting up "in real life" for a date. Great. Now they just had to learn a few major differences.

First and foremost, Grindr is not a gay Tinder[1]; if anything, Tinder is a straight Grindr (though Tinder is also used by LGBTQs). Grindr debuted in 2009 just as early adopters were buying their first iPhones. The Internet Personals, Dating & Matchmaking Industry—which was concerned mainly with websites at the time—awarded Grindr "Best Mobile Dating App" at their annual trade shows in 2011, 2012, and 2013. It wasn't until 2015–2017 that the mainstream platforms Tinder and Bumble stole the show, and the award from Grindr.

Second, Grindr displays all nearby users in order of their *exact proximity* to one's iPhone. Some Tinder users describe this aspect as "creepy" and indeed, it's rather invasive. When you sign on, you see a grid of users

---

[1]Grindr consistently referred to itself a network for "gay men" ("the world's largest") from 2009 through 2018, at which point the app broadened its recognition of and support for trans and queer users (see Chapter 1).

© The Author(s) 2019
A. DJ Shield, *Immigrants on Grindr*,
https://doi.org/10.1007/978-3-030-30394-5_2

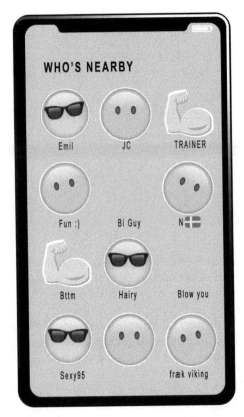

Fig. 2.1 A Grindr user's welcome screen offers a grid of users who are recently active, ordered by their exact proximity (*Note* Grindr did not grant permission to use the welcome "cascade" from their 2017 press kit. This "welcome screen" is a rough mock-up. The emojis represent different types of profile photos, as described in the "Guide to reading the skeleton profile" [Fig. 3.5]. Tapping on one of these thumbnail photos brings access to the user's full profile [e.g. Emil])

(Fig. 2.1): the first is the closest (Emil), the second is the second closest (JC), and so on. The default setting provides details on that exact distance; but even those who hide their exact distance will still be sandwiched between users who do provide these data (i.e. if Emil is 50 meters away, and TRAINER is 100 meters away, then one knows JC is within the 50-to 100-meter radius). Next, Grindr does not facilitate matches; users are *not* asked to "swipe right" for yes, and "swipe left" for no. Rather, all users are visible and contactable to all other users (unless they've been personally blocked).

There are a few other differences. Grindr is an independent profile: one can link to one's Facebook, Instagram, or Twitter, but no information is drawn directly from these sources. Especially since 2017, Grindr has tried to become a lifestyle brand, offering editorial content, gay-themed emojis, and merchandise.

For this book, it's important to note that Grindr has—since 2009, when the profile only allowed one photo, 50 words, and half a dozen drop-down menus—suggested that users identify by race ("ethnicity") and has offered a limited list of nine options (detailed and scrutinized in Chapter 6). These initial drop-down menus also addressed age, height, weight, relationship status, and "Looking For"; by 2015, Grindr added "Body Type" and "Tribe" (see Chapter 6, footnote 7); by 2017, they added sexual "Position" (i.e. top/vers/bottom, or in European parlance, active/versa/passive), "HIV Status," and "Last Tested Date"; by 2018, they added "Gender" and "Pronouns" to further recognize trans and non-binary users (Chapter 1); and in 2019, menus were added for "Meet at" and "Accepts NSFW pics," the latter of which seems to be a response to discussions around consent and x-rated photos. (NSFW or Not Safe For Work, is code for photos of a sexual nature, which can only be sent by private message). Since 2009, all users' profile photos (which are considered "public" to other Grindr users) have needed to be approved on a case-by-case basis, and cannot include a variety of things considered sexual; from 2019, users could include multiple (non-sexual) profile photos.

Grindr makes some claims about its members that circulate in most media coverage of the app. In 2014, Grindr claimed to have had "nearly 10 million users in over 192 countries."[2] But since then, they have tended to provide a lower number, albeit of "daily active users": 2 million in 2015, and over three million in 2017. These active users allegedly averaged "54 minutes" daily according to the 2017 press kit (down from "1.5 average

---

[2] Lara O'Reilly, "How Gay Hook-Up App Grindr Is Selling Itself to Major Brand Advertisers," *Business Insider Australia*, 27 November 2014, https://www.businessinsider.com.au/grindr-ceo-joel-simkhai-on-advertising-pitch-deck-2014-11.

daily hours" in 2014).[3] Since 2019, Grindr no longer offers figures about number of users or their average daily usage time.

In Scandinavia, Grindr has become a household name, and not only for gay men. In 2015, for example, the popular Danish television show "Rita"—about a high-school teacher and single mother—included an episode where Rita invited her son to speak about being gay: "Well my name is Jeppe, I'm 18 years old, and I'm a homosexual," he began (in Danish), before asking if the students had any questions. A female student asked Jeppe how he knew whether or not he could hit on a guy, and he responded, "Well, you can always [just] give it a try. Or you can try to find someone on Grindr." Another student promptly asked him to explain Grindr, and Jeppe took out his phone: "Grindr is an app, a little like Facebook. But only for homosexuals." For Jeppe's character, Grindr was his literal "gaydar," a technological apparatus that could pinpoint his potential gay matches in his immediate surroundings.[4]

The wildly popular Norwegian television show "Skam"—in which real teenage actors portrayed real teen issues—started its 2016 season with a beloved character (Isak) coming out. For Isak, downloading Grindr was like a step into his first gay bar: exciting, confusing, and a little overwhelming.[5] For both Jeppe and Isak, the online space enabled exploration of gay desire or connection with like-minded peers. For Grindr's tenth birthday, a young journalist at Denmark's largest daily newspaper attested to Grindr's significance in his own coming out, and in connecting to other local gays.[6] Grindr has become a matter-of-fact part of many gay men's lives, not least in Scandinavia.

This chapter overviews the emerging scholarly field of "Grindr Studies," then historicizes Grindr culture within a longer history of gay men's online

[3] The average daily user's number of daily logins has reportedly doubled from 9 to 18 during this period. Grindr, "Fact Sheet [2015]"; Grindr, "Fact Sheet [2017]."

[4] In the episode, Jeppe then signs onto the app, only to see that the class teacher—who had not said anything about his sexual orientation—was also signed on; the two of them have a brief tryst after school in the classroom, which Rita catches.

[5] Isak's relationship with the app is short-lived, as he begins to date another classmate whom he meets in an after-school activity.

[6] Rasmus Helmann, "'Er du den sutteglade fyr, jeg søger?': Efter ti år er appen Grindr mere end bare et kødkatalog" [After Ten Years: Grindr Is More Than Just a Meat Catalog], *Politiken*, 7 January 2019, https://politiken.dk/kultur/art6937614/Efter-ti-%C3%A5r-er-appen-Grindr-mere-end-bare-et-k%C3%B8dkatalog.

spaces. Throughout the chapter, I present my own personal history navigating online gay spaces since the late 1990s, with attention to concurrent scholarly literature on sexuality and race online.

GRINDR STUDIES

In *Gaydar Culture: Gay Men, Technology and Embodiment in the Digital Age* (2010), media scholar Sharif Mowlabocus explored user profiles, private messages, chat rooms, and discussion forums primarily on the British website Gaydar.co.uk, in order to map the terrain of "gay men's digital culture" (his preferred term throughout the book). Mowlabocus underscored that "gay male subculture (offline) and gay men's digital culture (online) are part and parcel of the same thing."[7] In his final chapter, he invited the readers to look ahead to a new development in gay men's online cruising: mobile-phone platforms. Mowlabocus introduced the reader to Grindr, a networking "app" that was only available on phones with geo-location technologies (GPS) and data/WiFi access.[8] The app described in his book was glitchy; it shut down, lost messages, and was largely unknown. But Mowlabocus was adept to observe the ways early Grindr adopters used the platform—for example, while waiting at a bus stop—and argued that the nature of mobile, online cruising might change dramatically.

In the decade following *Gaydar Culture*, a number of scholarly works on gay men's digital cultures did indeed address geo-locative socio-sexual apps (e.g. Grindr, Scruff, Jack'd, Blued) and their effects on gay men's cultures, online and offline.[9] As Mowlabocus predicted, mobile apps had

[7] Sharif Mowlabocus, *Gaydar Culture: Gay Men, Technology and Embodiment* (Farnham: Ashgate, 2010), 15.

[8] Much of this chapter also looks at the cruising possibilities via Bluetooth, though this technique ("Bluejacking") did not develop into a major method of mobile cruising. Mowlabocus, *Gaydar Culture*, 186–187, 194–195.

[9] Aside from the literature cited below, and in the rest of this chapter, other scholarly works that informed my review of geo-social apps and gay men's digital cultures include following: Jed R. Brubaker et al., "Departing Glances: A Sociotechnical Account of 'Leaving' Grindr," *New Media & Society* 18, no. 3 (2014), 373–390; Kane Race, "Speculative Pragmatism and Intimate Arrangements: Online Hook-Up Devices in Gay Life," *Culture, Health & Sexuality* 17, no. 4 (2014): 496–511; Kane Race, "'Party and Play': Online Hook-Up Devices and the Emergence of PNP Practices Among Gay Men," *Sexualities* 18, no. 3 (2015): 253–275; Jean Burgess et al., "Making Digital Cultures of Gender and Sexuality With Social Media," *Social Media + Society* 2, no. 4 (2016).

the power to transform the relationship between physical space and online cruising. Various scholars have supported this hypothesis, for example by arguing that geo-locative platforms challenge the idea that a physical "gay space" needs to be distinct from a straight space since the "grids of the Grindr interface can be overlaid atop any space."[10]

A notable study to underscore the mobile, geo-social aspects of Grindr was "Seeing and being seen: Co-situation and impression formation using Grindr, a location-aware gay dating app" (2015), by Courtney Blackwell, Jeremy Birnholtz, and Charles Abbott. Their study began by challenging the historiography that online spaces and communities "transcend geography" by connecting like-minded users regardless of their physical location. In the age of Grindr, geography mattered more than ever: "The ubiquity of location-aware mobile devices means that today's online interactions are deeply intertwined with offline places and relationships."[11] Blackwell et al. asked how "Grindr co-situates geographically proximate users in a way that transcends and conflates socially defined places and neighborhoods." But not all gay men felt comfortable with Grindr's geo-locative feature, as it had "the potential to cause tension, as people may not wish to be immediately identifiable to anybody nearby who downloads Grindr, and may not wish to be thought of as seeking sex on a mobile app."[12]

Blackwell et al. also presented optimistic narratives about how the geo-social virtual space could augment one's experience in offline spaces. For example, one interviewee spoke to them about being at a non-gay bar, where he:

> [in the interviewee's words] "was feeling very very alienated from everyone else there because… it was a very very straight feeling space". However, with Grindr he was able to locate and chat with another co-situated gay man who was down the street at another straight bar.[13]

---

[10]Yoel Roth, "Zero Feet Away: The Digital Geography of Gay Social Media," *Journal of Homosexuality* 63, no. 3 (2015): 437–442. See also David Gudelunas, "There's an App for That: The Uses and Gratifications of Online Social Networks for Gay Men," *Sexuality & Culture* 16 (2012): 347–365.

[11]Courtney Blackwell et al., "Seeing and Being Seen: Co-Situation and Impression Formation Using Grindr, a Location-Aware Gay Dating App," *New Media & Society*, 17 (2015): 1117.

[12]Brett A. Bumgarner, "Mobilizing the Gay Bar: Grindr and the Layering of Spatial Context," paper presented at the *Conference of the International Communication Association*, London, UK, 17–21 June 2013; cited in Blackwell et al., "Seeing and Being Seen," 1122.

[13]Blackwell et al., "Seeing and Being Seen," 1126.

Neither the interviewee nor his Grindr contact was located in a gay space physically. But Grindr was able to become "a gay place" that "was accessed from and layered on top of a range of physical places."[14] Gay men in all sorts of "mainstream" (heterosexual) spaces might use the app to connect to a gay network. Similarly and in a European context, Alexander Dhoest, Lukasz Szulc, and Bart Eeckhout argued that geo-social apps like Grindr provided "new possibilities of overlaying physical spaces with LGBTQ-related data."[15] Location-aware apps changed users' relationship with their immediate surroundings.

Related, new research has also questioned Grindr's role in the closing of (offline) LGBTQ spaces. To begin with the dominant theory: some scholars argued that platforms like Grindr "displace (when deployed) the regular need for specific physical gay meeting venues… reducing the motivation and frequency of long distance leisure commuting" to urban gay spaces.[16] Also outside of academia, this has been a popular topic: "Gay Dance Clubs on the Wane in the Age of Grindr," proclaimed the journalist Michael Musto in the New York Times in 2016. Musto—who had reported on gay life in New York for decades—noticed a decline in weekly dance parties, and—after speaking with club promoters and performers—kept hearing the same things: "In this digital age, clubs have been usurped by the right swipe"; "why pay an expensive cover charge and deal with rude bouncers when you can just swipe on your iPhone?"; "social media changed the landscape of going out."[17] Similarly, a bartender told a reporter in New Orleans the same thing: "You could ask any bartender in New Orleans whether the apps have affected business in gay bars, and they would all say yes."[18]

[14] Ibid.

[15] Alexander Dhoest et al., "Introduction," in *LGBTQs, Media, and Culture in Europe*, eds. Alexander Dhoest et al. (London: Routledge, 2017), 2.

[16] Alan Collins and Stephen Drinkwater, "Fifty Shades of Gay: Social and Technological Change, Urban Deconcentration and Niche Enterprise," *Urban Studies* 54, no. 3 (2017): 765–785.

[17] Michael Musto, "Gay Dance Clubs on the Wane in the Age of Grindr," *The New York Times*, 26 April 2016, https://www.nytimes.com/2016/04/28/fashion/gay-dance-clubs-grindr.html.

[18] Chris Staudinger, "Loading More Guys: Shining a Light on Gay Dating in the App Age," *Antigravity*, May 2017, http://www.antigravitymagazine.com/2017/05/loading-more-guys-shining-a-light-on-gay-dating-in-the-app-age/.

These various claims led geographers Ryan Centner and Martin Zebracki to organize two panels on urban gay spaces at the 2017 Royal Geographical Society (with the Institute of British Geographers) Conference.[19] Importantly, the panels underscored the role of gentrification (not just socio-sexual apps) in shifting the gay urban landscape. Greggor Mattson noted that gay bar decline can be uneven: in the United States, bars in smaller cities and/or frequented by women and people of color are hardest hit.[20] Wouter Van Gent and Gerald Brugman argued that gay urban spaces might be less important to white, middle-class men (in Amsterdam and New York), but these spaces are central to the identity formation of men with immigration background.[21]

Somewhat related, Grindr studies also differ from previous studies of gay men's digital cultures by emphasizing the near-constant accessibility of mobile apps. Cultural studies scholar Kane Race (University of Sydney) has noted how geo-social apps like Grindr and Scruff enable gay men to engage with the app casually at various times of the day by sending things like a "tap" on Grindr or a "woof" on Scruff, which Race describes as "signal[s] of interest," "noncommittal token[s] of appreciation," and gestures that—along with other quick communications—can

> ...punctuate, enhance, distract, enliven, infiltrate, frustrate or otherwise interfere with the mundane rhythms and activities of everyday life.[22]

---

[19]Ryan Centner and Martin Zebracki, "Gay Male Urban Spaces After Grindr & Gentrification," call for papers for the Annual Conference of the Royal Geographical Society with Institute of British Geographers 2017, http://www.zebracki.org/cfp-rgs-ibg-2017-gay-male-urban-spaces/.

[20]Greggor Mattson, "Centering Provincial Gay Life," Paper at the Annual Conference of the Royal Geographical Society with Institute of British Geographers 2017, http://conference.rgs.org/AC2017/338.

[21]Wouter Van Gent and Gerald Brugman, "Emancipation and the City: The Fragmented Spatiality of Migrant Gay Men in Amsterdam & New York," Paper at the Annual Conference of the Royal Geographical Society with Institute of British Geographers 2017, http://conference.rgs.org/AC2017/306.

[22]Kane Race, *The Gay Science: Intimate Experiments with the Problem of HIV* (London: Routledge, 2018), Chapter 7 (page numbers not yet available). As the book mainly explores contemporary issues related to HIV, Race observes that people are more likely to include personal information about HIV status and safer sex practices on web-based profiles (and thus less so on apps, where people tend to check in casually).

An app integrates social media and/or the act of cruising into one's mobile life and practices. These various Grindr studies confirm Mowlabocus' prediction that mobile apps could transform gay men's relationship to online cruising and offline spaces.

Grindr studies, however, also point to continuities between earlier gay men's digital cultures (e.g. web sites) and mobile app cultures. First, there are continuities with regard to self-presentation strategies. Often grounding their analyses in the early works of Erving Goffman on self-presentation—namely the "front stage, back stage" theories from the 1950s—various scholars have examined when and how gay men show face photos,[23] how they discuss masculinity,[24] how they avoid being perceived to be a "slut"[25] in their public profiles or within the online culture more generally, and so forth. Some of this research has been cross-cultural: for example, Lik Sam Chan used statistical analysis of men's photos on Jack'd (similar to Grindr) to conclude that "Chinese MSM were less likely to show their faces on Jack'd than American MSM because of the stronger stigma of homosexuality in China."[26] This is an interesting analysis, but the geo-social aspect of the platform is not key to his research questions; in this regard, one can see that there are continuities between the chat- and web-based digital research that developed in and since the 1990s, and today's geo-social apps.

Another continuity is that researchers in public health have used Grindr to observe gay men's behaviors regarding topics like safer sex or drug use;

---

[23] E.g. Brandon Miller, "'Dude, Where's Your Face?' Self-Presentation, Self-Description, and Partner Preferences on a Social Networking Application for Men Who Have Sex with Men: A Content Analysis," *Sexuality & Culture* 19, no. 4 (2015): 637–658; Lik Sam Chan, "How Sociocultural Context Matters in Self-Presentation: A Comparison of U.S. and Chinese Profiles on Jack'd, a Mobile Dating App for Men Who Have Sex With Men," *International Journal of Communication* 10 (2016): 6040–6059. An interesting study in Taiwan theorized Scruff (similar to Grindr) as a synopticon, where the many headless torsos observe the few who show their faces on profiles: Cheng-Nan Hou, "An Aggregated Interface of Xingtian Gods in Synopticon: Theorizing the Picture of Using Western Gay LBRTD App in a Chinese Perspective," paper presented at the Conference of the International Communication Association, Fukuoka, Japan, 9–13 June 2016.

[24] Miller, "'Dude, Where's Your Face"; Light, "Networked Masculinities", Light, "Introducing Masculinity Studies to Information Systems Research."

[25] Chan, "How Sociocultural Context Matters in Self-Presentation"; Terri D. Conley, "Perceived Proposer Personality Characteristics and Gender Differences in Acceptance of Casual Sex Offers," *Journal of Personality and Social Psychology* 100 (2011): 309–329.

[26] Lik Sam Chan, "How Sociocultural Context Matters," 6040, 6052.

related, public health researchers have used mobile apps to recruit potential interviewees, as they did also via earlier gay men's platforms.[27]

Finally, a crucial continuity is that Grindr studies continue to interrogate the roles of race and racism in gay men's digital cultures. Studies on "sexual racism" today tend to have a socio-sexual-media component, and Jesus G. Smith focused on platforms specifically geared at gay men in his book chapter "Two-faced Racism in Gay Online Sex: Preference in the Frontstage or Racism in the Backstage?" in the edited volume *Sex in the Digital Age*.[28] In his ethnographic work on socio-sexual platforms in Texas, Smith observed that white users tended to "disguise racist desire in multiracial spaces" through the language of "preferences."[29]

The concept of intersectionality—as it arose from black feminist critique—emphasizes that discrimination on multiple axes (e.g. race and sex) can be synergistic: an individual does not merely experience the additive aspects of discriminations (e.g. racism plus sexism) but can feel a larger weight as these systems of power operate in various contexts.[30] Research on race in gay men's digital cultures is inherently intersectional, and must acknowledge how multiple power structures interact with an individual. In order for one to historicize race in Grindr cultures today, one must look at intersectional studies of gay men's digital cultures in the decades prior, as this chapter does.

Just as many Grindr studies draw from Mowlabocus' work on gay website cultures, so too did Mowlabocus build his arguments from observations of gay men's chat rooms and message boards in the previous decades.

[27] E.g. Earl Burrell et al., "Use of the Location-Based Social Networking Application GRINDR as a Recruitment Tool in Rectal Microbicide Development Research," *AIDS and Behavior* 16, no. 7 (2012): 1816–1820.

[28] Jesus G. Smith, "Two-Faced Racism in Gay Online Sex: Preference in the Frontstage or Racism in the Backstage?" in *Sex in the Digital Age*, eds. Paul Nixon and Isabel Düsterhöft (New York: Routledge, 2018), 135–136.

[29] Smith, "Two-Faced Racism," 144.

[30] Kimberlé Crenshaw, "Demarginalizing the Intersection of Race and Sex: A Black Feminist Critique of Antidiscrimination Doctrine, Feminist Theory and Antiracist Politics," *University of Chicago Legal Forum*, 1989, no. 1 (1989): 139–167; Patricia Hill Collins, *Black Feminist Thought: Knowledge, Consciousness, and the Politics of Empowerment*, 2nd ed. (New York, NY: Routledge, 2000); (in a Danish context) Dorthe Staunæs, "Where Have All the Subjects Gone? Bringing Together the Concepts of Intersectionality and Subjectification," *NORA—Nordic Journal of Feminist and Gender Research* 11, no. 2 (2003): 101–110; Andrew DJ Shield, "Grindr Culture: Intersectional and Socio-Sexual," *Ephemera: Theory & Politics in Organization* 18, no. 1 (2018).

Thus we take a trip back to the early 1990s in order to overview an historiography of gay men's digital cultures and race online. In doing so, the reader will also get a look into my own life coming-of-age as a white, gay, U.S. American with internet access.

Historicizing Grindr Culture

Thinking Beyond Web 1.0 and Web 2.0: An Overview of Periodization

I divide my experiences with online media into three periods: 1995–2003 could be "the mainstreaming of online socializing"; 2004–2009 could be "the mainstreaming of social-networking profiles and social media"; and 2010–2019 could be "the mainstreaming of mobile platforms and geo-social media," or "the transition of social media platforms onto mobile (often geo-locative) smartphone apps." While I begin with my general first impressions of online cultures as a pre-teen (1995–1997), I generally focus on how my gay identity overlapped with online media during these three periods. The reader will see that there were rarely moments of dramatic change with regard to how my online and offline worlds interacted; rather, I integrated technological developments into my life in small and continuous increments.

One often hears of a division between the textual internet of (so-called) Web 1.0 and the user-generated-content-driven internet of (so-called) Web 2.0, which coincided with the development of multimedia platforms like Facebook and YouTube circa 2004–2006; some media scholars even refer to Web 2.0 as a "revolution" that sparked "all sorts of new styles and modes of interconnection."[31] Yet as media scholars like Nancy Baym caution—and as the following personal narrative also shows—"one must wonder what content on the textual internet and much of Web 1.0 was *not* generated by users."[32] Indeed, even in the 1990s my internet experience included making internet profiles, building networks of friends, and sharing media with these networks. At the same time, I observed a change in the ways especially "mainstream" audiences socialized around 2004–2006 with the

[31] Some refer to Web 2.0 as "revolution" that sparked such as "online dating" in the early 2000s: Robert V. Kozinets, *Netnography: Redefined* (Los Angeles: Sage, 2015), 7.

[32] Nancy K. Baym, *Personal Connections in the Digital Age*, 2nd ed. (Malden, MA: Polity Press, 2015), 12 (of the digital version of Chapter 1, as downloaded from the Danish Royal Library).

popularization of profile-network sites, particularly Facebook. Like Baym, I shy away from the labels Web 1.0 and Web 2.0; after all, it's still the same network of cables and the same http:// addresses. But my periodization does acknowledge the tremendous developments in the ways people used the internet around 2004–2006, and then since 2010 with the proliferation of mobile-phone applications.[33] Nodding to media scholars Nichole Ellison and danah boyd, my periodization recognizes not only technological advances, but also large-scale changes in social behaviors online.[34]

Before My Time

In *Gaydar Culture*, Mowlabocus argued that "gay men have integrated platforms such as the Internet into their everyday lives as a direct consequence of the immediate history of gay male subculture."[35] An important component of this immediate history was the *printed* gay/lesbian periodical, which served not only to raise consciousness about LGBTQ identifies and politics, but also to connect LGBTQ people to one another via contact ads.[36] Although the popularity of these printed ads dwindled with the rise of internet technologies, there are marked similarities in the ways users communicated in printed ads and online.

Anyone who has read my historic work knows my fascination with twentieth-century gay and lesbian personal advertisements. However, printed ads—and magazines more generally—were not part of my gay coming-of-age. That being said, it is possible to draw some connections between printed personal ads, early internet web forums and profiles, and

[33] Ibid.

[34] "While the technical and business aspects of Web 2.0 are significant in and of themselves, more germane to this discussion are the cultural shifts that came with Web 2.0": Nicole B. Ellison and danah boyd, "Sociality Through Social Network Sites," in *The Oxford Handbook of Internet Studies*, ed. William H. Dutton (Oxford: Oxford University Press, 2013), 151–172.

[35] Mowlabocus, 24 (and see Chapter 2 more generally). See also Jan Willem Duyvendak and Mattias Duyves, "Gai Pied After Ten Years: A Commercial Success, A Moral Bankruptcy?" *Journal of Homosexuality* 25, nos. 1–2 (1993): 205–213.

[36] Andrew DJ Shield, "'Suriname—Seeking a Lonely, Lesbian Friend for Correspondence': Immigration and Homo-Emancipation in the Netherlands, 1965–79," *History Workshop Journal* 78, no. 1 (2014): 246–264; Andrew DJ Shield, *Immigrants in the Sexual Revolution: Perceptions and Participation in Northwest Europe* (Cham, Switzerland: Palgrave Macmillan, 2017), Chapter 7.

Grindr profiles today.[37] An interesting stop on the jump from printed ads to web posts—known to few today—was the minitel.

In 1992, Dutch scholar Mattias Duyves became one of the first to analyze gay men's digital cultures when he studied a pre-worldwide-web technology called the minitel[38] with regard to its potential in connecting gay men.[39] The minitel allowed for anonymity—as users could communicate without phone numbers or postal addresses—and thus mirrored aspects of cruising parks, toilets, piers, bars, and other "offline" spaces. (Male cruising subcultures have been documented—largely in police reports—since the 1700s in the Netherlands, France, and England,[40] and the 1800s in Denmark.[41]) Entitled "The minitel: the glittering future of a new invention," Duyves' article failed to predict the imminent extinction of the technology; but Duyves was sharp to observe that the "glittering future" of gay and queer cruising would move online.

[37]For example, in the ways users self-identify (e.g. with regard to labels about ethnicity, coloring, masculinity, stature); the spectrum of relationships that users seek (e.g. friendship, romance, casual sex, logistical information); and the fact that users who communicate through the medium often seek to meet in person. See also: H.G. Cocks, *Classified: The Secret History of the Personal Column* (London: Random House Books, 2009); and more generally about the relationship between historic media and social media: Lee Humphreys, *The Qualified Self: Social Media and the Cataloguing of Everyday Life* (Cambridge: MIT Press, 2018).

[38]The Minitel was a pre-worldwide-web, closed-network videotext system that was popular particularly in France in the late 1980s and early 1990s, mainly for those seeking directories of phone numbers and addresses. See also: Anna Livia, "Public and Clandestine: Gay Men's Pseudonyms on the French Minitel," *Sexualities* 5, no. 2 (2002): 201–217; Julien Mailland and Kevin Driscoll, *Minitel: Welcome to the Internet* (Cambridge, MA: MIT Press, 2017).

[39]Mathias Duyves, "The Minitel: The Glittering Future of a New Invention," *Journal of Homosexuality* 25, nos. 1–2 (1993): 193–203. With the Minitel, one did not need to correspond via mailed letters to home addresses; nor did one need to exchange long and personal letters and photographs. Duyves wrote that the Minitel "influenced gay communication immediately, heavily and constantly."

[40]Theo van der Meer, "Sodomy and the Pursuit of a Third Sex in the Early Modern Period," in *Third Sex, Third Gender: Beyond Sexual Dimorphism in Culture and History*, ed. Gilbert Herdt (New York: Zone Books, 1994); Randolph Trumbach, "Renaissance Sodomy, 1500–1700" and "Modern Sodomy: The Origins of Modern Homosexuality, 1700–1800," in *A Gay History of Britain*, ed. Matt Cook (Westport, CT: Greenwood, 2007); Jeffrey Merrick, *Order and Disorder Under the Ancien Régime* (Newcastle: Cambridge Scholars Publishing, 2007).

[41]Wilhelm von Rosen, "A Short History of Gay Denmark 1613–1989: The Rise and the Possibly Happy End of the Danish Homosexual," *Nordisk Sexologi* 12 (1994): 125–136.

The Minitel and other early internet technologies—chat rooms, message boards, and eventually dating sites—connected the correspondence culture of (printed) personal ads with the anonymous cruising central to so many gay male (often urban) cultures.[42] Understanding these historical precedents to Grindr culture contextualize users' practices online today.

PERIOD 1, 1994–2003: THE MAINSTREAMING OF ONLINE SOCIALIZING

First Impressions of Online Media and Its Social Technologies

There are several origin stories of "the internet" (e.g. beginning with the U.S. Department of Defense in 1969), but this is not one of them.[43] Others have written about their early internet usage which far precedes mine: Baym, for example, was already in the 1970s as a teenager chatting anonymously with other uses of a computer network developed at the university in her town.[44] When I was born in 1984 in Massachusetts, there was already a vast network of cables and computers connecting government offices and research facilities into a "cyberspace" that brought together "hobbyists, intellectuals, and academics" via email, message boards, and some gaming dungeons.[45]

I lived in a single-parent household in a largely affluent Boston suburb where some of my friends' parents worked for technology companies or at universities like M.I.T., and I knew a few people with computers in their homes in the early 1990s. My mother bought our first personal computer in 1992, an Apple Macintosh, similar to the ones that my public (i.e. state) school started to amass. At home and at school, these computers

---

[42] On lesbian experiences: Tamara Chaplin, "Lesbians Online: Queer Identity and Community Formation on the French Minitel," *Journal of the History of Sexuality* 22, no. 3 (2014): 451–472.

[43] E.g. Kevin Driscoll, "Hobbyist Inter-Networking and the Popular Internet Imaginary: Forgotten Histories of Networked Personal Computing, 1978–1998" (PhD diss., University of Southern California, 2014); or Baym, *Personal Connections in the Digital Age*, 9–10 (of the digital file of Chapter 1).

[44] Baym, *Personal Connections in the Digital Age*, 9 (of the digital file of Chapter 1).

[45] Lisa Nakamura, *Cybertypes: Race, Ethnicity, and Identity on the Internet* (New York and London: Routledge, 2002), 114.

only provided "offline" support: word processing, semi-educational computer games, and—when the mouse became more widespread—some basic drawing programs.[46]

For me, the internet began in 1995 while visiting family friends in New York who worked for IBM. They had a dial-up modem and America Online (AOL), a software that transformed the confusing and black-and-white world of the internet into a user-friendly interface with clickable buttons and colorful graphics that gave access to email, chat rooms, direct messaging, buddy lists, message boards, "portals" with AOL's content, and other features. With the adults' help (and after some pleading), I was allowed to sign in with one of their screen names where I could click into the "Kids" portal. The portal had games and written content, but I was mostly intrigued by the chat room.

I had never before used a computer to communicate with a stranger, and was very excited to do so. Once inside,[47] I posted first to the general group to introduce myself, probably with something like "Hi I am 10 years old and have a pet turtle!!" I followed the group's incongruous conversations, and wound up chatting one-on-one (via Instant Message, or IM) with a few other users (with the adults nearby, half-monitoring[48]). When I announced to the chat room that I had to leave, one user wrote "bye, [screen name]" which warmed me. The computer felt like an entirely different machine now that I knew it could facilitate personal connections with people from across the United States (or even the world).

The chat room experience was so memorable that when I returned to school, I wrote a (prescient) creative fairy tale based on Cinderella about two socially awkward and not-particularly attractive people (Cinderella and

---

[46] At my school, these computers arrived gradually: first one per grade, then one per classroom, then 3–4 per classroom by 1995. Non-mouse computer games in school included Oregon Trail, Word Munchers, and Number Munchers. One teacher recounted that a few years prior, there was one computer at the whole school, which he helped roll to a vaulted room at the end of every week.

[47] It took persistence to enter my these early chat rooms, as they tended to be "full" (at thirty users or so) and one had to mindlessly click on the chat room button repeatedly until a user left.

[48] My friends' parents reacted differently to fears they had about children chatting with strangers online. At first, one friend's father insisted on sitting with us and approving every message we sent; one time, he wouldn't let us mention the name or even *the breed* of my friend's dog (out of privacy concerns). My mother probably told me to behave cautiously in chat rooms (e.g. not providing my full name), but I don't recall being monitored.

the Prince) who met and fell in love on the internet. Intrigued fiction-readers can refer the footnote.[49]

My sister went off to college in 1996, and took our first computer with her.[50] My mother replaced our home computer with a newer Macintosh (with a CD drive!) and decided it was time to get the internet. Following the lead of our friends in New York (and other friends and family), my mother bought a subscription to AOL, for which we initially had to pay *by the minute* for internet access (though this changed within a year or so).[51] Since we only had one phone line, I was limited to short periods online, usually in the afternoons after school and before my mother came home from work.

The idea of "surfing the web" (outside of AOL's portals) was pretty uninteresting to me: each photograph downloaded painfully slowly, sound files were limited to the electronic blips of Midi music, and videos were non-existent. I associated the worldwide web with boring business websites and colorless message boards. AOL's "online media" did not replace the news-papers, radio, or television that we consumed at home.[52] AOL had its own content, but it was not our primary reason to use the platform. Instead, the "online media" we consumed in the 1990s was primarily "social."

[49] In the illustrated story (entitled "**Cind.E.r**"), Cinderella—who was shy, and not beau-tiful—fantasized about marrying the Prince. The night of the Prince's ball—when he would choose a Princess—Cinderella's evil stepmother and stepsisters abandoned her. So Cin-derella—lonely and bored—was met by her Fairy Godmother who granted her one wish: a computer; with internet.

Cinderella made the screen name "Cind.E.r" and went into a chat room. But the chat room was empty, since everyone was at the ball! Everyone, except for one other user: "Prints2". Meanwhile, the Prince—who it turned out was also ugly and shy—had skipped his own ball so he could sit in his room and play online. That night, Cind.E.r and Prints2 chatted, bonded, fell in love, and then—just as the Prince "came out" about his true identity—the clock struck midnight and— *poof!*—Cinderella's computer disappeared. The Prince's men had to go door-to-door asking every young maiden to guess the Prince's screen name. Cinderella was the perfect match, and they lived happily ever after. Andrew Shield, "Cind.E.r," unpublished, 1995.

[50] She was able to hook it up to her university's Ethernet, which was free to all students.

[51] We had to "dial up" to get online, which took anywhere from one to five minutes, and culminated in a nonsense cacophony of blips and beeps and static that somehow resembled a song that I can still sing in my head today.

[52] At my mother's house, *The Boston Globe* was (and still is) delivered each morning, National Public Radio and local public radio was (and still is) played in the background from morning till evening, and network television was the main source for local news and entertainment (and still is, augmented by cable television and streaming services).

As I entered high school (1999), and throughout, the majority of my classmates' internet use centered on socializing with classmates, keeping in touch with friends from summer camp, and maintaining "offline" connections through email and IM. As far as I knew, most of my friends did not use online spaces to connect with strangers like I did.

Gay Chat Rooms

As a teenager, I was particularly interested in chatting with gay strangers about the topics I was too afraid to discuss with my "real" friends: feelings, desires, and questions about sexuality. From time to time, I found gay-themed chat rooms on AOL, but they were chaotic: there were those looking for "cybersex" (i.e. sexy chat conversations); those hoping to find someone in their physical proximity, so they could meet in real life; those looking to chat about gay culture and politics; and so forth.[53]

I was participating in what communication scholar Howard Rheingold had dubbed "virtual communities" (in his 1993 book), which were online spaces that fostered interpersonal relationships and social networks.[54] Within these communities,[55] there were new ways that participants expressed social cues to each other, as Baym was researching (in 1995), including the ways users conveyed emotion, facial expressions, physical body language, and movements within text-only environments.[56] LGBTQ AOL users flocked to these virtual communities disproportionately: of *Wired* magazine's Top 10 AOL Chatrooms in 1994, three were

[53] As a 14- or 15-year-old, I provoked different reactions from others: most were usually polite, but some accused me of being a police officer, or told me to leave the room because I was ruining it for the adults. But I never lied about my age, mainly in the hopes of meeting another teenager like myself.

[54] Howard Rheingold, *The Virtual Community: Homesteading on the Electronic Frontier* (Reading, MA: Addison-Wesley, 1993), 5.

[55] Scholarship on online communities has continued to develop: see e.g. Debra Ferreday, *Online Belongings: Fantasy, Affect and Web Communities* (Bern: Peter Lang, 2009); and on activist communities, see Thomas Poell and José van Dijck, "Social Media and Activist Communication," in *The Routledge Companion to Alternative and Community Media*, ed. Chris Atton (London: Routledge, 2015), 527–537.

[56] Nancy K. Baym, "The Emergence of Community in Computer-Mediated Communication," in *CyberSociety: Computer-Mediated Communication and Community*, ed. Steven G. Jones (Thousand Oaks, CA: Sage, 1995), 152.

for men-seeking men, one was for lesbians, and one more for swingers (many of whom were likely bisexual or queer).[57]

In 1999, I "met" Alex in one of these gay chatrooms, and we chatted for hours. Although we lived far away (he in the South, I in the North U.S.), we had a lot in common: we were both closeted teenagers living in suburbs, we both liked French class, we both attended Hebrew school, and we both desperately desired a gay best friend. He sent me a link to his school's webpage, with a science team photo that had his face (and even last name, which we both knew we were not supposed to share with strangers online). His face was tiny in the pixelated, scanned photograph, but I could squint and make sense of what he looked like.[58] Alex and I chatted online daily for two years. We knew all about each other's friends, family, teachers, crushes, and eventually hook-ups. (Later in life, we became Facebook friends, but never felt compelled to meet in real life.)

Also theorizing virtual communities, scholar David Shaw was one of the first to focus on gay chat rooms, which he argued could provide insight into gay men's identities and communities. Interestingly, Shaw was early to note that these communities were not entirely virtual, as face-to-face meetings "remain[ed] the ultimate goal" for many users.[59] Through interviews with and observations of gay men who chatted online, Shaw showed that although many men felt relieved to be in a space where words mattered more than physical bodies, "all of the men actively transgress the bounds of bodilessness" such as by meeting face-to-face, or in the case of Alex, by exchanging photographs."[60] Shaw did not address how gay men's experiences online intersected with other systems of power—racism, ageism, ableism—but his attention to the relationship between the physical body and the online community could be considered an early critique of the

[57] David Shaw, "Gay Men and Computer Communication: A Discourse of Sex and Identity in Cyberspace," in *Virtual Culture: Identity and Communication in Cybersociety*, ed. Steven Jones (London: Sage, 2002).

[58] Unfortunately, I could not link him to any photographs of myself, so I had to get his home address and *snail-mail* him *printed photographs*. This, in retrospect, is hilarious to me.

[59] Shaw, "Gay Men and Computer Communication," 133.

[60] Ibid., 135.

internet as a place where one's body, race, or abilities were invisible (i.e. the Cyberutopia hypothesis).[61]

No to "Cyberutopia": Race Still Matters Online (and Gender, Sexuality Too!)

During these early years of online expression in gay chat rooms and profile sites, I was rarely attuned to my race, or rather, to my whiteness. I benefitted from the fact that whiteness was the unmarked norm in many of these online spaces; the burden of racial identification fell on people of color, and not myself. I had little idea that scholars of digital media were heatedly researching the various ways that race was both absent and omnipresent within online cultures, including gay online cultures.

First, we begin with the concept of "cyberutopia": the idea that in an online world, ideas (and virtual avatars) could transcend bodies. In 1995, sociologist Sherry Turkle wrote *Life on the Screen: Identity in the Age of the Internet*, which included a theory of the "multiple self" online: the online "identity can be fluid and multiple, [as] a signifier no longer clearly points to a thing that is signified."[62] Turkle was optimistic that people could have a "fluid sense of self" online, and could play with diverse identifications. Turkle's work reflected the optimism that many had in the 1990s: that users could play with race, gender, or sexuality online, as bodies became less important; in doing so, online participants would bring postmodern ideas about subjective identities to life. Yet even the so-called utopian scholars— who were naïve with some assertions about disembodied figures—were also cautious with their optimism. Sandy Stone, for example, noted already in 1995 that "no refigured virtual body, no matter how beautiful, will slow the death of a cyberpunk with AIDS"; thus, "even in the age of the techno-social subject, life is lived through bodies."[63]

---

[61] See also Daniel Tsang, "Notes on Queer 'n Asian Virtual Sex," *Amerasia Journal* 20, no. 1 (1994): 117–128; Nina Wakeford, "Cyberqueer," in *Lesbian and Gay Studies: A Critical Introduction*, ed. Andy Medhurst and Sally R. Hunt (London: Cassell, 1997), 20–38.

[62] Sherry Turkle, *Life on the Screen: Identity in the Age of the Internet* (New York: Simon & Schuster, 1995), 49.

[63] Allucquère Rosanne Stone, *The War of Desire and Technology at the Close of the Mechanical Age* (Cambridge, MA: MIT Press, 1995); Mark Poster, *The Second Media Age* (Cambridge, MA: Polity Press, 1996), 113; see also Nakamura, *Cybertypes*, 115.

While Turkle, Stone and others nuanced their celebration of cyberutopia, internet companies oversimplified this idea as they (re)branded themselves in the 1990s. The most notorious offender (as identified in scholarly critiques of cyberutopia) was the 1997 commercial for the internet provider MCI, which proclaimed, "There is no race. There is no gender. There is no age. There are no infirmities. There are only minds. Utopia? No, Internet."[64]

Thus in 2000, media scholars Lisa Nakamura, Beth Kolko, and Gilbert Rodman responded to both scholarly and industry depictions of the race-less and bodiless internet with their anthology *Race in Cyberspace*: "In spite of popular utopian rhetoric to the contrary, we believe that race matters no less in cyberspace than it does 'IRL' (in real life)."[65] Yes, users could construct their identities online, and they did so by choosing nicknames (e.g. for email addresses, chat rooms, and other virtual communities), making avatars, and designing personal websites. But "within such a constructivist environment," the editors wrote, "the construction of identities becomes even more important."[66] Thus, racial identities, logics, and prejudices saturated online cultures, including the nicknames people chose, the limited types of avatars, and the language people used when communicating.

As Beth Kolko wrote, race may be socially constructed, but it is not something that can be either discarded or selected:

> The functions of primordial racelessness and racial voluntarism, while firmly based in a humanist ethos (i.e. "we're all the same under the skin") risk dismissing the very real effect of race in people's lives.... One does not choose the color of one's skin, and although racial identity is constructed, it is never simply chosen.[67]

---

[64] "Anthem," produced for MCI by Messner Vetere Berger McNamee Schemetterer, 1997; available as "MCI TV Ad 1997," YouTube.com, uploaded on 12 October 2010, last accessed Fall 2017 via https://www.youtube.com/watch?v=ioVMoeCbrig. See also discussions in Nakamura, *Cybertypes*, 88–95, including of AT&T's 1996 ad, "Imagine a world without limits."

[65] Beth Kolko, Lisa Nakamura, and Gilbert Rodman, "Introduction," in *Race in Cyberspace*, ed. Kolko, et al. (New York: Routledge, 2000), 4. The anthology addressed diverse topics, such as how white schools in the U.S. had more computer access in the 1990s, which affected the demographics of online participants; or how indigenous Hawaiians worked to preserve their language and culture online.

[66] Kolko et al., "Introduction," 6.

[67] Beth Kolko, "Erasing @race: Going White in the (Inter)Face," in *Race in Cyberspace*, ed. Beth Kolko et al. (New York: Routledge, 2000), 193.

Race—like gender and sexuality—could be "routed around" in a digital culture, meaning that one did not need to disclose these aspects of one's identity; but the "default" assumption was that a given user was "white, male, and heterosexual" until proven otherwise.[68] Overall, there was in 2000 "very little scholarly work that deal[t] with how our notions of race are shaped and challenged by new technologies such as the Internet."

Gay Dating Profiles

In high school, everyone I knew had AOL profiles, where we filled out some of the eight open-ended questions (name, location, marital status, hobbies, quotations). In fact, it was via the advanced search feature on AOL profiles that I connected with my first gay-identified friend "in real life" in 2000; I rollerbladed to the town center and chatted with him on a bench, and a week later, with the support of online friend Alex, rollerbladed directly to his home.

Around this time, I made my first dating profile on PlanetOut.com, a news and community-building website for LGBTQ people (which merged with Gay.com soon after, and no longer exists). According to their website in 2000, there were 150,000 people who had dating profiles, and 700,000 registered users who could interact with each other via message boards and community forums.[69] This online space resembled the culture described in *Gaydar Culture*, but it also resembled the culture of gay chat rooms to which I had grown accustomed; in fact, Mowlabocus cited Shaw's ethnography of chat rooms, and described *Gaydar Culture* as "an extension of, and a response to, his [Shaw's] 1997 article."[70] For example, Mowlabocus also emphasized that users of Gaydar and related websites had the end-goal of physical interaction.

But beyond hoping to meet people in real life, I also found PlanetRomeo to be a space where I could browse the faces, hobbies, and personalities of various gay men, lesbians, and bi and trans people, albeit voyeuristically.

---

[68] David Silver, "Margins in the Wires: Looking for Race, Gender, and Sexuality in the Blacksburg Electronic Village," in *Race in Cyberspace*, ed. Kolko et al. (New York: Routledge, 2000), 143.

[69] "PlanetOut's Online Personal Service Hits 150,000 Milestone," PlanetOut.com, 9 August 2000, last accessed Fall 2017 via Wayback Machine.

[70] Mowlabocus, 7.

Media scholar danah boyd noted that the process of stealthily lurking on others' online profiles could actually increase one's social and cultural capital[71]: "Social voyeurism passes time while providing insight into society at large."[72] PlanetOut.com benefitted my social capital in this way, as I learned about gay and lesbian communities, niche sub-communities, vocabularies, and codes by lurking on profiles for users in the Boston area.

In 2003 during the last months of high school, I joined the social/dating platform XY.com, which was affiliated with a printed magazine *XY* (founded in 1996) with content specifically for gay *youth*.[73] On the online platform, there were hundreds of young guys (usually age 16–21) in the greater Boston area with whom I could chat, flirt, befriend.

Through AOL, PlanetOut, and XY, I met a handful of people "in real life" from 2000–2003. The only high-school friend I knew who met friends online, and dared to meet them offline, was a queer woman, musician, and LiveJournal blogger. Ellison and boyd have referred to LiveJournal as "retrospectively viewable as a cross between blog platforms and SNSs [social network sites]," and thus one of the earliest popular social media.[74] One day she gave me a tutorial of LiveJournal, where she showed me that if she clicked on the hyperlink for "Ani DiFranco," for example, she could see all the other users who shared her interest in this folk-rock icon. Not surprisingly, many of these DiFranco fans were also (young) queer women, and so she followed or connected with them. (One became a bridesmaid at her wedding!) Scholar Marion Wasserbauer has shown this still remains

---

[71] Pierre Bourdieu, "The Forms of Capital," in *Hand-Book of Theory and Research for the Sociology of Education*, ed. J.G. Richardson (New York: Greenwood, 2011 [1985]), 241–258. With some attention to this topic in the context of gay men's dating websites: David Gudelunas, "Online Personal Ads: Community and Sex, Virtually," *Journal of Homosexuality* 49, no. 1 (2005): 62–87.

[72] Danah boyd, "Why Youth < 3 Social Network Sites: The Role of Networked Publics in Teenage Social Life," in *Youth, Identity, and Digital Media*, ed. David Buckingham (The John D. and Catherine T. MacArthur Foundation Series on Digital Media and Learning) (Cambridge, MA: MIT Press, 2008), 127.

[73] The colorful, glossy periodical resembled the teen magazines my female friends read, like *YM*, which were filled with photos of cute teen guys, quizzes, and confessions. The XY profile was very basic: one photo, and a box of open text.

[74] Ellison and boyd, "Sociality Through Social Network Sites," 157.

true today: queer women build sexual identities as they connect to other queer women (often online) over shared interests in female music icons.[75]

Race, Identity Tourism and Gay Chats

In 2002, Nakamura published *Cybertypes: Race, Ethnicity, and Identity on the Internet*, which explored how race was portrayed online; an important part of this work was her critique of "identity tourism," or "passing"[76] as another identity, online.[77] Especially in the text-heavy 1990s and early 2000s, chat rooms and online gaming spaces *did* allow people to pretend to be another race (or sex), which was thought-provoking for some. But the act of pretending to be another race (or sex, etc.) was not necessarily revolutionary, nor synonymous with the challenging of stereotypes: Nakamura highlighted the example of non-Japanese people "masquerading as exotic samurais or horny geishas" in online gaming cultures, which showed that racist, sexist, and anachronistic depictions of Japanese people—promulgated in Western film and television—took on new forms in online subcultures.[78]

Further, Nakamura's *Cybertypes* provided one of the earliest critiques of racial drop-down menus and check-boxes on profile-based websites (Chapter 6 of this book). For example, she noted that many people did not fit the pre-described racial categories in drop-down menus, and that certain racial identities (e.g. mixed identities) were often impossible to select.

Early literature on race in gay men's digital cultures benefitted from the research of those like Nakamura—who argued *against* cyberutopian ideas by arguing that race mattered in all online environments—and those like Shaw—who argued *against* the idea that online communities transcended space, since gay men chatting online often sought to meet face-to-face. Yet a predecessor to both was Daniel C. Tsang, perhaps the first to approach the intersections of race and gay men's online cultures with his 1994 article,

---

[75] Marion Wasserbauer, "'I Think I'm Quite Fluid with Those Kinds of Things': Exploring Music and Non-Heterosexual Women's Identities," in *LGBTQs, Media, and Culture in Europe*, ed. Alexander Dhoest et al. (London: Routledge, 2017), 80–97.

[76] It is important to link the concept of "passing" to the history of light-skinned Americans of African descent "passing" as white in order to access certain privileges afforded only to whites, e.g. in the antebellum and Jim-Crow-era U.S.

[77] Nakamura, *Cybertypes*, 139.

[78] Ibid., xv–xvi, 5, 32–47.

"Notes on Queer 'N Asian in Virtual Sex," which problematized racism in gay online message boards.

Tsang's online ethnographic work engaged with an identity tourism that contrasts Nakamura's "exotic samurais or horny geishas": he, like many gay men of color to follow him, decided to experiment online as white. For his research, Tsang posted on gay message boards as either Asian (his racial identity) or Caucasian, and published about the higher response rate that he received as the Caucasian man.[79] Despite these grim results, Tsang was also optimistic about some aspects of online dating, namely that message boards allowed users to express their racial and ethnic identities in their own words (rather than by checking a box).[80]

Also conducting their research on text-based message boards, Voon Chin Phua and Gayle Kaufman published their 2003 article, "The Cross-roads of Race and Sexuality: Date Selection Among Men in Internet 'Personal' Ads." The article looked at 2400 dating profiles of white-, black-, Asian-, and Latino-identified men in the United States with specific attention to how users posted about their racial preferences. Phua and Kaufman differentiated between (i) those who sought homogamy (i.e. the same race as themselves), (ii) those who sought one specific other race, (iii) those that specified 2–3 races, and (iv) those who specified that they were open to meeting people of all races. The authors deliberated those who sought homogamy: *was this racist?* Phua and Kaufman avoided the word "racist" and indeed sympathized that many men preferred homogamy due to a desire for a shared language or cultural background. But at the same time, the authors presented a more critical hypothesis: "[P]references for homogamy are sometimes structurally reinforced through lack of exposure to people of different cultures and xenophobia."[81] (Discussion of "sexual racism" becomes more prominent especially in the following decade.)[82]

---

[79] Tsang.

[80] Or as Mowlabocus summarized: "Text-based representations of the self allow cultural specificities to come to the fore, bypassing the essentialising category of 'asian-american' and providing users with a greater sense of cultural identity." Mowlabocus, *Gaydar Culture*, 11–12.

[81] Voon Chin Phua and Gayle Kaufman, "The Crossroads of Race and Sexuality: Date Selection Among Men in Internet 'Personal' Ads," *Journal of Family Issues* 8 (November 2003): 984.

[82] E.g. Denton Callander et al., "Is Sexual Racism Really Racism? Distinguishing Attitudes Toward Sexual Racism and Generic Racism Among Gay and Bisexual Men," *Archives of Sexual Behavior* 44 (2015): 1991–2000.

Tsang was not the only researcher engaging in ethnographic work that doubled as "identity tourism." In the late 1990s and early 2000s, sociologist Andil Gosine engaged with experimental fieldwork on Gay.com, although he would not publish it for several years. A seasoned user of Gay.com's website and chat rooms, Gosine decided to log in with ethnic/racial self-presentations that were different from his Indian-American identity.[83] Of all his online identities, "the most fun to inhabit" was "Robbie":

> Robbie fit my own physical description except, importantly, that he was blonde and blue-eyed. I enjoyed the most attention from other online chatters than in any other representation of myself. I was overwhelmed with requests for private window conversations and many times I was chatting separately but simultaneously with five or six of the thirty users in the room. Changing only information about hair and eye color to indicate a white identity, I was invited to participate in conversations with many more men and had an altogether different experience than when my descriptor indicated that I was non-white.[84]

As media scholar Richard Dyer wrote about whiteness in 1997: white people can "blithely carry on as if what they say is neutral and unsituated—human not raced."[85]

With Dyer's assertion in mind, Gosine reflected on *why* he desired to "play" or "pass" as white on Gay.com: presenting himself as white online was not just for fun, nor was it because he desired *to be* white; rather, he wanted to experience the digital space *without race*.[86] Indeed, my whiteness was likely a crucial factor in my ability to connect with gay men in chat rooms, on dating websites, and consequently in real life in the Boston area. The fact that I was unaware of this supports the assertions made by Gosine and Nakamura, among others, that racial awareness has always been central to the lives of (queer) people of color online.

---

[83] Andil Gosine, "Brown to Blonde at Gay.com: Passing White in Queer Cyberspace," in *Queer Online: Media Technology and Sexuality*, ed. Kate O'Riordan et al. (New York: Peter Lang, 2007), "Brown to Blonde," 141.

[84] Gosine, "Brown to Blonde," 147.

[85] Richard Dyer, *White* (New York: Routledge, 1997), 4.

[86] Gosine, "Brown to Blonde," 150.

Gay Porn

At school in 1997, a librarian tried to teach us how to use the internet for research, and introduced us to search engines like Altavista.[87] I glanced over to my classmate, who had immediately stumbled onto a porn website. Like many curious teenagers, I too took an interest in the world of pornography.[88] For the sake of brevity, I will not dwell on gay porn's (largely positive) role in my sexual education.[89] Rather, I will defer again to Dyer, who had already written this defense of (pre-digital) gay pornography in 1985:

> Homosexual desire has been constructed as perverse and unspeakable; gay porn does speak/show gay sex. Gay porn asserts homosexual desire, it turns the definition of homosexual desire on its head, says bad is good, sick is healthy and so on. It thus defends the universal human practice of same-sex physical contact (which our society constructs as homosexual). It has made life bearable for countless millions of gay men.[90]

If I had read that defense during my dial-up internet days, I would have concurred: gay porn did make life a little more bearable during those years. And better, I did not have to sneak into a corner store to steal it, as some

---

[87] The first thing I ever searched was "Andrew Shield," and I found a professional sports photographer in Australia with a beautiful, colorful website filled with surfers and wind boarders. He's still at it: andrewshield.com.au and on Instagram as andrewshield.

[88] In the 1990s, most porn sites illegally circulated scanned images from printed magazines. For a mediocre film depicting this early era of internet porn: *Middle Men*, dir. George Gallo (Hollywood, CA: Paramount Pictures, 2009). See also Jeffrey Escoffier, *Bigger Than Life: The History of Gay Porn Cinema from Beefcake to Hardcore* (Philadelphia: Running Press, 2009).

[89] This education was augmented by my public-school health classes and the syndicated radio show *Love Line*. On the sensitive topic of how and what young teenagers (might) learn from watching porn—and note that I have some concerns with the conclusions in this study—see Ine Beyens et al., "Early Adolescent Boys' Exposure to Internet Pornography: Relationships to Pubertal Timing, Sensation Seeking, and Academic Performance," *The Journal of Early Adolescence* 35, no. 8 (2015). Beyens' research has asserted that teenagers learn from the porn they watch; but she measured for banal factors, like the idea that both partners should climax, or that partners need to change positions multiple times during a sexual encounter.

[90] Richard Dyer, "Male Gay Porn: Coming to Terms," *Jump Cut (A Review of Contemporary Media)*, no. 30 (March 1985), https://www.ejumpcut.org/archive/onlinessays/JC30folder/GayPornDyer.html.

teenagers surely did when Dyer wrote this tract. Rather, I could find free images that "assert[ed] homosexual desire" from the comfort of my home.

PERIOD 2, 2004–2009: THE MAINSTREAMING OF SOCIAL-NETWORKING PROFILES AND SOCIAL MEDIA

From the "Face Book" to thefacebook.com

Upon arrival at Brown University in 2003, I received a key to my dorm room, an ID card, and the "Face Book," which was a *printed booklet* that had the name, high school, and small black-and-white thumbnail portrait of each of the 1400 incoming students in our class (excluding the handful who forgot or refused to submit a photograph). There I sat frozen in time with this one photograph, the staged yearbook portrait I grew to loathe. My classmates and I cherished our Face Books, which we dog-eared and highlighted as we "stalked" classmates and crushes.[91]

Despite the analog Face Book that structured my social voyeurism, I was partially aware of profile-based websites, to which some of my friends belonged. As danah boyd summarized about her 2004 research on Friendster (an early social network site): the platform "gained traction among three groups of early adopters who shaped the site—bloggers, attendees of the Burning Man arts festival, and gay men."[92] Indeed, a handful of my friends who first discussed Friendster were also LiveJournal bloggers; otherwise, Friendster had a niche among the soon-to-be-named-"hipster" crowd more generally. Similarly, a handful of friends were active on Make-OutClub, an early social-networking and dating site for those interested in underground ("indie" and "emo") art and music. Another friend was active with SuicideGirls, a site and virtual community that featured tattooed and pierced pin-up models, as well as (goth, punk, metal) lay users, who wrote posts, communicated in message boards, and periodically held offline events. These examples from my social circles show that online social networking beyond email and IM was considered "alternative" in 2003,

---

[91] The Face Book was also made available online, which facilitated searching if one knew the first name of a classmate; but students had no ability to change their photo or update personal information.

[92] danah boyd, and Nicole B. Ellison, "Social Network Sites: Definition, History, and Scholarship," *Journal of Computer-Mediated Communication* 13, no. 2 (2007): 216.

and was most attractive to niche audiences (i.e. gay, emo, indie, goth, punk, metal). But a more mainstream audience was about to get targeted: college students.

For most people my age, the "mainstreaming" of social-networking sites coincided almost immediately with the arrival of Facebook—or www. thefacebook.com at the time—a profile site for anyone with an elite university email address (2004), and then for anyone with any university email address (2005), and then for everyone with any email address (since 2006). Facebook had started at Harvard a few months before it trickled to Brown in April 2004.[93]

In its first 48 hours at Brown, thousands of students made Facebook profiles.[94] At this time, Facebook profiles were very simple: one small profile photo, a few drop-down menus (e.g. "interested in:" men and/or women; "looking for:" friendship, dating, random play, whatever I can get), and a few open-ended questions.[95] But overall the effects that Facebook had on my offline life were gradual. Many of the more dramatic changes came incrementally from 2005–2009, such as the ability to share photos, to tag friends in posts, to browse a "news feed" of friends' recent activity, or to create event invitations.

But there was one social change I felt instantly: I now had immediate access to many classmates' sexual orientation.[96] (The default privacy

---

[93] For an interesting dramatization of Facebook's foundation in the context of printed "face books" and early social networking and dating sites, see the first third of the 2010 film *The Social Network*. David Fincher et al., *The Social Network* (Culver City, CA: Sony Pictures Home Entertainment, 2011).

[94] Most heard about it immediately through word-of-mouth, but some knew about it already from friends at other Ivy League schools. For many years, one' Facebook URL was actually the number that the user joined at a university. A few of my friends resisted joining, either because they declared loyalty to Friendster (or other websites), or because they were hesitant to share their face and other personal information on the internet. Upon making my profile, I amassed over a hundred "friends" in one day.

[95] Finally, students could link to their classes, which had the effect of transforming the physical bodies seated in a lecture hall into a digital page through which one could browse one's classmates' profiles.

[96] Prior to Facebook, I had three options for figuring out if someone was openly gay: ask the person directly; ask someone who knew the person; or guess, based on behavior, dress, or eye contact. This changed with Facebook, as this anecdote shows: On my first day on Facebook, I stumbled across a friend of a friend of a friend who I recognized immediately: my mailroom crush! Before the arrival of Facebook, the best that I could hope for was that I would run into him at a party and strike up a conversation. But now, I could learn his name (Zach), his class

settings—which few people adjusted—meant that anyone at Brown could view the profile of anyone else at Brown without restriction.) Facebook's search function was rather invasive at this time; it was easy to perform an advanced search for male Facebook users who were "Interested in: Men." With the click of a button or two, I readily had a list of four-dozen gay male classmates, many of whom I had never seen at the LGBTQ student group. The "gay community" at Brown—a debatable concept—was no longer a gathering of people at monthly meetings; it could now be enumerated through a Facebook search.[97]

In the summer of 2005, I made a profile on MySpace, which had a loyal user base of Providence-area hipsters, partly because—as Ellison and boyd have also shown—MySpace attracted indie rock bands and their fans by showcasing music pages.[98] It was socially acceptable to connect with strangers on MySpace, and the home page encouraged new users to gather friends by offering a list of "Cool new people" on their home screen. The day I joined MySpace, a guy messaged me from Pennsylvania who had also just joined MySpace and stumbled across my profile. We started writing back and forth. We met in person four months later. We dated for five years.

During these years, Australian media scholar Ben Light began studying how conceptions of masculinity circulated on men's social network sites (like PlanetOut),[99] as well as how gay men became targeted as a consumer

year ('06), his relationship status (Single), and his avowed sexual orientation: "Interested in: Women." Damn! A brief moment of heartbreak. But maybe I could find someone else?

[97] During orientation week, I began to meet members of the LGBT student group to make gay friends or a boyfriend, and I gradually stopped checking my XY and PlanetOut profiles. Over the next years, I browsed a few new gay websites, which in many ways resembled PlanetOut, except that (at least it felt like) there were more users exchanging more messages and more digital photos than before. I learned about a few websites that were more "cruise-y," like Manhunt.net (f. 2001), Gay.com's chatrooms, and Cragislist's personal ads. When I traveled to Europe for the first time, I also used Gaydar (f. 1999).

[98] boyd and Ellison, "Social Network Sites," 220. MySpace also allowed for more individualization with colors and fonts (via basic HTML) than Facebook, and did not require a university affiliation (as Facebook did at the time).

[99] Ben Light, "Introducing Masculinity Studies to Information Systems Research: The Case of Gaydar," *European Journal of Information Systems* 16, no. 5 (2007): 658–665; and Ben Light, "Networked Masculinities and Social Networking Sites: A Call for the Analysis of Men and Contemporary Digital Media," *Masculinities and Social Change* 2, no. 3 (2013): 245–265.

group[100]; and Mowlabocus was researching his book-length ethnography of gay men's web communities.

Race and Social Media, Continued

Like the aforementioned ethnographies by Tsang and Gosine, early-2000s research on gay men's digital cultures continued to utilize "identity tourism" as a method for uncovering sexual racism. In 2009, Russel Robinson enacted a study involving eight profiles on Adam4Adam: for white, Latino, Asian, and black men, both "tops" and "bottoms",[101] controlled for their stats otherwise.[102] He found that white and Latino profiles tended to receive the most responses (20–60 messages), followed by Asians and black men; and black bottoms received the fewest responses (only 4).[103] This relates to topics about sexual stereotypes, including racialized notions about how black and Asian men are expected to perform sexually.[104]

Despite over a decade of attention to race and queer sexuality online in North American contexts, there was still a paucity of research in European settings. A Romanian study of gay men's personal ads in 2009 quickly noted that race was "conspicuously absent" from profile texts, which led

---

[100]Ben Light et al., "Gay men, Gaydar and the Commodification of Difference," *Information Technology and People* 21, no. 3 (2008): 300–314. For example, p. 304: "Through the use of Gaydar.co.uk individuals write a version of themselves and of this gay community into being. However, because of the desire to commodify 'the difference' that is gay, predominantly white men, online and offline, such inscriptions become monolithic caricatures that are obdurate and enrol even those who do not participate in such arrangements at all or only by proxy."

[101]These terms generally relate to anal sex (i.e. penetrator and recipient) but also sometimes relate to sexual personality more generally. In Europe, it is also common to hear "active" and "passive."

[102]In contrast to the experiments performed by Tsang and Gosine, Robinson engaged with a platform that was highly visual, and where most users expected to see at least one photograph. Thus, in order to control the variables on his eight profiles, Robinson needed to select a photograph of a racially ambiguous man who could pass as white, Latino, Asian, and Black. Russell Robinson, "Structural Dimensions of Romantic Preferences," *Fordham Law Review* 76 (2008): 2786–2820.

[103]Ibid. See also Shaka McGlotten, *Virtual Intimacy. Media, Affect, and Queer Sociality* (Albany, NY: State University of New York Press, 2014), 73.

[104]E.g. "Mandingo: The Stereotyped Hypersexual Black Male 'Buck'"; in McGlotten, 68.

the authors to wonder if and when "racial tension between Roma and Romanians" might be present online.[105]

As social media blossomed, I was slightly more attuned to (my) race; for example on MySpace, my friend humorously went by the name "Just Black Kris" and I wondered if I should also acknowledge my race in some tongue-in-cheek way. But whiteness tended to remain the unmarked norm in many spaces. This was not the case in all online spaces, however, as African-Americans carved niches on social media, for example Twitter. So-called "Black Twitter" was not a distinct social media platform, but rather a way of conceiving of black (mainly African-American) niches, subcultures, networks, hashtags, trending topics, and identities on Twitter. Media scholar André Brock documented the history, culture, and identity of Black Twitter, with origins in hashtags like #YouKnowYoureBlackWhen circa 2009.[106]

But as digital cameras proliferated (including on mobile phones), many profile-based websites stopped asking users to identify by race, since race could be discerned visually instead. Race continued to saturate the online cultures of social media sites, sometimes in tacit ways. Looking at Facebook and MySpace around 2008–2010, boyd observed something interesting about the demographics of these social network sites: they became *racialized*.[107] More specifically, as Facebook attracted white, middle-class teenagers (especially after 2006), these users began to describe MySpace differently: one of boyd's 14-year-old suburban informants referred to MySpace as "ghetto" when reasoning her switch to Facebook. boyd described a "white flight" from MySpace to Facebook, and concluded that social media "reflected a reproduction of social categories that exist in schools throughout the United States" with regard to race, ethnicity, and socio-economic status.[108] And around 2009–2010, Nakamura explored

[105] S. Bartoş et al., "Differences in Romanian Men's Online Personals by Sexualities," *The Journal of Men's Studies* 17 (2009): 153.

[106] André Brock, "From the Blackhand Side: Twitter as a Cultural Conversation," *Journal of Broadcasting & Electronic Media* 56, no. 4 (2012): 529–549. See also "Who Said What, When About Black Twitter Part 1–2009–2012," last accessed Fall 2017 via, https://raceandict4d.wordpress.com/2013/11/15/who-said-what-when-about-black-twitter-part-1-2009-2012/.

[107] danah boyd, "White Flight in Networked Publics? How Race and Class Shaped American Teen Engagement with MySpace and Facebook," in *Race After the Internet*, ed. Lisa Nakamura et al. (London: Routledge, 2011), 203–222.

[108] boyd, "White Flight," 203–204.

how the internet reinforced the raced and sexed body, and homed in on online gaming platforms, where global economic inequality underpinned much of the racism that saturated these online communities (e.g. racist speech directed at Chinese players of *World of Warcraft*).[109]

Scholar of media and race Gavan Titley observed that much academic research on racism online in Europe focused on right-wing and extremist platforms; so Titley called on scholars to "unsettle the idea that extremists sites, and thus extremist groups, form the exceptional loci of racism in contemporary Europe."[110] The aforementioned articles can serve as models to guide research on race and (non-extremist) racism on mainstream social media.

Online queer cultures also flourished in parts of East Asia,[111] and contemporaneous scholars explored female queer communities in Hong Kong,[112] gay sissyness in Taiwanese cyberspaces,[113] and other studies (e.g. in Japan).[114] Additionally, there were a handful of studies about gay profiles

[109]Lisa Nakamura, "Race and Identity in Digital Media", in *Mass Media and Society*, 5th ed., ed. James Curran (Sage, 2010), i.e. the specific roles that some Chinese players assumed (e.g. "gold miners") and the racist invectives hurled at these players. See also Lisa Nakamura, *Digitizing Race Visual Cultures of the Internet* (Minneapolis: University of Minnesota Press, 2008).

[110]Gavan Titley, "No Apologies for Cross-Posting: European Trans-Media Space and the Digital Circuitries of Racism," *Crossings: Journal of Migration & Culture* 5, no. 1 (2014): 51.

[111]Chris Berry et al., eds. *Mobile Cultures: New Media in Queer Asia* (Durham, NC: Duke University Press, 2003).

[112]Joyce Y.M. Nip, "The Queer Sisters and its Electronic Bulletin Board: A Study of the Internet for Social Movement Mobilization," *Information, Communication and Society* 7, no. 1 (2004): 23–49.

[113]D.C. Lin, "Sissies Online: Taiwanese Male Queers Performing Sissinesses in Cyberspaces," *Inter-Asia Cultural Studies* 7, no. 2 (2006): 270–288.

[114]See also Mowlabocus, *Gaydar Culture*, 12; Lukasz Szulc, "The Geography of LGBTQ Internet Studies," *International Journal of Communication* 8 (2014).

in the Middle East and North Africa—specifically Tunis[115] and Beirut[116]—that explored online sexual identities and communities, but without explicit attention to questions of race.[117]

Akhil Katyal conducted extraordinary research about gay men's digital cultures in India.[118] In one section, Katyal explored the opportunities that gay dating platforms presented to same-sex-desiring men in rural areas who moved to cities like Delhi based on their positive experiences chatting online. Gay men's digital cultures—which existed also increasingly in the Global South—helped sexual minorities form LGBTQ identities, share niche media, and meet up for sex; but more, these online cultures could link LGBTQ individuals with information and networks that could assist with (e.g. urban) migration.

PERIOD 3, 2010–2019: THE TRANSITION TO MOBILE (AND GEO-LOCATIVE) SMARTPHONE APPS

Initiation into Grindr Culture

At the start of 2010, I still had a flip-phone that enabled calls, text messages, and lower-quality photographs; by the end of the year, I was intimately connected to my new toy with its large screen and access to a market of "apps." Within a week of acquiring my first smartphone, I had downloaded Grindr, an app I had heard about through word-of-mouth jokes among gay early adopters. I lived in New York at the time, but I downloaded Grindr while traveling in Utah for the Sundance Film Festival. The town of Park City, Utah was quite small, and there were no explicitly gay bars; but I was

[115] Collins, Rodney, "Efféminés, Gigolos, and MSMs in the Cyber-Networks, Coffee-houses, and 'Secret Gardens' of Contemporary Tunis," *Journal of Middle East Women's Studies* 8, no. 3 (2012): 89–112.

[116] Matthew Gagné, "Queer Beirut Online: The Participation of Men in Gayromeo.com," *Journal of Middle East Women's Studies* 8, no. 3 (2012): 113–137.

[117] See also the other articles in the special issue on "Queering Middle Eastern Cyber-scapes," ed. Adi Kuntsman and Noor Al-Qasimi; Adi Kuntsman et al., "Introduction," *Journal of Middle East Women's Studies* 8, no. 3 (2012): 1–13.

[118] Akhil Katyal, "Playing a Double Game: Idioms of Same Sex Desire in India" (PhD diss., University of London, 2009). See also Rahul Mitra and Radhika Gajjala, "Queer Blogging in Indian Digital Diasporas: A Dialogic Encounter," *Journal of Communication Inquiry* 32, no. 4 (2008): 400–423.

new in town and wanted to make some local gay friends, and maybe get invited to a party related to Sundance. That's where Grindr came in.

Thrillingly, I was outside the home when I first used Grindr; I was at a bar, with a beer, and time to kill. The first thing I saw was the grid of all other active users (i.e. users who had signed on within the last hour) arranged in order of their exact proximity. Upon tapping into a user's profile, I could actually see his distance: "*Only 50 feet away? Where?!*" The look and feel of Grindr at the time was surprisingly similar to today. Eventually, I started chatting with another Sundance attendee who was at his hotel down the street. I invited him to join me at the bar, and he arrived twenty minutes later. Upon chatting further, I learned that he was a director of photography who had been invited to a private party for people in the industry (which I was not), and I joined him. The evening was a blast, and—was this embarrassing to admit?—I had Grindr to thank.

A few months later, I downloaded Scruff, a similar app that claimed a more niche audience of "scruffy" (i.e. bearded and hairy) guys and their admirers. But my transition to Grindr or Scruff was not immediate, and I continued to utilize web-based platforms for gay men, such as the male-for-male message boards on Craigslist(.org) and the profiles on the website Adam4Adam.com.[119] Also in academia, the transition was not immediate: media scholar Shaka McGlotten's 2013 book *Virtual Intimacies* paid much attention to Craigslist and Adam4Adam, which McGlotten still described as "**new** digital media technologies" that "facilitated a **new** era of casual or anonymous hook-ups."[120] Thus even in 2013, most media scholars still categorized text-based message boards and web-situated profile sites as part of the "new media" landscape of gay men's digital cultures, which shows that the transition to mobile, geo-social apps was gradual.

---

[119] Grindr's geo-social feature—while novel—was also a limitation. Limited to viewing only the 100 closest users (on my free version), I could seldom view people in another neighborhood of dense Manhattan, let alone another borough of New York.

[120] McGlotten, 2. Emphasis added.

Race in Grindr Studies, Continued

McGlotten also shared autoethnographic reflections on his use of Grindr, where he observed "depressing evidence of antiblack racism in online dating."[121] Adding to the critique of cyberutopia, McGlotten concluded, "Online spaces reproduce and perhaps even heighten forms of racial injury, including ordinary microaggressions as well as overt structural forms of racism."[122] Along the lines of Sedgwick's "queer affect," McGlotten referred to "black affect" with regard to three specific feelings and emotions on gay social media: anxiety ("a state of heightened awareness" of race online), paranoia (similar to anxiety, but more "delusional") and optimism ("refusals" and "challenging" hegemonic ideas about race and sex, so as to "open and inspire a more spacious imagining" of blackness online).[123]

Many Grindr users, myself included, were acutely aware that until 2017, Grindr's and Scruff's promotional materials advertised their cultures as *white-majority* spaces. Images in app stores and press kits featured sample grids with a majority of white thumbnail-sized faces, as well as sample profiles from poster boys who identified unambiguously as "White" via the "ethnicity" menu. In 2017, Grindr's poster boy was more visually ambiguous and the thumbnail photos in the sample grid (which should have been Fig. 2.1) represented a more diverse array of user photos.

Most research on race and racism within Grindr studies comes from the United States, as the introduction to this chapter outlined. Outside of the United States, scholars have paid some attention to the role of mobile and/or geo-locative technologies among gay immigrants, but race is not always a lens of analysis. An article concerning diasporic Chinese in Australia and their use of the smartphone app LINE (a "mainstream" app that nevertheless hosts numerous networks for gay-identified, Chinese-speaking users) makes interesting points about diasporic gay communities and sexual identity formation, but there is little attention to the users' racial positions in Australia; after all, LINE mainly facilitates communication *between*

---

[121] These and other works showed "depressing evidence of antiblack racism in online dating": Ibid., 147.

[122] Ibid., 63.

[123] Ibid., 66, 76.

Chinese-speaking users.[124] Chan's aforementioned comparison of Jack'd users in China and the United States "did not consider race for the reason that it concerns profiles created by Chinese MSM living in China,"[125] ninety-nine percent of whom identified as Asian.[126] Rising scholars Runze Ding and Oscar Tianyang Zhou may change this trend in their forthcoming work on Chinese queer online cultures.

Also in Europe, new research on socio-sexual platforms aimed at gay men has taken a variety of angles, but race has not always been foregrounded. One study of Scruff users in London, for example, mentions a variety of interviewees by pseudonym. The author describes interviewee "Hassan" as "rather nervous" talking about his Scruff usage at a public café, due in part to Hassan's "negative interactions on the app as well as a precarious personal situation."[127] Attuned to questions of race and migration background, I wondered what Hassan's negative interactions might have looked like within a gay digital environment, and how they differed from other informants like "James." The author lamented that Hassan's "unwillingness to engage discursively makes the interaction quite uninformative and unpleasant for me," which again made me wonder what factors contributed to Hassan's unwillingness to speak about the gay men's digital culture.[128]

Race, migration status, and perceived religion are intimately tied to immigrants' and ethnic minorities' experience in gay men's digital cultures, not least in Europe. One example of this type of research is anthropologist

---

[124]Elija Cassidy and Wilfred Yang Wang, "Gay Men's Digital Cultures Beyond Gaydar and Grindr: LINE Use in the Gay Chinese Diaspora of Australia," *Information, Communication & Society*, 2018.

[125]Chan, 6054.

[126]Ibid., 6054, 6047.

[127]Kristian Møller Jørgensen, "The Media Go-Along: Researching Mobilities with Media at Hand," *MedieKultur: Journal of Media and Communication Research* 32, no. 60 (2016): 41.

[128]Ibid., 47. See also: Kristian Møller et al., "Bleeding Boundaries: Domesticating Gay Hook-Up Apps," in *Mediated Intimacies: Connectivities, Relationalities and Proximities*, ed. Rikke Andreassen et al. (London: Routledge, 2017), 213: "All participants in the sample are… white and cis-gendered men."

Wim Peumans' detailed 2014 account of one Vietnamese-Belgian's experiences with racism and discrimination on gay socio-sexual media, entitled "No Asians Please."[129]

Scholarly research on online cultures has shifted in relation to new technologies: 1990s research focused on the translation of offline social codes to online spaces like chat rooms and web forums; research in the first decade of the 2000s asked how the boom in social-networking platforms affected users' conception of online content; and studies of the last ten years have underscored how online cultures have changed due to our near-constant access to online media via mobile phones. Yet nevertheless, we can see several undercurrents throughout these decades of research. Among scholars of gay men's digital cultures, one recurring trend is the notion that online communication is often done in anticipation of eventually meeting offline. Among scholars of race online, research has continued to underscore that (offline) bodies matter online, that racist speech and viewpoints surface in many online cultures, and that whiteness permeates many online spaces as the unmarked norm. Most generally, media scholars with a cultural bent have consistently viewed online spaces as "fields" for conducting ethnographic work: for gathering data about user self-presentations, for collecting texts for discourse analysis, for recruiting interviewees. Thus in Chapter 3, I outline the ethnographic methods and ethical reflections that have guided this research on race and ethnicity in a socio-sexual online culture.

Bibliography

Bartoş, Sebastian, Voon Chin Phua, and Erin Avery. "Differences in Romanian Men's Online Personals by Sexualities." *The Journal of Men's Studies* 17 (2009): 145–154.

Baym, Nancy K. "The Emergence of Community in Computer-Mediated Communication." In *CyberSociety: Computer-Mediated Communication and Community*, edited by Steven G. Jones, 138–163. Thousand Oaks, CA: Sage, 1995.

Baym, Nancy K. *Personal Connections in the Digital Age*, 2nd ed. Malden, MA: Polity Press, 2015.

Berry, Chris, Fran Martin, and Audrey Yue, eds. *Mobile Cultures: New Media in Queer Asia*. Durham, NC: Duke University Press, 2003.

---

[129]Wim Peumans, "'No Asians, Please': Same-Sex Sexualities and Ethnic Minorities in Europe," in *Hand Picked: Stimulus Respond*, ed. Jack Boulton (London: Pavement Books, 2014), 128–139.

Blackwell, Courtney, Jeremy Birnholtz, and Charles Abbott. "Seeing and Being Seen: Co-Situation and Impression Formation Using Grindr, a Location-Aware Gay Dating App." *New Media & Society* 17 (2015): 1117–1136.

Boston, Nicholas. "Libidinal Cosmopolitanism: The Case of Digital Sexual Encounters in Post-Enlargement Europe." In *Postcolonial Transitions in Europe: Contexts, Practices and Politics*, edited by Sandra Ponzanesi and Gianmaria Colpani, 291–312. London: Rowman & Littlefield, 2015.

Bourdieu, Pierre. "The Forms of Capital." In *Hand-Book of Theory and Research for the Sociology of Education*, edited by J.G. Richardson, 241–258. New York: Greenwood, 2011 [1985].

boyd, danah. "White Flight in Networked Publics? How Race and Class Shaped American Teen Engagement with MySpace and Facebook." In *Race After the Internet*, edited by Lisa Nakamura and Peter A. Chow-White, 203–222. London: Routledge, 2011.

boyd, danah. "Why Youth <3 Social Network Sites: The Role of Networked Publics in Teenage Social Life." In *Youth, Identity, and Digital Media*, edited by David Buckingham. The John D. and Catherine T. MacArthur Foundation Series on Digital Media and Learning. Cambridge, MA: MIT Press, 2008.

boyd, danah, and Nicole B. Ellison. "Social Network Sites: Definition, History, and Scholarship." *Journal of Computer-Mediated Communication* 13, no. 2 (2007): 210–230.

Brock, André. "From the Blackhand Side: Twitter as a Cultural Conversation." *Journal of Broadcasting & Electronic Media* 56, no. 4 (2012): 529–549.

Brubaker, Jed R., Mike Ananny, and Kate Crawford. "Departing Glances: A Sociotechnical Account of 'Leaving' Grindr." *New Media & Society* 18, no. 3 (2014): 373–390.

Bumgarner, Brett A. "Mobilizing the Gay Bar: Grindr and the Layering of Spatial Context." Paper presented at the Conference of the International Communication Association, London, UK, 17–21 June 2013.

Burgess, Jean, Elija Cassidy, Stefanie Duguay, and Ben Light. "Making Digital Cultures of Gender and Sexuality with Social Media." *Social Media + Society* 2, no. 4 (2016).

Burrell, Earl, Heather Pines, Edward Robbie, Leonardo Coleman, Ryan Murphy, Kirsten Hess, and Pamina Gorbach. "Use of the Location-Based Social Networking Application GRINDR as a Recruitment Tool in Rectal Microbicide Development Research." *AIDS and Behavior* 16, no. 7 (2012): 1816–1820.

Callander, Denton, Christy E. Newman, and Martin Holt. "Is Sexual Racism *Really* Racism? Distinguishing Attitudes Toward Sexual Racism and Generic Racism Among Gay and Bisexual Men." *Archives of Sexual Behavior* 44 (2015): 1991–2000.

Cassidy, Elija, and Wilfred Yang Wang. "Gay Men's Digital Cultures Beyond Gaydar and Grindr: LINE Use in the Gay Chinese Diaspora of Australia." *Information, Communication & Society* 2, no. 6 (2018): 851–865.

Centner, Ryan, and Martin Zebracki. "Gay Male Urban Spaces After Grindr & Gentrification." Call for papers for the Annual Conference of the Royal Geographical Society with Institute of British Geographers 2017, http://www.zebracki.org/cfp-rgs-ibg-2017-gay-male-urban-spaces/.

Chan, Lik Sam. "How Sociocultural Context Matters in Self-Presentation: A Comparison of U.S. and Chinese Profiles on Jack'd, a Mobile Dating App for Men Who Have Sex With Men." *International Journal of Communication* 10 (2016): 6040–6059.

Chaplin, Tamara. "Lesbians Online: Queer Identity and Community Formation on the French Minitel." *Journal of the History of Sexuality* 22, no. 3 (2014): 451–472.

Cocks, H.G. *Classified: The Secret History of the Personal Column.* London: Random House Books, 2009.

Collins, Patricia Hill. *Black Feminist Thought: Knowledge, Consciousness, and the Politics of Empowerment,* 2nd ed. New York, NY: Routledge, 2000.

Collins, Rodney. "Efféminés, Gigolos, and MSMs in the Cyber-Networks, Coffee-houses, and 'Secret Gardens' of Contemporary Tunis." *Journal of Middle East Women's Studies* 8, no. 3 (2012): 89–112.

Collins, Alan, and Stephen Drinkwater. "Fifty Shades of Gay: Social and Techno-logical Change, Urban Deconcentration and Niche Enterprise." *Urban Studies* 54, no. 3 (2017): 765–785.

Conley, Terri D. "Perceived Proposer Personality Characteristics and Gender Differences in Acceptance of Casual Sex Offers." *Journal of Personality and Social Psychology* 100 (2011): 309–329.

Crenshaw, Kimberlé. "Demarginalizing the Intersection of Race and Sex: A Black Feminist Critique of Antidiscrimination Doctrine, Feminist Theory and Antiracist Politics." *University of Chicago Legal Forum* 1989, no. 1 (1989): 139–167.

Dhoest, Alexander. "Media, Visibility and Sexual Identity Among Gay Men with a Migration Background." *Sexualities* 19, no. 4 (2016): 412–431.

Dhoest, Alexander, and Lukasz Szulc. "Navigating Online Selves: Social, Cultural and Material Contexts of Social Media Use by Diasporic Gay Men." *Social Media + Society* 2, no. 4 (2016): 1–10.

Dhoest, Alexander, Lukasz Szulc, and Bart Eeckhout. "Introduction." In *LGBTQs, Media, and Culture in Europe,* edited by Alexander Dhoest, Lukasz Szulc, and Bart Eeckhout, 1–12. London: Routledge, 2017.

Driscoll, Kevin. "Hobbyist Inter-Networking and the Popular Internet Imaginary: Forgotten Histories of Networked Personal Computing, 1978–1998." PhD diss., University of Southern California, 2014.

Duyvendak, Jan Willem, and Mattias Duyves. "Gai Pied After Ten Years: A Commercial Success, A Moral Bankruptcy?" *Journal of Homosexuality* 25, no. 1–2 (1993): 205–213.

Duyves, Mathias. "The Minitel: The Glittering Future of a New Invention." *Journal of Homosexuality* 25, nos. 1–2 (1993): 193–203.

Dyer, Richard. "Male Gay Porn: Coming to Terms." *Jump Cut (A Review of Contemporary Media)*, no. 30 (March 1985): 27–29. https://www.ejumpcut. org/archive/onlinessays/JC30folder/GayPornDyer.html.

Dyer, Richard. *White*. New York: Routledge, 1997.

Ellison, Nicole B., and danah boyd. "Sociality Through Social Network Sites." In *The Oxford Handbook of Internet Studies*, edited by William H. Dutton, 151–172. Oxford: Oxford University Press, 2013.

Escoffier, Jeffrey. *Bigger Than Life: The History of Gay Porn Cinema from Beefcake to Hardcore*. Philadelphia: Running Press, 2009.

Ferreday, Debra. *Online Belongings: Fantasy, Affect and Web Communities*. Bern: Peter Lang, 2009.

Fincher, David, Scott Rudin, Dana Brunetti, Michael De Luca, Ceán Chaffin, Aaron Sorkin, et al. *The Social Network*. Directed by David Fincher. Culver City, CA: Sony Pictures Home Entertainment, 2011.

Gagné, Matthew. "Queer Beirut Online: The Participation of Men in Gay-romeo.com." *Journal of Middle East Women's Studies* 8, no. 3 (2012): 113–137.

Garde-Hansen, Joanne, and Kristyn Gorton. *Emotion Online, Theorizing Affect on the Internet*. Basingstoke: Palgrave Macmillan, 2013.

Gosine, Andil. "Brown to Blonde at Gay.com: Passing White in Queer Cyberspace." In *Queer Online: Media Technology and Sexuality*, edited by Kate O'Riordan and David J. Phillips, 139–154. New York: Peter Lang, 2007.

Gross, Larry. "Foreword." In *Getting It on Online: Cyberspace, Gay Male Sexuality, and Embodied Identity*, edited by John Edward Campbell, i–xiv. London: Harrington Park Press, 2004.

Gudelunas, David. "Online Personal Ads: Community and Sex, Virtually." *Journal of Homosexuality* 49, no. 1 (2005): 62–87.

Gudelunas, David. "There's an App for That: The Uses and Gratifications of Online Social Networks for Gay Men." *Sexuality & Culture* 16 (2012): 347–365.

Helmann, Rasmus. "'Er du den suttegladel fyr, jeg søger?': Efter ti år er appen Grindr mere end bare et kødkatalog" [After Ten Years: Grindr Is More Than Just a Meat Catalog]. *Politiken*, 7 January 2019, https://politiken.dk/kultur/ art6937614/Efter-ti-%C3%A5r-er-appen-Grindr-mere-end-bare-et-k%C3% B8dkatalog.

Hou, Cheng-Nan. "An Aggregated Interface of Xingtian Gods in Synopticon: Theorizing the Picture of Using Western Gay LBRTD App in a Chinese Perspective." Paper presented at the Conference of the International Communication Association, Fukuoka, Japan, 9–13 June 2016.

Humphreys, Lee. *The Qualified Self: Social Media and the Cataloguing of Everyday Life*. Cambridge: MIT Press, 2018.

Katyal, Akhil. "Playing a Double Game: Idioms of Same Sex Desire in India." PhD diss., University of London, 2009.

Kolko, Beth. "Erasing @race: Going White in the (Inter)Face." In *Race in Cyberspace*, edited by Beth Kolko, Lisa Nakamura, and Gilbert Rodman. New York: Routledge, 2000.

Kolko, Beth, Lisa Nakamura, and Gilbert Rodman. "Introduction." In *Race in Cyberspace*, edited by Beth Kolko, Lisa Nakamura, and Gilbert Rodman. New York: Routledge, 2000.

Kozinets, Robert V. *Netnography: Redefined*. Los Angeles: Sage, 2015.

Kuntsman, Adi. *Figurations of Violence and Belonging: Queerness, Migranthood and Nationalism in Cyberspace and Beyond*. Oxford, UK: Peter Lang, 2009.

Kuntsman, Adi, and Noor Al-Qasimi. "Introduction." *Journal of Middle East Women's Studies* 8, no. 3 (2012): 1–13.

Light, Ben. "Introducing Masculinity Studies to Information Systems Research: The Case of Gaydar." *European Journal of Information Systems* 16, no. 5 (2007): 658–665.

Light, Ben. "Networked Masculinities and Social Networking Sites: A Call for the Analysis of Men and Contemporary Digital Media." *Masculinities and Social Change* 2, no. 3 (2013): 245–265.

Light, Ben, Gordon Fletcher, and Alison Adam. "Gay men, Gaydar and the Commodification of Difference." *Information Technology and People* 21, no. 3 (2008): 300–314.

Lin, D.C. "Sissies Online: Taiwanese Male Queers Performing Sissinesses in Cyberspaces." *Inter-Asia Cultural Studies* 7, no. 2 (2006): 270–288.

Livia, Anna. "Public and Clandestine: Gay Men's Pseudonyms on the French Minitel." *Sexualities* 5, no. 2 (2002): 201–217.

Mailland, Julien, and Kevin Driscoll. *Minitel: Welcome to the Internet*. Cambridge, MA: MIT Press, 2017.

Mattson, Greggor. "Centering Provincial Gay Life." Paper at the Annual Conference of the Royal Geographical Society with Institute of British Geographers 2017. http://conference.rgs.org/AC2017/338.

McGlotten, Shaka. *Virtual Intimacy: Media, Affect, and Queer Sociality*. Albany, NY: State University of New York Press, 2014.

Merrick, Jeffrey. *Order and Disorder Under the Ancien Régime*. Newcastle: Cambridge Scholars Publishing, 2007.

Miller, Brandon. "'Dude, Where's Your Face?' Self-Presentation, Self-Description, and Partner Preferences on a Social Networking Application for Men Who Have Sex with Men: A Content Analysis." *Sexuality & Culture* 19, no. 4 (2015): 637–658.

Mitra, Rahul, and Radhika Gajjala. "Queer Blogging in Indian Digital Diasporas: A Dialogic Encounter." *Journal of Communication Inquiry* 32, no. 4 (2008): 400–423.

Møller, Kristian, and Michael Nebeling Petersen. "Bleeding Boundaries: Domesticating Gay Hook-Up Apps." In *Mediated Intimacies: Connectivities, Relationalities and Proximities*, edited by Rikke Andreassen, Michael Nebeling Petersen, and Katherine Harrison, Tobias Raun, 208–224. London: Routledge, 2017.

Mowlabocus, Sharif. *Gaydar Culture: Gay Men, Technology and Embodiment.* Burlington, VT: Ashgate, 2010.

Musto, Michael. "Gay Dance Clubs on the Wane in the Age of Grindr." *The New York Times*, 26 April 2016, https://www.nytimes.com/2016/04/28/fashion/gay-dance-clubs-grindr.html.

Nakamura, Lisa. *Cybertypes: Race, Ethnicity, and Identity on the Internet.* New York and London: Routledge, 2002.

Nakamura, Lisa. *Digitizing Race Visual Cultures of the Internet.* Minneapolis: University of Minnesota Press, 2008.

Nakamura, Lisa. "Race and Identity in Digital Media." In *Mass Media and Society*, 5th ed., edited by James Curran. London: Sage, 2010.

Nip, Joyce Y.M. "The Queer Sisters and Its Electronic Bulletin Board: A Study of the Internet for Social Movement Mobilization." *Information, Communication and Society* 7, no. 1 (2004): 23–49.

O'Riordan, Kate. "Queer Theories and Cybersubjects: Intersecting Figures." In *Queer Online: Media Technology and Sexuality*, edited by Kate O'Riordan and David J. Phillips, 13–30. New York: Peter Lang, 2007.

Peumans, Wim. "'No Asians, Please': Same-Sex Sexualities and Ethnic Minorities in Europe." In *Hand Picked: Stimulus Respond*, edited by Jack Boulton, 128–139. London: Pavement Books, 2014.

Phua, Voon Chin, and Gayle Kaufman. "The Crossroads of Race and Sexuality: Date Selection Among Men in Internet 'Personal' Ads." *Journal of Family Issues* 8 (November 2003): 981–995.

Poell, Thomas, and José van Dijck. "Social Media and Activist Communication." In *The Routledge Companion to Alternative and Community Media*, edited by Chris Atton, 527–537. London: Routledge, 2015.

Poster, Mark. *The Second Media Age.* Cambridge, MA: Polity Press, 1996.

Race, Kane. "'Party and Play': Online Hook-Up Devices and the Emergence of PNP Practices Among Gay Men." *Sexualities* 18, no. 3 (2015): 253–275.

Race, Kane. "Speculative Pragmatism and Intimate Arrangements: Online Hook-Up Devices in Gay Life." *Culture, Health & Sexuality* 17, no. 4 (2014): 496–511.

Race, Kane. *The Gay Science: Intimate Experiments with the Problem of HIV.* London: Routledge, 2018.

Raynes-Goldie, Kate. "Aliases, Creeping, and Wall Cleaning: Understanding Privacy in the Age of Facebook." *First Monday* 15, no. 1 (2010).

Rheingold, Howard. *The Virtual Community: Homesteading on the Electronic Frontier.* Reading, MA: Addison-Wesley, 1993.

Roth, Yoel. "Zero Feet Away: The Digital Geography of Gay Social Media." *Journal of Homosexuality* 63, no. 3 (2015): 437–442.

Shaw, David. "Gay Men and Computer Communication: A Discourse of Sex and Identity in Cyberspace." In *Virtual Culture: Identity and Communication in Cybersociety,* edited by Steven Jones, 133–146. London: Sage, 2002.

Shield, Andrew DJ. "'Suriname—Seeking a Lonely, Lesbian Friend for Correspondence': Immigration and Homo-Emancipation in the Netherlands, 1965–79." *History Workshop Journal* 78, no. 1 (2014): 246–264.

Shield, Andrew DJ. "Grindr Culture: Intersectional and Socio-Sexual." *Ephemera: Theory & Politics in Organization* 18, no. 1 (2018): 149–161.

Shield, Andrew DJ. *Immigrants in the Sexual Revolution: Perceptions and Participation in Northwest Europe.* Cham, Switzerland: Palgrave Macmillan, 2017.

Silver, David. "Margins in the Wires: Looking for Race, Gender, and Sexuality in the Blacksburg Electronic Village." In *Race in Cyberspace,* edited by Beth Kolko, Lisa Nakamura, and Gilbert Rodman. New York: Routledge, 2000.

Smith, Jesus G. "Two-Faced Racism in Gay Online Sex: Preference in the Frontstage or Racism in the Backstage?" In *Sex in the Digital Age,* edited by Paul Nixon and Isabel Düsterhöft, 134–145. New York: Routledge, 2018.

Staudinger, Chris. "Loading More Guys: Shining a Light on Gay Dating in the App Age." *Antigravity,* May 2017, http://www.antigravitymagazine.com/2017/05/loading-more-guys-shining-a-light-on-gay-dating-in-the-app-age/.

Staunæs, Dorthe. "Where Have All the Subjects Gone? Bringing Together the Concepts of Intersectionality and Subjectification." *NORA—Nordic Journal of Feminist and Gender Research* 11, no. 2 (2003): 101–110.

Stone, Allucquère Rosanne [Sandy]. *The War of Desire and Technology at the Close of the Mechanical Age.* Cambridge, MA: MIT Press, 1995.

Szulc, Lukasz. "Domesticating the Nation Online: Banal Nationalism on LGBTQ Websites in Poland and Turkey." *Sexualities* 19, no. 3 (2016): 304–327.

Szulc, Lukasz. "The Geography of LGBTQ Internet Studies." *International Journal of Communication* 8 (2014): 2927–2931.

Titley, Gavan. "No Apologies for Cross-Posting: European Trans-Media Space and the Digital Circuitries of Racism." *Crossings: Journal of Migration & Culture* 5, no. 1 (2014): 41–55.

Trumbach, Randolph. "'Renaissance Sodomy, 1500–1700' and 'Modern Sodomy: The Origins of Modern Homosexuality, 1700–1800'." In *A Gay History of Britain,* edited by Matt Cook, Westport, CT: Greenwood, 2007.

Tsang, Daniel. "Notes on Queer 'N Asian Virtual Sex." *Amerasia Journal* 20, no. 1 (1994): 117–128.

Turkle, Sherry. *Life on the Screen: Identity in the Age of the Internet*. New York: Simon & Schuster, 1995.

Van Der Meer, Theo. "Sodomy and the Pursuit of a Third Sex in the Early Modern Period." In *Third Sex, Third Gender: Beyond Sexual Dimorphism in Culture and History*, edited by Gilbert Herdt. New York: Zone Books, 1994.

van Gent, Wouter, and Gerald Brugman. "Emancipation and the City: The Fragmented Spatiality of Migrant Gay Men in Amsterdam & New York." Paper at the Annual Conference of the Royal Geographical Society with Institute of British Geographers 2017, http://conference.rgs.org/AC2017/306.

von Rosen, Wilhelm. "A Short History of Gay Denmark 1613–1989: The Rise and the Possibly Happy End of the Danish Homosexual." *Nordisk Sexologi* 12 (1994): 125–136.

Wakeford, Nina. "Cyberqueer." In *Lesbian and Gay Studies: A Critical Introduction*, edited by Andy Medhurst and Sally R. Hunt, 20–38. London: Cassell, 1997.

Wasserbauer, Marion. "'I Think I'm Quite Fluid with Those Kinds of Things': Exploring Music and Non-heterosexual Women's Identities." In *LGBTQs, Media, and Culture in Europe*, edited by Alexander Dhoest, Lukasz Szulc, and Bart Eeckhout, 80–97. London: Routledge, 2017.

"Remember that if you choose to include information in your public profile … that information will also become public": Methods and Ethics for Online, Socio-Sexual Fieldwork

As an increasing number of scholars embark on research projects in a field that could be called "Grindr studies"—that is, studies related to socio-sexual media, especially (but not limited to) platforms aimed at gay men—this chapter lays out some methods for doing research about and via Grindr and related platforms. Fortunately there is a great body of research about online ethnography and internet research ethics, from which this chapter draws.[1] But what is unique about research in a socio-sexual platform like Grindr? What sensitivities should the researcher consider when studying or contacting research participants via sexually saturated profile platforms?

The chapter touches on three main topics. First, we explore the possibility of using Grindr for quantitative data about the demographics and behaviors of Grindr users in a bounded field. Second, we consider the meaning of "participant observation" on Grindr, including whether or not one should announce oneself in the field or remain "covert." How can a researcher

---

[1] For starters: Katrin Tiidenberg, "Research Ethics, Vulnerability, and Trust on the Internet," in *Second International Handbook of Internet Research*, ed. J. Hunsinger et al. (Dordrecht: Springer, 2018).

© The Author(s) 2019
A. DJ Shield, *Immigrants on Grindr*,
https://doi.org/10.1007/978-3-030-30394-5_3

archive profiles perceived to be "private" in an ethical manner?[2] Specifically, this section presents new strategies for presenting individuals' private profiles "visually" without divulging personally identifiable information. Third, the chapter considers how one could use a socio-sexual platform to recruit interviewees for face-to-face conversations; here, in particular, one must seriously consider how announced presence as a researcher in the field might affect user behavior.

USING GRINDR FOR QUANTITATIVE DATA

For researchers who are interested in gathering quantitative data about a population via Grindr, there are several ways to do so. But a caveat: it is tedious to glean quantitative data from Grindr, and either requires filters (of users) and manually counting thumbnail images, or even more tiresomely, requires reading and/or manually tracking individual profiles. Thus, one must first bound one's field of study to a reasonable size.

Quantitative data can tell the researcher a little about the demographics of Grindr users in a given region, such as the number of active users at a given time of day, or even the frequency with which users tend to log into the app on a given day. But there is a major limitation with the data gleaned from filters or profile texts: these data only reliably tell the researcher how users in the field *report* their data. One cannot, for example, use the data to say what the average age or racial demographics of a field are; but one can use Grindr's data to report on the likelihood that users in a field utilize Grindr's age or "ethnicity" menus, and what selections are the most popular. This section outlines a few ways researchers can use an app like Grindr to collect quantitative data, and presents some readings from the greater Copenhagen area.

The bounded field for this book was a 36-kilometer radius from the Copenhagen University Southern campus, a radius that covers the greater Copenhagen metropolitan area, as well as Malmö, Sweden (Chapter 1). To diversify my data—and to increase the likelihood that diverse users would view my researcher profile (detailed later)—I traveled to various locations within this radius to gather data, including Copenhagen city

[2]On "perceived privacy," see discussion of Annette Markham and Elizabeth Buchanan, "Ethical Decision-Making and Internet Research: Recommendations from the AOIR Ethics Working Committee" (Paper approved by the AOIR Ethics Committee, 2012), http://www.aoir.org/reports/ethics2.pdf, 9–10.

center (a bustling area with many hotels and gay establishments), Nør-rebro/Nordvest (a neighborhood of outer Copenhagen characterized by decades of immigration), Høje Taastrup (a suburb of Copenhagen that includes neighborhoods with long immigrant histories), Charlottenlund (a suburb of Copenhagen with many diplomats and au pairs), and Malmö city center, among other places. By changing locations, researchers of geo-social platforms can ascertain trends in user self-presentations, behaviors, or demographics in sub-regions of one's bounded field.

One easy piece of quantitative data to glean from Grindr is the total number of active users within a radius. For example, if one seeks to know the total number of users in one's 4 (or 3.99) km radius, one merely browses through the grid until one finds the first profile listed as 4 km away, then one can manually count the number of profiles listed in one's grid before that profile. (For users of Grindr's free version, one can only view 100 profiles at a time, so this is easier with the paid version if the number exceeds 100.) Usage data can suggest the popularity of a given platform in a region, but an increase in the number of users in a radius does not always indicate that new users signed on for the first time that day; the increase could also mean that new users traveled into the radius (i.e. from more than 4 km away) and signed on from a new location closer to Copenhagen's city center.

On two particularly taxing days, I performed this task hourly so as to document the most popular usage times as well as the average number of users signed on throughout the day in Copenhagen's city center (Fig. 3.1). The graph—from a Wednesday—shows that between 7:00 in the morning and midnight, usage increased steadily (with only one drop between 18:00 and 19:00) until 22:00, at which point the usage peaked at 641 users ($r = 4$ km). Throughout the period 8:00–24:00, the average was 590 users at a given interval ($r = 4$ km). I repeated this method on a Saturday a few months later and found a different peak—between 17:00 and 18:00—in which there were 703 active users ($r = 4$ km); throughout that day, there was an average of 646 users at a given interval.

A tip for the researcher who is using the free version of Grindr: using the (free) age filter, you can view far more than the initial 100 profiles in your grid. You can even use one-year intervals, like "18 to 18," which displays the 100 closest people who mark their age as 18. Repeating this for every age, you can view thousands of profiles in your region.

Based on ten age-interval readings in Copenhagen City Center, I found that the Grindr population broke down roughly into thirds: one-third were 18–27, one-third were 28–37, and one-third were over 38 (Fig. 3.2).

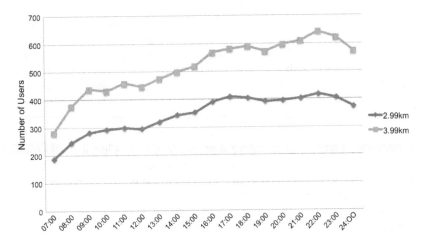

Fig. 3.1 The number of Grindr users signed on throughout a typical weekday in Copenhagen City Center (3- and 4-kilometer radii in Copenhagen) (This graph refers to data from Wednesday, 7 December 2016 based on radii from my data-collection point in Copenhagen South. The data from Saturday, 25 March 2017 from the same collection point shows comparable data, with differences described in text)

Looking at the 36-kilometer radius, there were similar results. It is also through this method that one can estimate *the total number of active users in a bounded field,* even if that number exceeds the limit of 600. By counting the total users in all age brackets, I found that there were on average 1660 active Grindr users in my 36-kilometer radius.

If one were to trust that users self-reported their true ages, then these data would provide a decent estimate about the age demographics of Grindr users in the area. If one approaches these data more cynically, then the data tell the researcher those ages that are understood to be the most desirable in a Grindr culture. For example, when I performed this search using one-year intervals, I found that the most popular reported age was 28; this could mean that there were indeed more 28-year-olds on Grindr than any other group; but these data could also hint to the fact that those aged 29–32 (or so) are hesitant to update their ages. In Chapter 6, I present similar data for and analyze the "ethnicity" menu.

There are also more complex ways of gathering quantitative data from profile platforms like Grindr, and these methods require more meticulous

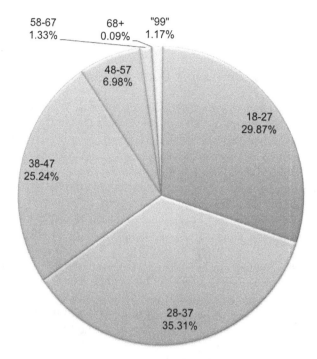

Fig. 3.2 A typical age distribution on Grindr in Copenhagen City Center (based on ten readings throughout a weekend in December 2016, with average of $N = 564$ per reading, within a 4-kilometer radius from my collection point in Copenhagen South. Frequent users [e.g. those signed in at all ten intervals] are over-represented in the statistics. This does not invalidate the statistics, however, since these graphs are meant to inform the reader about Grindr's typical demographics at any given time, and are not meant to elucidate the demographics of the entire population of Grindr users in Copenhagen)

attention to individual profiles. For example, by viewing every profile within a 4-km radius individually, and tallying data, a researcher could identify the percentage of Grindr users who provide a face photo versus a body photo versus another type of photo. Within the field of Grindr studies, Lik Sam Chan performed such a quantitative analysis on 204 men's profiles from the United States and 204 profiles from China, and reported that "64.2% of the U.S. profiles had at least one photo showing a face, but only 36.8% of the Chinese profiles had at least one such photo," from which Chan concluded that the stigma toward homosexuality was stronger in China than in the United States.[3] This method can also be used to find statistics about textual items not in the drop-down menu, such as percentage of users who identify as a newcomer, or the languages in which users post their profiles.

An extremely labor-intensive data-collection method involves tracking individual profiles within a certain radius and over a given day, a method that could help ascertain behaviors like the frequency with which users log on throughout a day. Tracking profiles requires assigning unique names to each user. The following data look at the frequency of Grindr use throughout a given day among a subgroup[4] within my 4 km radius; there were 178 unique profiles tracked throughout this day (Fig. 3.3).

The subgroup followed the general patterns of usage identified in Fig. 3.1, with lowest usage in the morning (i.e. 7:00–10:00), and highest in the late evening (i.e. 22:00–23:00). At 8:00, I began by tracking 32 people in the subgroup by assigning them unique names and listing them in a spreadsheet manually. At 10:00, I checked back and saw that 14 of these 32 users were still active in my 4 km radius, and thus I marked them as "returning" users; the other 18 users from 8:00 had likely signed off, though some may have left the 4 km radius. Additionally, there were 26 new people in the subgroup for whom I needed to assign new unique names. Thus by 10:00, I had tracked 58 cumulative users in this subgroup. I repeated this procedure in two-hour intervals until midnight, at which point I had tracked a total of 178 unique profiles (Fig. 3.3).

If one were to look only at the number of active users in this subgroup at any one interval, one would only encounter 32 to 64 users; thus, the cumulative number (178) suggests that time-of-usage differs between Grindr users. These data are extremely useful for understanding the mercurial state of a Grindr grid. Figure 3.1 establishes that a user signed into Grindr at 8:00 would encounter fewer users per square kilometer than in the evening. But Fig. 3.3 adds nuance: not only will the density be different, but the composition of users can change entirely. Even at peak usage times, a user's

[3] Lik Sam Chan, "How Sociocultural Context Matters in Self-Presentation: A Comparison of U.S. and Chinese Profiles on Jack'd, a Mobile Dating App for Men Who Have Sex With Men," *International Journal of Communication* 10 (2016): 6040–6059.

[4] This "subgroup" was those who selected something other than "White" from Grindr's "ethnicity" menu; this data is not meant to suggest that this subgroup's behaviors differ from the "overall" population on Grindr.

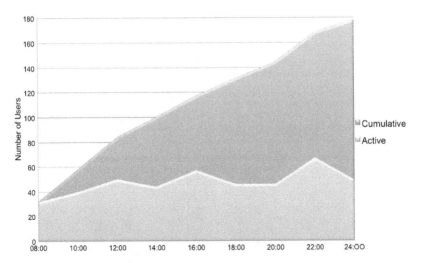

Fig. 3.3 Accumulation of distinct profiles throughout a typical day in Copenhagen City Center. In red, the active users (in a subgroup); in blue, the cumulative number of unique users (in this subgroup) (This graph refers to data from Wednesday, 7 December 2016 based on a 4-km radius from my data collection point in Copenhagen South)

Grindr grid only shows a fraction of the users who will sign on at some point that day.

A user signed on continuously from 8:00 to 24:00 will see 3–4 times more unique users than a user signed on at only one interval during the day. Using this logic, the average of 1660 users I measured in my 36-kilometer radius might only represent one-third or one-quarter of those signed on cumulatively throughout the day; thus, I estimate that there are 4980–6640 users signed onto Grindr throughout a given day in the greater Copenhagen area, including Malmö.

As I tracked unique users at nine intervals throughout that day, I was also able to track the frequency with which users returned to Grindr. After a full day of tracking unique profiles, my data found that almost half of the cumulative unique users (82 of 178) only appeared in my data at one interval.[5] Next, just over one-quarter of the tracked users appeared in my

[5] These were mostly users who had signed on only once in the daytime, but also included commuters who signed on only once from my radius.

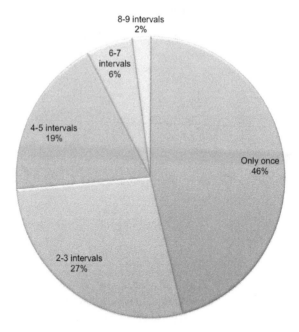

Fig. 3.4 Frequency with which Grindr users check their app throughout a day (This graph refers to the same data described with Fig. 3.3)

data at 2 or 3 different intervals. The last 27% of the pie chart represents the most frequent users: 33 unique users (19%) were signed on at 4 or 5 intervals throughout the day; 10 users (6%) were recorded within my radius at 6–7 intervals; three users were recorded at 8 intervals, and one user (not myself!) was recorded during all nine intervals (Fig. 3.4).

There are a few difficulties with tracking unique profiles for quantitative data. Notably, a handful of users updated their profiles during the day. One user changed his name from "Latin visiting" (at 12:00) to "Vistin. Drink?" (at 18:00) to "Latin. Now" at midnight; but because he maintained the same profile photo, I was able to keep track of daily behaviors. However, if he had also changed the profile photo, I might have counted him as two or three unique profiles instead of one returning user.[6] Nevertheless, this

---

[6]Additionally, I could have tracked profiles once an hour for better accuracy. As profiles only remain on the grid for one hour, I might have missed some users (i.e. who signed on

method of tracking unique profiles also allows for other data about group behaviors, such as the common times for users' first sign-ins of the day, or the most popular times for users to return to Grindr after an initial sign-in. Within the field of Grindr studies, researchers tend to favor qualitative data and analyses; thus the next section centers on qualitative methods.

QUALITATIVE DATA VIA COVERT PARTICIPATION

Covert Participation Online: Theory and Tips

When researching an online platform, "participant observation" can take many forms and can serve many useful purposes for data collection. This chapter overviews and evaluates both "covert" and "overt" participant observation in an online field such as Grindr. I recommend covert participant observation always for quantitative data, but often for qualitative data collection. Overt participant observation—that is, when researchers announce their presence in a field—works best for interviewee recruitment (see next section). Covert participation is similar to *lurking*; in internet slang, a *lurker* is someone who reads online discussions with no intention to interact. Online media scholar Annette Markham describes lurking as "a common and socially acceptable form of non-active participation" among researchers and participants alike.[7]

An example of (nearly) covert participation in Grindr studies is Lorenza Parisi and Francesca Comunello's study of Grindr usage in Rome and Milan, in which the researchers created a blank Grindr profile to examine the self-presentation strategies of Grindr users.[8] By using a blank profile in a bounded field with hundreds of Grindr users, the researchers' blank

from 12:10–12:30, and thus were in neither my 12:00 nor my 14:00 data set). Third—and relevant also for the other methods—is that one unique profile does not always correspond to one unique user. As mentioned with regard to relationship status, some Grindr profiles are shared by two users. Additionally, some Grindr users manage two different profiles (e.g. on an iPhone and an iPad) to cater to different needs.

[7] Annette N. Markham, "Fieldwork in Social Media: What Would Malinowski Do?" *Qualitative Communication Research* 2, no. 4 (2013): 440.

[8] Lorenza Parisi and Francesca Comunello, "Exploring Networked Interactions Through the Lens of Location-Based Dating Services: The Case of Italian Grindr Users," in *LGBTQs, Media, and Culture in Europe*, ed. Alexander Dhoest et al. (London: Routledge, 2017).

profile got lost in the larger population. By not announcing themselves as researchers, they decreased the likelihood that participants in their field altered their profiles or behaviors in response to the researchers' presence. If, however, they were in a less populated area, regulars might become curious about the presence of a new, anonymous (discreet?) user, and thus the researchers' presence becomes palpable.

As of 2019, paid Grindr subscribers can utilize an "incognito" mode that allows them to view profiles without appearing as an active user in others' grids. This is the best method for conducting truly covert participatory research.

Markham's methodological article "Fieldwork in Social Media: What Would Malinowski Do?" translates traditional ethnographic methods to an online setting, such as how to observe participants, conduct interviews, or collect field notes.[9] (Bronisław Malinowski, b. 1884, was a distinguished twentieth-century anthropologist who contributed to the methods of the discipline not least by coining the term "participant observation.") Markham's conception of "the field" and "participant observation" in the context of social media applies to much Grindr research, as she understands online spaces as both cultures and products of culture.

Taking a step back in the historiography: the many studies in the early 2000s that critiqued the "cyberutopian" view of the internet—that is, as a coherent space for disembodied communication—were written in tandem with new methodologies for doing ethnographic work in digital subcultures.[10] Christine Hine's 2000 *Virtual Ethnography* was one of the earliest books to adapt traditional anthropological and sociological methods (e.g. content analysis) into methods for doing research online.[11] Hine's work inspired many internet studies in the following decades, including danah boyd's work on Facebook and MySpace[12]; Patricia Lange's research into

---

[9] Markham, "Fieldwork in Social Media."

[10] Jenny Sundén, "Desires at Play: On Closeness and Epistemological Uncertainty," *Games and Culture* 7, no. 2 (2012): 166.

[11] Christine Hine, *Virtual Ethnography* (London: Sage, 2000). For contemporaneous methodological publications, see, for example, Andreas Wittel, "Ethnography on the Move: From Field to Net to Internet," *Forum Qualitative Sozialforschung* [Forum: Qualitative Social Research] 1, no. 1 (2000): Article 21; or Daniel Miller and Don Slater, *The Internet: An Ethnographic Approach* (Oxford: Oxford University Press, 2000).

[12] Danah boyd, "Why Youth < 3 Social Network Sites: The Role of Networked Publics in Teenage Social Life," in *Youth, Identity, and Digital Media*, ed. David Buckingham (The

YouTube communities[13]; Mathew Gagné's study of GayRomeo.com in Lebanon[14]; Robert Kozinet's theorization of the method of "netnography"[15]; and several methodological articles by Annette Markham.[16]

The *field* in pre-digital anthropology was almost always a physical, bounded space (e.g. an island) that contained the object of study (e.g. a foreign tribe). Entering this field required not only a physical movement into the space, but also a cultural adjustment (e.g. clothes, language). A website or an app can also serve as "a (field) site for research," but the requirements for and upon entering the field differ greatly from the physical field site.[17] Entering an *online field* in the pre-app days did not usually require movement: a researcher could browse message boards, profiles, and hashtags from around the world without leaving one's home.[18] Also

John D. and Catherine T. MacArthur Foundation Series on Digital Media and Learning). Cambridge, MA: MIT Press, 2008).

[13] Patricia G. Lange, "Publicly Private and Privately Public: Social Networking on YouTube," *Journal of Computer-Mediated Communication* 13, no. 1 (2007): 361–380.

[14] Mathew Gagné, "Queer Beirut Online: The Participation of Men in Gayromeo.com," *Journal of Middle East Women's Studies* 8, no. 3 (2012): 113–137.

[15] Robert Kozinets, *Netnography: Doing Ethnographic Research Online* (Thousand Oaks: Sage, 2009); Robert Kozinets, *Netnography: Redefined* (Thousand Oaks: Sage, 2015).

Kozinets used the term "netnography" to define a set of online methods developed from Hine's. His 2009 book *Netnography: Doing Ethnographic Research Online* dealt with research for marketing purposes in web communities to which one had to gain access; he asserted that his "specified, distinct, common sense of methodological procedures and protocols" was more standardized, and thus would be more academically respected, than other online ethnographic methods (*Netnography: Doing*, 60). Even though he sought to streamline online ethnography so that researchers would not have to "reinvent the method" with every study, Kozinets reported that he received some critical feedback on his 2009 book by those who were not convinced that his methods differed substantially from Hine's; thus when he updated his book in 2015, Kozinets addressed this concern directly, and defended his methods as unique from Hine's and others' (*Netnography: Redefined*, 4, 6). The 2015 book also addressed *social media* communities more directly, which he felt were "still a bit of a novelty" when writing the first book (*Netnography: Redefined*, 2, 3).

[16] Annette Markham, "How Can Qualitative Researchers Produce Work That Is Meaningful Across Time, Space, and Culture?" in *Internet Inquiry: Conversations About Method*, ed. Annette Markham et al. (Thousand Oaks, CA: Sage, 2009), 131–155; Markham, "Fieldwork in Social Media."

[17] Markham and Buchanan, 3.

[18] As long as the researcher had access to the internet, the cultural capital to be able to navigate and use the online space, and the ability to penetrate paid memberships, firewalls, or other entry requirements that excluded users from the online field. Markham, "Fieldwork in Social Media," 437–438.

in these online spaces, one usually did not need to worry about visibility in the field; it was easy to lurk in the field without anyone noticing your participant observation. In a gay digital context, examples of this type of unbounded field would include dating websites, message boards, and (as long as one could remain incognito) chat rooms. On PlanetRomeo, for example, there was no way to verify whether a user who listed himself as located in Copenhagen was indeed in Copenhagen; perhaps he was in a suburb of Copenhagen, in another part of Denmark, or anywhere in the world.

Deciding how much to participate in an online environment is up to the researcher on a case-by-case basis, and participation does not always necessitate becoming visible within one's field. Related, researchers could also conduct observations using their own personal profiles on a given platform (without necessarily announcing oneself as a researcher).

Regarding the ethics of conducting research in digital cultures, Markham and Elizabeth Buchanan ask: might "individuals cease to use [the platform]... because of the presence of researchers?"[19] On socio-sexual platforms, it is extremely likely that some users would be uncomfortable with the presence of a researcher,[20] and could even potentially change their habits accordingly. Those conducting ethnographic research via and about geo-social apps must decide if and how to present themselves, and whether announcing themselves in the field (e.g. via researcher profiles) would benefit their research (e.g. if connecting them to participants for in-depth chats, in-person interviews) more than it would risk altering users' behaviors or willingness to participate on the app.

[19] Markham and Buchanan, 10.

[20] I have never encountered researcher profiles in Copenhagen, as I did on gay websites (e.g. Adam4Adam) and message boards (e.g. Craigslist m4m) in New York (circa 2010–2012), when researchers tried to recruit interviewees or survey participants. I remember reading one profile of an angry Adam4Adam user who wrote that he did *not* consent to his data being used for any research, and was frustrated that the space was being used by researchers in this way.

Collecting Archives Ethically

Field notes are a way of archiving observations in the field (while participating) and traditionally would be written in a notebook that the anthropologist kept at all times. One can also gather field notes in an online setting: Markham suggests listening to informants in a field (i.e. through observation) and analyzing the recurring words and phrases used but adds some reflections on collecting online field notes:

> Collecting "naturally occurring" discourse was accomplished traditionally by listening and then later recalling in writing what was said, when, and to whom. In social media, we need to ask not only how to collect this, but ask more basically: What is naturally occurring discourse?[21]

A researcher must continually reflect on participation and observation in order to decide "what is relevant and what isn't" when collecting field notes.[22] On Grindr, profile texts are the most available "naturally occurring discourses" one can observe covertly.

One method for presenting ethnographic research on socio-sexual platforms ethically is to avoid studying individuals, and rather to talk about behaviors and trends more broadly. In their 2008 research on the gay male profile website Gaydar, Ben Light, Gordon Fletcher, and Alison Adam reflected on the ethics of presenting ethnographic field notes within this digital subculture. In their effort to remain "[m]indful of the ethical considerations for internet associated research," the researchers avoided studying individuals, but rather "approached Gaydar as an artefact that is informed by and influences contemporary cultural and social attitudes and beliefs."[23] The authors reflected on publishing or citing individual profiles on Gaydar: "We have made a conscious decision not to reproduce quotes from private member profiles... to ensure that no 'private' data are made unwittingly or unnecessarily made 'public' for arguably marginal benefit."[24]

In addition to ethics, the researcher who worked on platforms such as Grindr should consider the legal obligations too. In agreeing with Grindr's

[21] Markham, "Fieldwork in Social Media," 439.

[22] Ibid.

[23] Ben Light et al., "Gay Men, Gaydar and the Commodification of Difference," *Information Technology and People* 21, no. 3 (2008): 304.

[24] Light et al., "Gay Men, Gaydar," 304.

Terms of Services, all Grindr users pledge *not* to "collect, attempt to collect, store, or disclose without permission the location or personal information about other Users"; further, they agree *not* to "disseminate any information or material which a reasonable person could deem to be objectionable, defamatory."[25] That being said, Grindr's Privacy Policy (a second document) provides the following caveat:

> **Remember that if you choose to include information in your public profile, and make your profile public, that information will also become public.** As a result, you should carefully consider what information to include in your profile.[26]

Despite Grindr's warning that the platform is a "public" space accessible to anyone with a smartphone, Grindr researchers must acknowledge that users perceive and expect the space to be private.[27] Grindr researchers must always reflect on how users in the field might react if they feel their privacy has been violated; they should also consider if and how their research could put a person at risk of harm, physically or psychologically.[28]

Outing Grindr users and disseminating other objectionable material from Grindr users are not hypothetical: it happened rather egregiously

---

[25] Grindr, "Grindr Terms and Conditions of Service," effective date: 30 March 2017; accessed Autumn 2017 via https://www.grindr.com/terms-of-service:

> 8.3 YOU UNDERSTAND AND HEREBY ACKNOWLEDGE AND AGREE TO THE FOLLOWING TERMS REGARDING PROHIBITED CONDUCT AND USES LISTED BELOW:
> 8.3.1 You will NOT use the Grindr Services or any information displayed within the Grindr Services to "stalk," harass, abuse, defame, threaten or defraud other Users; violate the privacy or other rights of Users; or collect, attempt to collect, store, or disclose without permission the location or personal information about other Users;
> …
> 8.3.12 You will NOT post, store, send, transmit, or disseminate any information or material which a reasonable person could deem to be objectionable, defamatory, libelous, offensive, obscene, indecent, pornographic, harassing, threatening, embarrassing, distressing, vulgar, hateful, racially, or ethnically or otherwise offensive to any group or individual, intentionally misleading, false, or otherwise inappropriate, regardless of whether this material or its dissemination is unlawful;

[26] Grindr, "Privacy Policy", last accessed January 2018 via https://www.grindr.com/privacy-policy. Emphasis added.

[27] Markham and Buchanan, 6.

[28] Ibid., 8–10.

at the Rio Summer Olympics 2016, when a (heterosexual male) journalist for *The Daily Beast* logged onto Grindr, got hit on, then penned a piece about it. The journalist included this sub-par self-reflection on the ethics of conducting research on Grindr:

> For the record, I didn't lie to anyone or pretend to be someone I wasn't—unless you count being on Grindr in the first place—since I'm straight, with a wife and child. I used my own picture (just of my face...) and confessed to being a journalist as soon as anyone asked who I was.[29]

"Of course being on Grindr in the first place is a lie," responded a journalist from *Slate*, who slammed Hines' article as "Sleazy, Dangerous, and Wildly Unethical."[30] A writer at the *Boston Globe* called the piece "reckless sexual tourism," and noted the journalist's role in potentially "outing and jeopardizing the safety of multiple athletes."[31] The article was removed from the site within a day.

Digital media scholar Stefanie Duguay assessed the assumptions that "sexuality is no big deal these days" (hint: it is), and that a Grindr profile is meant to be shared like a tweet (hint: it is not). Duguay also addressed the assumption that "personal information on dating apps is readily available and therefore can be publicized":

> Many arguments about data ethics get stuck debating whether information shared on social media and apps is public or private. In actuality, users place their information in a particular context with a specific audience in mind. The violation of privacy occurs when another party re-contextualizes this information by placing it in front of a different audience.[32]

---

[29]Nico Hines, ellipses in original, as cited and critiqued in Bob Finger, "Straight *Daily Beast* Reporter Fascinated By Men Who Fuck Men," *Jezebel*, 11 August 2016, https:// jezebel.com/straight-daily-beast-reporter-fascinated-by-men-who-fuc-1785146830.

[30]Mark Joseph Stern, "This *Daily Beast* Stunt Is Sleazy, Dangerous, and Wildly Unethical," *Slate*, 11 August 2016, http://www.slate.com/blogs/future_tense/2016/08/11/ the_daily_beast_s_olympics_grindr_stunt_is_dangerous_and_unethical.html.

[31]Michael Andor Brodeur, "How a Writer's Reckless Sexual Tourism Put Olympians at Risk," *Boston Globe*, 12 August 2016, via http://www.bostonglobe.com/ lifestyle/style/2016/08/12/how-writer-reckless-sexual-tourism-put-olympians-risk/ Wa48PZ7OmSsYvs6zNnFirI/story.html.

[32]Stefanie Duguay, "Three Flawed Assumptions the Daily Beast Made About Dating Apps," *Social Media Collective Research Blog*, 16 August 2016, https://socialmediacollective. org/2016/08/16/three-assumptions-the-daily-beast-made-about-dating-apps/.

While Duguay chastises the *Daily Beast* journalist for his article, she also uses the incident as a learning moment for researchers. After all, Duguay had also observed researchers who shared dating profiles—whether in articles or during conference presentations—without permission from the users. Duguay called on internet researchers to examine how these unethical practices could be harmful to users.

Grindr users expect privacy, and violating that perceived privacy could potentially result in user discontinuation of the app; further, outing an individual as LGBTQ could potentially put that individual at harm. Within the field of hook-up app studies, the general consensus is that researchers should avoid presenting material that could be traced directly to individuals. Light et al.'s strategy was to avoid quoting individuals' profiles entirely. However, this book *does* rely on analyses of individuals' profile texts, and argues that a researcher *can* do so ethically and legally, even without explicit permission from the users. For example, the researcher can manually re-type each profile into a "skeleton profile" that includes personally identifiable information (whether in a spreadsheet or a document). By doing so, the researcher can maintain an "archive" of relevant profile texts without actually storing screenshots of the original Grindr profiles that more easily link to an individual Grindr user.

During the period of research, I archived 600 "skeleton" profiles that related to newcomer identification, race, or logistical uses of Grindr, and coded them into one (or sometimes more than one) of the following categories:

i. Identifying as tourist
ii. Identifying as international student
iii. Identifying as international immigrant
iv. Identifying as (Danish/Swedish) internal migrant
v. Looking for or offering housing
vi. Looking for or offering jobs; or looking for clients
vii. Referring to racial-sexual preferences
viii. Referring to anti-racism
ix. Referring to other anti-discrimination
x. Clarifying a racial and/or ethnic minority position in text (beyond merely selecting from the drop-down menu)

These ten categories structure the analytic chapters: Chapter 4 draws from the profiles in categories i through vi; Chapter 5 draws from those in categories vii through ix; and Chapter 6 draws from those categorized as x.

Presenting Archives Ethically

Those who seek to present users' profiles on Grindr or related apps will inevitable encounter the following ethical dilemma: (1) you wish to present as much as possible from a given profile, so that readers can contextualize the keywords and phrases circulating in the larger culture of the app; (2) you seek to avoid divulging personally identifiable information; and (3) you do not want to fictionalize profiles, or to create "archetypical" profiles that resemble those in the field.

You can generally cite profile texts without fear that these texts will be linked to an individual. This is because, fortunately, the content on apps like Grindr are not yet searchable on web engines like Google, nor are texts searchable within the platform Grindr. (By contrast, quoting a blogger or Twitter user anonymously can be trickier.) You must reflect on the various constellations of items that might be considered personally identifiable information in these profile texts. Perhaps a "student from London" is not personally identifiable, but a "veterinary student from London, living by the Meatpacking District for the spring" is. As a researcher, you must decide for yourself what might be personally identifiable, and whether you should ask a user for explicit permission to quote his/her/their text. Related, you must also consider how many drop-down menus will be included alongside the text; perhaps the "student from Paris" is also over 2 meters tall and Asian-identified; this constellation of information might be personally identifiable.

For this book, I redacted specific information about individuals' studies, jobs, and extended families in Scandinavia, unless the information was relevant to the analysis, and (hopefully) not personally identifiable. Drawing also from the fact that sexuality is often considered private, I generally redacted sexual inclinations (e.g. "I'm an oral sub pig who likes to service dom tops") unless relevant to the analysis. In some cases, I also redacted redundant or otherwise distracting text (e.g. "if I don't respond, it means I'm not interested").

Regarding drop-down menus, I convey to the reader which menus a user answered, but I do not always divulge their answers. For the purpose of this book, "height" and "weight" were never relevant to my analysis; further, these menus could become personally identifiable information when read in tandem with other text and menus. Thus if users report their height or weight, their responses appear as a grey bar. I also tended to redact responses to sexual "position" and "HIV status."

On the other hand, I always retained a user's answer to the "ethnicity" menu, as this response conveys to the reader how discourses of race and ethnicity circulate within Grindr culture. Related, I generally retained the user's response to "Looking for" (e.g. friendship, a relationship) and "tribe" (e.g. geek, jock) as these responses further contextualize the discourses of self-presentation within Grindr culture.

I did not fictionalize profiles, but I altered them regarding names and (slightly) ages. While I generally retain a user's reported age, I sometimes adjusted this by 1–2 years; and if the user included a name, I changed it to another name that still indicates the name's origin: "Mikkel" might become "Søren," or "Ibrahim" might become "Ahmed," as with interviewees' pseudonyms. The handle to a linked social media profile is not included.

Profile photos, in most cases, are the most definitive piece of personally identifiable information. Even if one does not include a face—or even if a researcher attempts to blur a user's face—the photo might still provide personal details such as tattoos, birthmarks, the setting of the photograph (e.g. the user's apartment), patterns of body hair, scars, and so forth. This book excludes all visual self-presentations.

How to Read the "Skeleton Profile"

The profile "skeletons" in Chapters 4 through 6 provide the reader with a glance into the textual discourses and self-presentations of Grindr users, but should not tell enough information that a reader could identify an individual based on the skeleton profile. Profile photos have been replaced by one of the following:

- The **expressionless emoji** indicates that the user included a full face photo. Unlike the smiley face (☺), this emoji does not indicate emotion. The yellow emoji is recognized as a non-racialized face.
- The **expressionless emoji in sunglasses** indicates that the user included an obscured face photo, such as by wearing sunglasses. Users

might obscure their faces in other ways: photos cropped above the smile, photos where the user is looking so far to the side that the face is almost not visible, full-body photos where the face is small and hard to decipher, even photos where the user has included a filter with puppy-dog ears and tongue.

- The **flexing-arm emoji** indicates that the user shared only a shirtless torso, which I found to be the most common type of non-face photo. I used the same emoji if the user showed another non-face body part (e.g. legs, back). Again, all Grindr photos are screened, and explicit photos are forbidden.
- If the Grindr user shared an unrelated image (e.g. a landscape) or no image at all, then the skeleton profile includes **no emoji**.

As of 2018, the Grindr profile contained the following elements: (1) the profile photo (since 2019, multiple photos are allowed); (2) the display name (about 12 letters), followed by the user's age, if chosen to be displayed; (3) the user's open profile text (250 characters); (4) the user's responses to Grindr's ten drop-down menus; and (5) links to the user's Facebook, Instagram, or Twitter. All elements are optional.

Here is what the reader can glean from this skeleton profile (note: numbers correspond with the pink numbers in Fig. 3.5):

1. The **type of photo** (here: an obscured face photo).
2a. The **display name/headline** (which also appears in the thumbnail view of the profile).
2b. The **age**, if made visible.
3a. **Profile text**, which I present in English; if the text was translated, I indicate so in the caption.
3b. Grey bars represent **redacted text**.
4. **Drop-down menu** options: again, a grey bar indicates redacted text. If the user left the menu blank, the menu does not appear on the skeleton profile (e.g. ethnicity).
5. **Cross-media links:** users can link to Facebook, Instagram and Twitter. In Copenhagen, users more often link to Instagram (the icon in this sample profile) than to the other platforms.

Critical discourse analysis focuses on the power behind words and phrases (e.g. related to race, immigration status) and can thus help explain

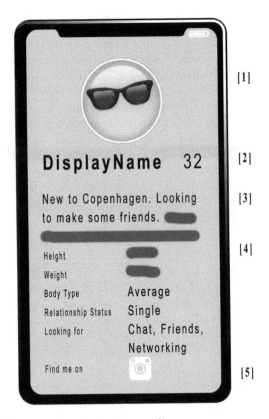

Fig. 3.5   Guide to reading the skeleton profile

how processes of belonging and exclusion occur through words and menus within Grindr culture.[33] Discourse analysis has a long history in feminist studies, as feminist scholars showed how societal norms around gender circulated in texts (or signs and other communicative practices) to reify

---

[33]Discourse analysis aims to "investigate and analyse power relations in society" through language, and to understand and critique the "normative perspectives" within that society; thus language becomes an articulation of social powers. Marianne W. Jørgensen and Louise J. Phillips, *Discourse Analysis as Theory and Method* (Thousand Oaks: Sage, 2002), 2.

patriarchy, sexism, or heterosexism.[34] But language does not merely reflect power and privilege: language can also challenge dominant discourses and act as "counterpowers" or counter-hegemonic discourses.[35] For example, "queer" activists worked to deconstruct and re-signify the word queer, breaking its association with defective oddness and transforming it into a word for pride and community.[36] Grindr profile texts related to subject position (e.g. by those who identify as an immigrant, person of color) and counter-hegemonic discourses (e.g. by those that challenge the "ethnicity" drop-down menu) are central to this research.

INTERVIEWEE RECRUITMENT VIA GRINDR

Overt Participant Observation

The data discussed thus far—quantitative data, profile texts—can be collected covertly. For some other data, one will have to announce one's presence in the field. If one wishes to correspond with Grindr users for research purposes, one should consider if, ethically, one should also identify oneself as a researcher. A common reason to identify oneself is for recruitment to a study. This final section first overviews some practices for recruiting interviewees via Grindr or related platforms; second, highlights the imperative of researcher self-reflection; and third, looks at some of the practical steps of conducting interviews on and about Grindr.

[34] This feminist method built from a 1970s turn toward linguistic analysis and semiotics more generally: Charlotte Kroløkke and Anne Scott Sørensen, *Gender Communication Theories & Analyses, from Silence to Performance* (Thousand Oaks, Sage: 2005), 51. See especially Chapter 3, "Feminist Communication Methodology." Discourse analysis can also highlight "the process of positioning and being positioned" (i.e. with regard to race, sex, or sexual orientation) in a text or conversation: Kroløkke and Sørensen, 58.

[35] Kroløkke and Sørensen, 54. Judith Butler's work is central to this turn in feminist perspectives of discourse, as she centers her analyses on gender, performativity and subversion. See Judith Butler, *Gender Trouble: Feminism and the Subversion of Identity* (New York: Routledge, 1990).

[36] Kroløkke and Sørensen, 57.

Interviewee Recruitment

Using gay social media to recruit interviewees for scientific research is not unprecedented.[37] But there is no standard practice for announcing oneself as a researcher in the field. Some have used university logos as their profile photos, while others have used their own personal Grindr profiles and merely "came out" as a researcher via one-on-one messages.

Being a gay male is not a prerequisite for conducting interviews via or about Grindr and related platforms.[38] Blackwell, along with two men, conducted interviews with Grindr users for the aforementioned study at Northwestern University. The authors reflected, "[P]articipants were sometimes surprised to learn the researcher was female, saying they expected a gay man."[39] Blackwell's position might have even benefitted the research, as the researchers reflected that "some participants provided more detail about Grindr and their behavior because they believed the female researcher knew little about it."[40]

In recruiting oral history participants for *Immigrants in the Sexual Revolution* via chat rooms and dating sites geared primarily at gay men, I found that users were most welcome to chatting with me (online) when I was open with them, for example, by sharing a clear photograph. Further, I encountered that many asked me immediately whether I was gay, then softened upon hearing the affirmative. From this, I learned that users of a socio-sexual platform were skeptical of researchers who only engaged with the platform to find objects of study. Thus, I sought to signal that I was also gay and familiar with the platform in my private time. At the same time, I avoided flirtation as a means of attracting attention; indeed as Blackwell et al. reflected, having a female researcher on the team minimized "potential sexual attraction" with interviewees, and can increase the likelihood of a truthful interview and objective analysis. More on sexual closeness to come.

---

[37] Courtney Blackwell et al., "Seeing and Being Seen: Co-Situation and Impression Formation Using Grindr, a Location-Aware Gay Dating App," *New Media & Society* 17 (2015): 1126; Earl Burrell et al., "Use of the Location-Based Social Networking Application GRINDR as a Recruitment Tool in Rectal Microbicide Development Research," *AIDS and Behavior* 16, no. 7 (2012): 1816–1820; Andrew DJ Shield, *Immigrants in the Sexual Revolution: Perceptions and Participation in Northwest Europe* (Cham, Switzerland: Palgrave Macmillan, 2017), 220.

[38] See also the work by two aforementioned researchers, Parisi and Comunello.

[39] Blackwell et al., 1126.

[40] Ibid., 1125.

Thus on my Grindr researcher profile, I identified myself as a "friendly, gay PhD student from NYC," who sought to meet people who were new in town to talk about their platonic and practical uses of Grindr: "If you're interested in being part of the study, write!" (Fig. 3.6) I filled out a few of the basic drop-down menus, and included a photograph of my smiling face. (Later I was told it looks like I am winking to the camera, but this was not intentional.) I also included a short synopsis in Arabic, a language

Fig. 3.6 My researcher profile on Grindr (2015–2016) (Those who speak Arabic will notice that only one line of the Arabic text is included here; the grey bar represents the Arabic text that was redacted for brevity. Although the "skeleton profile" is meant to preserve anonymity, I chose to use the same format for consistency, but I have included my original photo)

I studied for five years, which said, "Are you new here in Denmark? I am a doctoral student writing about Grindr. Want to talk to me about my research? Write!" I signed into the research profile from different locations around the greater Copenhagen area (detailed in the quantitative section of this chapter) and hoped that an interested person would stumble onto my profile and initiate correspondence. Sometimes I browsed nearby profiles, and if the user happened to identify as an immigrant or addressed something about race, I might write a short message like, "Hi there– Take a look at my profile. Would you be interested in participating in my research?" To anyone I contacted, or who contacted me, I would tell them that their (potential) interview would be anonymous, and I suggested meeting for a coffee for an hour.

Signaling I was gay was a method of positioning myself as an insider in this culture. Including a face photo—which Sharif Mowlabocus has noted is synonymous (in gay men's digital cultures) with authenticity, openness about one's sexuality, and investment in the (imagined) community[41]— further alleviated users' feelings that my presence was a disruption to the overall Grindr culture. I limited the frequency with which I signed onto the researcher profile to only those times I was actively recruiting participants, and I did so from a variety of locations. Grindr researchers must consider how their own self-presentation affects not only the recruitment process, but also the Grindr culture.

Twenty semi-structured interviews with immigrants who came to the greater Copenhagen area since 2009 are central to this book (see Table 1.1). I met most through the aforementioned researcher profile, in which I identified as a scholar investigating the various uses of gay dating platforms, particularly newcomers' experiences.[42] Drawing from anthropological imperatives of self-reflexivity in the field, the following section includes

---

[41] Sharif Mowlabocus, *Gaydar Culture: Gay Men, Technology and Embodiment* (Farnham: Ashgate, 2010), 103–106.

[42] In three cases, I met people face-to-face and invited them to participate in my research. The first instance was at Copenhagen's Trampoline House, a community center for refugees and asylum seekers. During a weekend of programming, I attended talks about LGBT Asylum and racial positions in Denmark, where I met two informants. We spoke afterward, where I mentioned my research and they expressed interest in participating; we exchanged contact information. In a second instance, I attended a talk about LGBTQ life in the Middle East, and contacted a speaker directly afterward. He was happy to speak to me about his socio-sexual media use. In one instance, I met someone at City Hall Square during Pride, then he contacted me later on my researcher profile for an interview. Otherwise, I never interviewed anyone who I met socially (e.g. at a bar or party, or through a friend).

reflections on my position as a researcher in relation to my informants. Self-reflexivity has always been central to work in gender studies; similar to the historiography of feminist discourse analysis, ethnographic studies with a focus on gender have often been led by women and LGBTQ people and have thus centered on systems of power (e.g. patriarchy, heterosexism).[43] Because of their close connection to these systems of power, gender researchers have been attuned to how their subject positions—in terms of gender, sexuality, and ideally other intersectional positions—affect their epistemological understandings of key concepts in a field, or challenge hegemonic ways of doing research in a field. Related, this section overviews the concept of "auto-ethnography" to show how doing research on a (e.g. marginalized) group to which one also belongs can challenge dominant understandings of that group, similar to the concept of "counterpowers" in discourse analysis.

Insider/Outsider Reflections

Feminist sociologist Sharlene Hesse-Biber defines reflexivity as "the process through which a researcher recognizes, examines, and understands how his or her own social background and assumptions can intervene in the research process," and thus it can be "the heart of the in-depth interview."[44] Researchers must reflect on their own subject positions—e.g. with regard to race, class, age, position as a researcher—and examine how these positions could bias the ethnographic process. As feminist researchers are accustomed to analyzing social interactions through the lens of gender, they have an advantage in understanding the relationship between subject positions and power; the same can be said for most scholars of cultural studies.[45] But from an intersectional perspective, a researcher can never be a full "insider" with regard to her informants: "one's insider/outsider status is fluid and can change even in the course of a single interview."[46]

---

[43] See, e.g., Gayle Letherby, "Dangerous Liaisons: Auto/Biography in Research and Research Writing," in *Danger in the Field: Ethics and Risk in Social Research*, ed. Geraldine Lee-Treweek and Stephanie Linkogle (London: Routledge, 2000).

[44] Sharlene Hagy Hesse-Biber, "The Practice of Feminist In-Depth Interviewing," in *Feminist Research Practice*, ed. Sharlene Hesse-Biber et al. (London: Sage, 2007), 129, 130.

[45] Hesse-Biber, 147.

[46] Ibid., 143.

For example with her fieldwork in Bangladesh, geographer Farhama Sultana noted that her subjects were warm and friendly to her as a "*deshi* girl"; but her class differences were obvious (watch, camera, notebook and thus literacy), and the fact that she had a "boyish haircut" (rather than "long flowing hair") meant locals (mis)interpreted her as masculine or pitiful.[47] Nadje Al-Ali has also reflected on how she has "*performed* being German or Iraqi" at various times, from conducting interviews to giving talks to navigating airport security.[48]

Those recruiting interviewees on sexually charged platforms must be attuned to issues such as flirtation and closeness, a topic addressed in Jenny Sundén's 2012 methodological article, "Desires at Play." The article explores "closeness and (queer) desire in new media ethnography" and drew from her larger work on the platform *World of Warcraft*.[49] She began with a candid and intimate example of a dilemma she faced while researching queer women and online gaming:

> I met her in a bar. ... We spent the night together. She woke up... "Is that *World of Warcraft* I see over there?" ... I must confess. I've been playing for two years now." We joked about me interviewing her, and how that hardly could be an ethical procedure....[50]

The next week, the two of them met again, not face-to-face for an interview, but in the virtual gaming world. As a highly skilled player, the woman was a "jump-start" to Sundén by skillfully introducing her to the spaces and peculiarities of the virtual world with "good humor and wit," and a little flirtation.[51] In doing so, Sundén hoped to develop new media research methods that foregrounded affective connections.

---

[47] Farhana Sultana, "Reflexivity, Positionality and Participatory Ethics: Negotiating Fieldwork Dilemmas in International Research," *ACME: An International Journal for Critical Geographies* 6, no. 3 (March 2015): 378–379.

[48] Nadje Al-Ali, *Secularism, Gender, and the State in the Middle East: The Egyptian Women's Movement* (Cambridge: Cambridge University Press, 2000), 36–37. See especially Chapter 1, "Up against conceptual frameworks: post-orientalism, occidentalism and presentations of the self."

[49] Sundén, 164.

[50] Ibid., 167–168.

[51] Ibid., 168.

Grindr researchers must seriously consider issues related to sexual closeness. To minimize flirtation, for example, I never sent photos (beyond my main profile photos) or complimented a user's physical appearance in order to get attention or gain trust. Nevertheless, some potential interviewees inferred that when I chatted with them, I sought not only to recruit them for my study, but also to cruise. One user wrote, after a mixture of comments about both my research and my appearance: "I'd like to get to know the man behind the research. What do you like sexually? For me, I like to be dominant." In this instance, I decided not to meet the person for an interview, based on my hunch that he would have persisted in looking for sex in conjunction with the interview.

Before announcing themselves in the field, Grindr researchers with personal profiles must reflect on the extent to which they are already known in the field. Fortunately, I had not been a frequent user of Grindr in Copenhagen prior to the study (but rather, in the United States). Nevertheless, I realize that participants in the field could have recognized me upon signing in as a researcher. Grindr researchers who have both a personal and researcher profile should avoid signing onto both accounts at the same time. Further, one should ask how one's visibility as a non-researcher might affect the way a user perceives one's researcher profile: Have I ever initiated conversation or flirted with a potential interviewee? Have I ever ignored or otherwise offended a potential interviewee? Did any interviewees contact me because they had been attracted to something in my non-researcher profile?

Aside from reflecting on one's own sexual closeness to potential interviewees, there are other positions to interrogate: "I am... a researcher," Hesse-Biber reflected after her interview with a fitness instructor, "who inhabits a social world different from" that fitness instructor; "I have a research agenda. I want to know 'a something.'" In reflecting on this subject position, Hesse-Biber identified herself as an outsider with regard to her informant's social world, even though she also shared some positions with that informant.[52] In my researcher profile, I used the term "PhD student" so as to slightly obscure this outsider position (i.e. as researcher). I suspected that many would perceive "student" to mean that I was a curious person who sought to learn something from the informants, and not

---

[52] Hesse-Biber, 114.

a professional researcher.[53] I used the term "friendly" in order to dispel any preconceived notion that researchers might be cold or impersonal. Those who were also students might have perceived me to be at their level, someone who shared their concerns: completing coursework and papers, living on a stipend, etc. One user initiated conversation with me by writing, "Student here. Just saw your profile and decided to write to you." Perhaps our shared identification as students motivated his message. Drawing from Svend Brinkmann and Steinar Kvale's notion of the "inter-view" as a conversation that is also a site of knowledge creation, I sought to show that I was someone with whom the interviewee could chat and co-create knowledge on our topics of interest, and not someone who viewed my interviewee as an object to observe and judge.[54]

With regard to my immigration status, I was an insider (to my immigrant informants) because we were all learning the intricacies of Scandinavian culture. We were all learning new languages, concepts, and social codes. Because of this shared status, I felt comfortable asking interviewees, "Where are you from?" and "How long have you lived in Denmark?" which are two questions that can be experienced as annoying or even racist when posed by Scandinavians.[55] Potential interviewees seemed comfortable answering these questions, and generally asked me the same. Eventually I also felt comfortable asking on what grounds interviewees had residency.

Writing that I was "from New York City" was a half-truth; I did indeed move to Copenhagen from New York City (where I had lived for six years), but I was not born or raised there. I chose the term deliberately rather than saying "[U.S.] American" or "from the United States," as I know that being a U.S. American can be controversial. When many of my friends and I studied abroad in Europe in 2005—shortly after George W. Bush had enlisted European support for the wars in Iraq and Afghanistan—I remember some said they were Canadian, and some even put Canadian

---

[53] However, someone more aware of the Danish system would know that a PhD student is a full-time staff member of the university (unlike in, say, the United States). Thus, they would have perceived me as someone in a more powerful position with regard to my role in knowledge creation.

[54] Sven Brinkmann and Steinar Kvale, *InterViews. Learning the Craft of Qualitative Research Interviewing* (London: Sage, 2015), 2.

[55] Especially when directed at Scandinavian-born racial minorities; see Chapter 6 and Paula Mulinari, "Racism as Intimacy—Looking, Questioning and Touching in the Service Encounter," *Social Identities* 2, no. 5 (2017): 600–613.

flags on their luggage and backpacks. Since late 2016, I have encountered many associations between Americans and Donald Trump, and I expect that some potential interviewees associated (non-Muslim) U.S. Americans with Islamophobia.[56] On the other hand, when I tell people I am from New York City, I rarely get the same first impression. For example, I met two young Iranian queers at a refugee pride event in Uppsala, Sweden, and when I said I was from New York City, their eyes lit up, they looked at each other, and said in unison, "Sex in the City!"

Saying I was from New York City seemed to be the least controversial way to convey my citizenship. But I was still an outsider in some ways, even as a fellow immigrant. The United States is a Western country; and while I don't share the rights and privileges of EU immigrants in Denmark, I do share some of the socio-economic connotations of being a Western immigrant. I have never experienced someone looking down on me because of my home country, as some of my interviewees conveyed. Finally, I did not always share the same cultural understanding of race as my informants, which is natural when conducting cross-cultural work.

On race and (my) whiteness: the first two chapters underscored that "race" (whether in Scandinavia, or more generally online) is relational; it is reproduced contingently in different socio-political contexts. As my personal history of social media showed (Chapter 2), I was rarely attuned to how my race (or rather, my whiteness) ingratiated me into various online contexts. Richard Dyer has remarked that white scholars (and people more generally) often lack self-reflection on their racial position; too often they view their perspective—even on race-related topics—as un-situated.[57]

In a U.S. American context, I have always identified as white, and I am always perceived to be white, resulting in that I experience white privilege on a daily basis.[58] Although most of my great-grandparents were born

---

[56]Recently I met a Syrian refugee—unrelated to this research—who upon learning that I was from the United States, asked me (perhaps jokingly) if I could change Trump's opinions about Syrian refugees. This was merely his first impression of me, a sort-of word association between "American," "Trump," and "immigration ban." So when this Middle Eastern refugee heard that I was from the United States, his first association was Islamophobia; but when two other Middle Eastern refugees heard that I was from New York City, they first thought about Sarah Jessica Parker on HBO.

[57]Richard Dyer, *White* (New York: Routledge, 1997).

[58]I was only deemed "suspicious" enough to be followed around in stores in 2000, during a brief period where I had dyed my hair blue; otherwise, I don't recall being harassed in commercial establishments or public spaces based on superficial reasons.

in the United States, my mother's side descends from Eastern European Jewish immigrants, and my father's side from British, Irish, and Greek immigrants. My features align more closely with those of a stereotypical Ashkenazi Jew (e.g. long face, big nose, dark hair, full beard) whereas my first and last names are fully Anglo. Moreover, I am "officially" white in the United States, meaning that I have always (and only) been encouraged to identify as white when filling out the census, university applications, or preliminary questions before standardized tests.[59]

However in Scandinavia, my whiteness is disputable. I assume that on a day-to-day basis, most people in Denmark perceive me as "white" in a broader sense (i.e. a person of European descent). Officially, no Danish document will ever ask me to define my race; I am in the category of immigrant from a "Western" country, which—like "immigrant from a non-Western country"—becomes racialized in public discourses. White Scandinavians have almost never made any reference to my ethnic background or race; but I also know that many immediately see me as something other than a "typical" Scandinavian (with fair hair, for example).

One exception relates to an incident in January 2016, immediately after Denmark and Sweden implemented border control for the first time since the 1950s. Passengers on trains from Copenhagen to Malmö had to show "nationally issued photo identification." Before getting on the train in Denmark, I showed my Danish residence card, which the Danish authorities approved; but upon arriving in Sweden, the Swedish authorities rejected the residence card, as it is only recognized as a national I.D. in Denmark (!). The Swedish police escorted me to a train returning to Denmark, and waited on the platform until the doors on the train closed and I was officially deported from Sweden. (Poignantly, I showed up three hours late to Malmö University's symposium, entitled "Current Themes in Migration Research: Where Do We Go from Here?") This "deportation," however, was not my experience with being racialized (per se). The following day, when I told this story to my colleagues, one white Danish man laughed

---

[59] But my experiences stand in contrast to those of my maternal grandmother, who—in New York in the 1930s—was encouraged by a schoolteacher to identify as "Jewish" rather than white or Caucasian on a standardized form. She also recalled that her name prohibited her from working in certain environments: at a job interview with a prestigious Manhattan publishing company, she was told, "Miss Jaffe, you understand the publishing business is not for you" (to which she told me "I understood, even then, what that meant"). See Karen Brodkin, *How Jews Became White Folks and What That Says About Race in America* (New Brunswick: Rutgers University Press, 1998).

and responded, "Well maybe if you had blue eyes, they would have let you through!" But the irony is: I *do* have blue eyes. Or blueish-greenish-grey. While it's possible that my colleague could not discern my eye color from across the lunch table, I realized that he used "blue eyes" as a metonym for something larger: "Well, maybe if you looked like a typical Scandinavian...."[60] Fortunately I *am* a foreigner, so this Othering did not bother me. (On the other hand, if I had been born in Denmark, this Othering would certainly frustrate me, and I might view the microaggression as a form of everyday racism: see Chapter 5.)

"You are white. Your skin is white," said Daniel (b. Nigeria) during our interview. "My skin is black." He said this flatly while making a point about how skin color affects one's experience on Grindr. "You will receive like 14 messages in one hour. And I would just get like 10 messages in 4 hours. That is… racism."

In Daniel's eyes, I experience the Grindr culture in Scandinavia with the privileges of a white person. My ruddy coloring, made paler by the Scandinavian winter; my light eyes; my names, which no one struggles to pronounce… For these reasons—in tandem with my position as a full-time university researcher, and as someone from a "Western" country—I inhabited an "outsider" status with many of my interviewees. This outsider status might have been a hindrance to interviewees' opening up to me, or it could have meant that interviewees clarified positions to me (e.g. about race and racism) that they thought I might not understand. Like Blackwell—the female researcher whose interviewees assumed she knew little about Grindr—I might have benefitted from some of my outsider positions, as interviewees sought to underscore how their experiences in Scandinavia differed from mine.

Semi-Structured Interviews

The interviews that I conducted for this research loosely followed a guide, but I intentionally strayed from a rigid path of questioning. According to Brinkmann and Kvale, this fluid approach to interview methodology allows for a more natural conversation flow between the researcher and interviewee.[61] Their notion of the "inter-view" is as an "inter-change of

---

[60] In the Danish language, saying that someone is "blue-eyed" can also mean that someone is naïve, but that's not what he meant here.

[61] Brinkmann and Kvale; see also Steinar Kvale, *Doing Interviews* (London: Sage, 2008).

views between two persons conversing about a theme of mutual interest," and thus as the site "where knowledge is constructed in the interaction between the interviewer and the interviewee."[62] To Hesse-Biber, the semi-structured interview allows room "for spontaneity on the part of the researcher and interviewee."[63] Interviews often felt like conversations in which the interviewee and I were both exploring complicated issues together; and in the course of our interviews, some even raised new questions themselves.

Before my first interview, I wrote twenty guiding questions, which focused on three main areas: (1) background information (e.g. on migration, coming out, and gay profile use); (2) what the individual sought to find via the platform(s); and (3) the individual's experiences with, and observations of, race-related communications on the platform(s).[64] Lastly, I encouraged users to say anything else about their experiences on Grindr or related platforms. Because I gathered background information, the interview also resembled oral history.[65]

Despite using an interview guide, I never asked questions in a mechanical order. For example, one open-ended question related to logistical uses of Grindr (e.g. finding rooms, jobs). If the interviewee had not considered using Grindr for these purposes, I did not immediately press the topic (e.g. asking "Why not?") but might transition to a more open and related question, such as "Have you considered using Grindr to make friends in Copenhagen?" But if the interviewee answered the question about housing in the affirmative, I might continue down that topic: "Can you tell me about the types of offers you received?" or "What was your living situation with the flat mate you found?" In some cases, prepared questions were tailored to specific individuals, for example, "I saw that you shared a link about 'sexual racism' in your profile. What were your reasons for that?"

Regarding interview dynamics, I sought to ask questions that would address sensitive topics—such as about experiences of exclusion on

[62] Brinkmann and Kvale, 2.

[63] Hesse-Biber, 116.

[64] During the initial interviews, I also asked questions about international correspondence on the platforms (e.g. receiving messages from men from Ghana while living in Denmark), but I dropped this research topic as I came to narrow my focus.

[65] Hesse-Biber, 118, 122–124.

Grindr—while maintaining a positive rapport with interviewees.[66] I maintained this positive rapport in part by allowing conversations to meander, which showed that I listened to interviewees and was interested in their experiences and opinions. Interviews ranged from 30 minutes to two hours, usually depending on the interviewee's loquacity. About half of the interviews were conducted at cafés in Copenhagen, and the other half over Skype; one interview took place in the informant's personal residence at the request of the informant and for privacy-related reasons.

All but one interviewee agreed to have the interview audio recorded.[67] I transcribed all interviews myself, which many ethnographers agree can have the added benefit of reflection on the interview process.[68] There were a few other reasons I transcribed all interviews myself: the sensitivity of many of the conversations; the fact that I like to include notes about tone, tempo, hesitations and pauses in the conversation; and my ear for interpreting English with foreign accents or errors. When transcribing, I also typed ethnographic observations that would not show up in the recording: hand gestures, facial expressions, details about the location, etc. Upon re-reading interviews, I highlighted key passages, using color-codes for certain topics, then created separate documents into which I copy-pasted key passages from the interviews by category. I was then able to analyze, compare, and contrast recurring themes in the interviews.

As many Grindr researchers will experience closeness with their interviewees—perhaps due to shared subject positions, or potential attraction—one must reflect on whether or not one feels compelled to seek support or approval from these interviewees. This was a question pondered by Sundén: she was admittedly "uncertain" whether her choice to work with someone with whom she had had an intimate relationship was academically sound: "Does desire per se make you less critical?" Sundén asked herself.[69] The

---

[66] Brinkmann and Kvale.

[67] Regarding the one exception, the interviewee did not want a recording due to concerns about privacy. I took notes by hand throughout the meeting, and typed up a mock transcript within an hour of the interview.

[68] E.g. Brinkmann and Kvale.

[69] Sundén, 173. See also Tobias Raun, "Out Online: Trans Self-Representation and Community Building on YouTube" (Ph.D diss., Roskilde University, 2012), 47. Raun asks himself: does one "censor oneself" if one feels too close with one's subjects? Or conversely, might one be "more critical of tensions" among the group one researches than an ethnographer with an outsider status?

answer is not immediately clear: although Sundén aimed to remain critical of her research field, she also circulated drafts of her writing to her informant and wrote that she was "relieved" and "flattered" to receive the informant's "blessing."[70] The literature in this section—much of which benefitted from the long feminist tradition of self-reflexivity in the field—encourages Grindr researchers to think about the benefits and risks in studying a group with which one shares many characteristics.

Conclusions

This chapter foremost provides new insights into methods for collecting empiric data via a geo-locative, socio-sexual platform like Grindr.

Quantitative Methods Are More Useful for Data About General Usage Than Population Demographics

Quantitative data can be gleaned from apps differently, depending on the technology and what information is available. On some platforms, one can use drop-down-menu filters to see the breakdown in reported ages or ethnic backgrounds of users in a bounded area. But these data will reflect users' self-reported values, which might be a lie; further, those who utilize these menus might not be representative of the total online population in the bounded area. Nevertheless, we learned that 1600–1700 people were active on Grindr in the greater Copenhagen area, including Malmö, at a given moment of a given evening. Yet the number of active users at any given time represents only a fraction of the total users who might sign on; thus, we estimated that there might be 5000 unique users cumulatively on a given day. Half of those users will only sign on once that day, but another quarter or so will sign on at four or more intervals throughout the day. These data provide some general background on the estimated size and behaviors of a population of Grindr users, but quantitative data on drop-down menus (e.g. "ethnicity") do not necessarily provide meaningful data about the (e.g. racial) demographics of Grindr users (as we explore in Chapter 6).

---

[70]Sundén, 174.

Covert Participation Is Recommended for Both Quantitative and Qualitative Data Gathering

Covert participant observation is the best method for gathering data on not just usage behavior, but also language trends. By using a blank profile, a researcher can likely go unnoticed in the "field" and can observe users' self-presentations without altering them. This method works best in areas that are densely populated with Grindr users; otherwise, in a sparsely populated area, regular users might notice the presence of an entirely blank profile, and might initiate communications enquiring about the researcher's identity. Researchers should consider investing in a paid Grindr membership if it still includes the "incognito" mode for browsing profiles; this aligns best with anthropological ideals of observing cultural patterns without altering them.

Users Perceive Their Grindr Profiles to Be "Private": Do Not Divulge Personally Identifiable Information Gleaned From an Individual Profile

If users feel their privacy is at risk because of the presence of an outside observer, they may stop using the platform altogether. Even though Grindr considers users' socio-sexual profiles to be "public" (i.e. that they are visible to other users of that platform), researchers should assume that Grindr users understand their profiles to be deeply "private." Thus all researchers who present data about an individual Grindr user—such as that user's profile text—should take precautions to ensure that the Grindr user is not personally identifiable. For example, unless a research project specifically concerns height and weight, there is no reason to include a user's height and weight if presenting the user's profile. Photographs, even when blurred, reveal personally identifiable information via setting or other visual cues. Thus for researchers interested in presenting socio-sexual profiles visually, the "skeleton profile" (Fig. 3.5) is one way to do so without divulging personally identifiable information.

Announcing One's Presence as a Researcher Has Benefit, but Only When Done with Sensitivity and Self-Reflection

Announced presence within an online field works best if the researcher seeks to recruit interviewees via the platform. Interviews could be conducted in-person, via online software, or even through the online platform from which the interviewee was recruited. Researchers must reflect on the words with which they choose to identify, as this may affect the likelihood that potential interviewees want to connect with them. A researcher's announcement should use language that puts readers at ease about the presence of the researcher, who may be perceived as an outsider.

I end by reviewing one additional method for conducting socio-sexual research online: deceptive overt participation. I do not condone this for formal academic research, but it has precedence. This method involves creating fake profiles on socio-sexual platforms in order to observe how people interact with various "types" of people. Chapter 2 overviewed several examples of this: Russel Robinson, for example, created eight different fake profiles to see how Adam4Adam.com users responded sexually to men with different races and sexual positions. Other scholars have used this method more informally: Andil Gosine created a fake profile for blond-haired, blue-eyed "Robbie" to see how Gay.com participants chatted differently with Robbie versus his personal profile in which he identified as Indian. Gosine did not declare this a scientific method; rather he used his anecdotal findings to justify future work about race in gay men's digital cultures. Future researchers conducting long-term, formal studies involving deceptive profiles must seriously reflect on their justifications for this method.

Outside of academia, "identity tourism" can be enticing to those paranoid that their subject positions negatively affect their experiences in a socio-sexual online culture. Looking ahead to Chapter 4, interviewee Daniel (from Nigeria) used this method to confirm his hypothesis that white Grindr users received friendlier responses—and more invitations for bareback sex—than black users in the greater Copenhagen area. Many readers will be sympathetic to Daniel's methods, as he sought to understand how certain self-presentation strategies might swell or diminish a newcomer's allure within Grindr culture.

BIBLIOGRAPHY

Al-Ali, Nadje. *Secularism, Gender, and the State in the Middle East: The Egyptian Women's Movement.* Cambridge: Cambridge University Press, 2000.

Blackwell, Courtney, Jeremy Birnholtz, and Charles Abbott. "Seeing and Being Seen: Co-Situation and Impression Formation Using Grindr, a Location-Aware Gay Dating App." *New Media & Society* 17 (2015): 1117–1136.

boyd, danah. "Why Youth <3 Social Network Sites: The Role of Networked Publics in Teenage Social Life." In *Youth, Identity, and Digital Media,* edited by David Buckingham. The John D. and Catherine T. MacArthur Foundation Series on Digital Media and Learning. Cambridge, MA: MIT Press, 2008.

Brodeur, Michael Andor, "How a Writer's Reckless Sexual Tourism Put Olympians at Risk." *Boston Globe,* 12 August 2016. http://www.bostonglobe.com/lifestyle/style/2016/08/12/how-writer-reckless-sexual-tourism-put-olympians-risk/Wa48PZ7OmSsYvs6zNnFirI/story.html.

Brodkin, Karen. *How Jews Became White Folks and What That Says About Race in America.* New Brunswick: Rutgers University Press, 1998.

Burrell, Earl, Heather Pines, Edward Robbie, Leonardo Coleman, Ryan Murphy, Kirsten Hess, Pamina Gorbach. "Use of the Location-Based Social Networking Application GRINDR as a Recruitment Tool in Rectal Microbicide Development Research." *AIDS and Behavior* 16, no. 7 (2012): 1816–1820.

Butler, Judith. *Gender Trouble: Feminism and the Subversion of Identity.* New York: Routledge, 1990.

Chan, Lik Sam. "How Sociocultural Context Matters in Self-Presentation: A Comparison of U.S. and Chinese Profiles on Jack'd, a Mobile Dating App for Men Who Have Sex With Men." *International Journal of Communication* 10 (2016): 6040–6059.

Duguay, Stefanie. "Three Flawed Assumptions the Daily Beast Made About Dating Apps." Social Media Collective Research Blog, 16 August 2016. https://socialmediacollective.org/2016/08/16/three-assumptions-the-daily-beast-made-about-dating-apps/.

Dyer, Richard. *White.* New York: Routledge, 1997.

Finger, Bob. "Straight *Daily Beast* Reporter Fascinated By Men Who Fuck Men." *Jezebel,* 11 August 2016, https://jezebel.com/straight-daily-beast-reporter-fascinated-by-men-who-fuc-1785146830.

Gagné, Mathew. "Queer Beirut Online: The Participation of Men in Gay-romeo.com." *Journal of Middle East Women's Studies* 8, no. 3 (2012): 113–137.

Grindr. "Grindr Terms and Conditions of Service." Terms of Service. Effective Date: 30 March 2017, last accessed Fall 2017 via https://www.grindr.com/terms-of-service.

Hesse-Biber, Sharlene Nagy. "The Practice of Feminist In-Depth Interviewing." In *Feminist Research Practice,* edited by Sharlene Hesse-Biber and P. Leavy, 111–148. London: Sage, 2007.

Hine, Christine. *Virtual Ethnography.* London: Sage, 2000.

Jørgensen, Marianne W., and Louise J. Phillips. *Discourse Analysis as Theory and Method.* Thousand Oaks: Sage, 2002.

Katrin Tiidenberg, "Research Ethics, Vulnerability, and Trust on the Internet." *Second International Handbook of Internet Research,* edited by J. Hunsinger et al. Dordrecht: Springer, 2018.

Kozinets, Robert. *Netnography: Doing Ethnographic Research Online.* Thousand Oaks: Sage, 2009.

Kozinets, Robert. *Netnography: Redefined.* Los Angeles: Sage, 2015.

Kroløkke, Charlotte, and Anne Scott Sørensen. *Gender Communication Theories & Analyses, from Silence to Performance.* Thousand Oaks, Sage: 2005.

Kvale, Steinar. *Doing Interviews.* London: Sage, 2008.

Lange, Patricia G. "Publicly Private and Privately Public: Social Networking on YouTube." *Journal of Computer-Mediated Communication* 13, no. 1 (2007): 361–380.

Letherby, Gayle. "Dangerous Liaisons: Auto/Biography in Research and Research Writing." In *Danger in the Field: Ethics and Risk in Social Research,* edited by Geraldine Lee-Treweek and Stephanie Linkogle. London: Routledge, 2000.

Light, Ben, Gordon Fletcher, and Alison Adam. "Gay Men, Gaydar and the Commodification of Difference." *Information Technology and People* 21, no. 3 (2008): 300–314.

Markham, Annette N. "Fieldwork in Social Media: What Would Malinowski Do?" *Qualitative Communication Research* 2, no. 4 (2013): 434–446.

Markham, Annette N. "How Can Qualitative Researchers Produce Work That Is Meaningful Across Time, Space, and Culture?" In *Internet Inquiry: Conversations About Method,* edited by Annette N. Markham and Nancy K. Baym, 131–155. Thousand Oaks, CA: Sage, 2009.

Markham, Annette, and Elizabeth Buchanan, "Ethical Decision-Making and Internet Research: Recommendations from the AOIR Ethics Working Committee." Paper approved by the AOIR Ethics Committee, 2012. http://www.aoir.org/reports/ethics2.pdf.

Markham, Annette, and Elizabeth Buchanan. "Ethical Concerns in Internet Research." In *The International Encyclopedia of Social and Behavioral Sciences,* 2nd ed. Elsevier, 2015.

Miller, Daniel, and Don Slater. *The Internet: An Ethnographic Approach.* Oxford: Oxford University Press, 2000.

Mowlabocus, Sharif. *Gaydar Culture: Gay Men, Technology and Embodiment.* Burlington, VT: Ashgate, 2010.

Mulinari, Paula. "Racism as Intimacy—Looking, Questioning and Touching in the Service Encounter." *Social Identities* 2, no. 5 (2017): 600–613.

Parisi, Lorenza, and Francesca Comunello. "Exploring Networked Interactions Through the Lens of Location-Based Dating Services: The Case of Italian

Grindr Users." In *LGBTQs, Media, and Culture in Europe*, edited by Alexander Dhoest, Lukasz Szulc, and Bart Eeckhout, 227–243. London: Routledge, 2017.

Raun, Tobias. "Out Online: Trans Self-Representation and Community Building on YouTube." PhD diss., Roskilde University, 2012.

Shield, Andrew DJ. *Immigrants in the Sexual Revolution: Perceptions and Participation in Northwest Europe*. Cham, Switzerland: Palgrave Macmillan, 2017.

Stern, Mark Joseph. "This *Daily Beast* Stunt Is Sleazy, Dangerous, and Wildly Unethical." *Slate*, 11 August 2016. http://www.slate.com/blogs/future_tense/2016/08/11/the_daily_beast_s_olympics_grindr_stunt_is_dangerous_and_unethical.html.

Sultana, Farhana. "Reflexivity, Positionality and Participatory Ethics: Negotiating Fieldwork Dilemmas in International Research." *ACME: An International Journal for Critical Geographies* 6, no. 3 (March 2015): 374–385.

Sundén, Jenny. "Desires at Play: On Closeness and Epistemological Uncertainty." *Games and Culture* 7, no. 2 (2012): 164–184.

Wittel, Andreas. "Ethnography on the Move: From Field to Net to Internet." *Forum Qualitative Sozialforschung* [Forum: Qualitative Social Research] 1, no. 1 (2000): Article 21.

CHAPTER 4

"I was staying at the camp, and I met this guy on Grindr, and he asked me to move in with him": Tourists, Immigrants, and Logistical Uses of Socio-Sexual Media

Newcomers play an important role in the Grindr culture of many major cities and tourist destinations. Regular Grindr users can grow tired of perusing the same profiles in their vicinity week after week, so the prospect of a fresh face is enough to lure them back to the app. Maybe the fresh face is a tourist passing through their town or city; maybe the new user has just come to terms with being gay, bi, trans, or queer; or maybe the person relocated from another country and has come to stay. The app's dynamic and changing home screen will always shift to accommodate a new user.

Grindr does not advertise itself as a tool for tourists and other newcomers, yet Grindr and related socio-sexual platforms play an important role in the exploration and adaptation processes of immigrants and tourists alike. For many newcomers, the most obvious connection on these platforms is a sexual one: the app might facilitate a sex date (hook-up) with a local, perhaps a casual one with "no strings attached" (NSA).

Within the culture of hook-up apps aimed primarily at gay men and queer people, sexual yearnings also blur with other desires. Maybe two Grindr users meet for a coffee or a swim in the harbor; when there's no "spark" or connection, what happens? Do the users go their separate ways, or might they become friends who continue to meet for non-sexual activities?

© The Author(s) 2019
A. DJ Shield, *Immigrants on Grindr*,
https://doi.org/10.1007/978-3-030-30394-5_4

111

Ali, who migrated from Iraq to the greater Copenhagen area in 2014, said in our interview that he met some of his best friends in Scandinavia via Grindr: "Either we dated and then became friends later or we were friends from the beginning."[1] After applying for political asylum and while waiting for his acceptance and permanent residence, Ali used the app to connect to locals: "Most of my gay friends are from Grindr," he reflected. Ali's narrative is just one of a number explored in this chapter that elucidates the socio-sexual[2] networking prevalent among some gay, bi, trans, and queer (GBTQ) migrants in the greater Copenhagen area. Other narratives show that beyond sexual, romantic, and/or platonic connections, many newcomers use Grindr and related apps for logistical help finding jobs, housing, or local information.

This chapter focuses on the cross-cultural interactions between gay immigrants and locals in the greater Copenhagen area, especially instances where gay immigrants seek platonic or logistical connections, through an analysis of newcomer profile texts and migrant narratives. In her introduction to *Queer Migrations*, Eithne Luibhéid argued that queer migrants' narratives can "reveal points of alliance, collaboration, and transformation" between queer migrants and local communities, or between one queer migrant community and another. These collaborations—or at times also "struggles"—enable queer migrants' to craft "identities, communities, cultural forms, and political activism" in a new locale.[3] But how do queer migrants connect to locals and to other queer migrants online? Since 2010, many of these cross-cultural communications have found a home "on app."

Grindr and related apps are critical sites for understanding cross-cultural connections forged between GBTQ migrants and locals. The first section presents and analyzes the ways people identify as newcomers on Grindr, and how they articulate their desired relationships: sexual, platonic, and/or

---

[1] Some material from this chapter—mostly empirics such as this quotation—was published first in Andrew DJ Shield, "New in Town: Gay Immigrants and Geosocial Dating Apps," in *LGBTQs, Media, and Culture in Europe*, ed. Alexander Dhoest et al. (London: Routledge, 2017), 244.

[2] From Chapter 1: "Grindr might best be described as a platform for socio-sexual networking, a term which emphasizes the processes of interpersonal communication among those open to forming erotic, platonic, and practical connections, sometimes simultaneously." This chapter expands on this definition.

[3] Eithne Luibhéid and Lionel Cantú, *Queer Migrations: Sexuality, U.S. Citizenship, and Border Crossings* (Minneapolis: University of Minnesota, 2005), xxxiii.

logistical. The section is primarily an analysis of Grindr profile texts collected by users based in or passing through the greater Copenhagen area 2015–2019, and as such focuses on recurring words or motifs, such as the tourist's fantasy for a local "guide." This first analytic section establishes the various practices of newcomers' self-identification and expression of (often blurred) desires on socio-sexual networking platforms.

In the second analytic section, we continue with an in-depth look at individual immigrants' experiences using Grindr (and related platforms) for socio-sexual networking. Based on interviews with immigrant Grindr users in the greater Copenhagen area (Table 1.1), this section establishes that the user experience varies tremendously with regard to connecting to locals and other migrants. Some immigrants have success finding dates and friends in their new locales, like Ali, but others express deep frustration in trying to forge connections via socio-sexual apps. In looking at these various narratives together, what trends emerge about the most successful relationships immigrants forge via Grindr?

This question about the "allure" of newcomers should linger on the reader's mind throughout the chapter, as queer migrants' identities vary tremendously and intersect with (mainstream attitudes about) race, socioeconomic status, sexual health, and other subject positions. As Luibhéid summarized, "[T]he gay citizen or tourist and the Third World immigrant function as binary figures" in which the former group represents modernity, and the latter queer figure becomes "literally inconceivable" in some European contexts.[4] Both the gay tourist and the queer ("Third World") immigrant are mobile and can inhabit the position of "newcomer" in locales, including urban Grindr cultures. But while the gay tourist's mobility is usually connected to social and economic privileges, the immigrant's mobility might be linked to social and economic disadvantages, such as involuntary movement as a refugee, economic migration to escape poverty or heavy unemployment, or even self-"exile" on account of sexual orientation, gender identity, or political activism.

---

[4] Luibhéid, xliv.

BACKGROUND: ON GAY COSMOPOLITAN TOURISM

Historically, there is a long northwest European tradition of wealthy young men taking extended tours to the Mediterranean basin during their bachelor years (i.e. after university and before the expectation of marriage), and historian Robert Aldrich has argued that these *fin-de-siècle* excursions—with their cross-cultural encounters—catalyzed many men's explorations of homosexuality.[5] Aldrich has also drawn connections between European colonialism and homosexuality, with numerous historic examples to show that officers could use their socially and economically privileged position in the colonies to enter homosexual relationships—either with other Europeans or with locals—far from sexually conservative mores of the European metropole.[6] Both the touring bachelor and the colonial officer—presumably white, male, educated, and financially secure—could take advantage of their mobile and privileged positions to escape the sexual conservatism of northwest Europe during an era of social stigmas and laws against male homosexuality.

In much of Europe today, by contrast, laws and taboos against homosexuality have vanished, and Europeans do not need to leave the continent to avoid social stigmas against homosexuality. Yet worldwide, tourism campaigns still flirt with gay tourists in order to attract so-called pink dollars,[7] and thus the idea of the wealthy and mobile (often white, male) homosexual persists.[8] In this age of gay cosmopolitan tourism, some tourists do indeed visit developing countries to engage in transactional sex with

---

[5] Robert Aldrich, *The Seduction of the Mediterranean: Writing, Art, and Homosexual Fantasy* (London: Routledge, 1993).

[6] Robert Aldrich, *Colonialism and Homosexuality* (London: Routledge, 2003).

[7] Gregory Mitchell, "TurboConsumers™ in Paradise: Tourism, Civil Rights, and Brazil's Gay Sex Industry," *American Ethnologist* 38, no. 4 (2011): 672. He defines "pink economy" as "markets shaped by LGBT culture," of which tourism is just a part. "Pink dollars" also relate to the idea that gay civil rights can be best achieved through economic claims.

[8] Further, gay tourism research draws on various other theories: Joseph Massad's conception of the Gay International (i.e. that white, especially male activists have projected an ethnocentric idea of "gay" identity onto other cultures worldwide), and Eve Sedgwick's assertion that competing sexual ideologies can coexist; see Joseph A. Massad, *Desiring Arabs* (Chicago: University of Chicago Press, 2007); Eve Kosofsky Sedgwick, *Between Men: English Literature and Male Homosocial Desire* (New York: Columbia University Press, 1985). See, for example, the use of this text by Mitchell (below).

locals; again, one sees parallels between these quick visits and Europeans' extended excursions to the Mediterranean and colonies a century prior.[9]

In *A Taste for Brown Bodies: Gay Modernity and Cosmopolitan Desire*, Hiram Pérez explores gay cosmopolitan tourism with a focus on the "fantasy of the exotic" of the local person of color.[10] Like Lubhéid, he underscored that gay cosmopolitan tourists' sexual partners—often economically disadvantaged and non-white—had a sexual orientation that was unintelligible: they were "gays who cannot properly be gay." Applying these ideas to cross-cultural connections in a European metropole, Fatima El-Tayeb used this exact phrase to explain European attitudes toward queer Muslims. Like the sexual partners of gay tourists visiting the developing world, queer Muslims in Europe could not be "properly" gay in the "homonormative western" sense.[11] As migrants, they were inherently "mobile"; but as (often) economically and socially disadvantaged people, they did not have the resources to live like a gay cosmopolitan tourist.

Similarly in Copenhagen and Malmö, one might contrast "proper" gays—gay Scandinavians and (often white, male, Western) gay tourists—with those who are sometimes understood outside of the normative gay paradigm: queer immigrants from Muslim-majority countries, from developing countries, and even (merely) from families with migration backgrounds. Geo-locative, socio-sexual apps can foster communications and relationships within and between these diverse GBTQs.

Since 2009, Grindr has catalyzed new types of cross-cultural interactions worldwide. In "Queer Cosmopolitanism in the Disaster Zone: 'My Grindr Became the United Nations,'" media scholar Jonathan Corpus Ong explored how low-income Filipino queers connected with (often white) foreign aid workers after a major cyclone (in Tacloban, the Philippines, November 2013). Filipinos who were unaccustomed to identifying with gay identities and networks embraced the sudden "cosmopolitanism" of

[9]Mitchell; Jasbir Puar, *Terrorist Assemblages: Homonationalism in Queer Times* (Durham, NC: Duke University Press, 2007).

[10]Hiram Pérez, *A Taste for Brown Bodies: Gay Modernity and Cosmopolitan Desire* (New York: New York University Press, 2015), 107–108.

[11]Fatima El-Tayeb, "'Gays Who Cannot Properly Be Gay': Queer Muslims in the Neoliberal European City," *European Journal of Women's Studies* 19 (February 2012): 89.

the aid zone, and connected with aid workers via Grindr.[12] Ong was not entirely critical of the cosmopolitan culture that blossomed on Grindr: for some, the new Grindr culture "open[ed] up opportunities for queer expression" in an otherwise "small town with strong Catholic values and an intensely repressive gossip culture."[13] But Ong emphasized that Grindr did *not* offer "a complete escape or free experimentation of sexual identities"; historic notions of racial hierarchy were embedded in Grindr communications. Locals desired white hook-ups—a "marker of prestige"—which hearkened to centuries of (Spanish and U.S. American) colonial history in which whiteness represented wealth and class.[14] Like the gay cosmopolitan tourist or even the colonial officer, the gay foreign aid worker was a privileged figure in homosexual, cross-cultural interactions.

Similarly in Scandinavia today, race and class might structure some cultural interactions on Grindr between (often white, advantaged) gay Scandinavians and (often non-white) immigrants from Muslim-majority and developing countries. Yet the binary between white/advantaged and non-white/disadvantaged must not be overly reified. In his ethnographic work on gay male (sex) tourism, anthropologist Gregory Mitchell underscored that white Europeans *and African-Americans* were two of the largest groups who engaged in transactional sex with locals (in Brazil).[15] Thus the Western tourist still embodied wealth and privilege, but not by extension whiteness. And Nicholas Boston's work on Polish gays who connect with black locals in London also complicates the notion that the economically disadvantaged migrant in Europe is a visible minority, or that the cosmopolitan local is white. Similarly in this book, immigrant narratives highlight the array of subject positions regarding race and socio-economic class, including Stepan (a Russian asylum seeker who can "pass" as Scandinavian) or Abdul (an educated student and "visible" minority from a wealthy family).

---

[12] Jonathan Corpus Ong, "Queer Cosmopolitanism in the Disaster Zone: 'My Grindr Became the United Nations'," *International Communication Gazette* 79, nos. 6–7 (2017): 656–673.

[13] Ibid., 658.

[14] Ibid., 668.

[15] African Americans & (white) Europeans were "two of the largest constituents of their customer bases." They represented "heroic and civilizing… paternalism," and provided locals with money, shopping trips, dinners, or drinks at bars: Mitchell, 671.

While race becomes the focus of subsequent chapters, this chapter centers on Grindr users' identification as newcomers, and immigrants' successes and failures connecting with locals for friendship and practical matters. This chapter builds the foundation for understanding socio-sexual networking in the greater Copenhagen area, allowing for discussion (in Chapters 5 and 6) about how racial difference facilitates or hinders cross-cultural, socio-sexual connections.

SOCIO-SEXUAL NETWORKING AND NEWCOMER IDENTIFICATION IN PROFILE TEXTS

Jobs, Housing, and Friends: Communicating Socio-Sexual Desire

Since its inception, Grindr has claimed in its outward promotions to be a "social network," and thus has distanced itself from established hook-up (sex) websites, even as it attracted members from these sites. Grindr's interface is not explicitly sexual.[16] Yet scholarly attention to Grindr and related platforms—which often focuses on public health concerns like HIV transmission—tend to emphasize the sexual component of networking platforms aimed at gay men.[17] This chapter treats Grindr's semi-public profiles and private exchanges as valuable sites for understanding sexual, non-sexual, and socio-sexual interactions including discursive practices on Grindr.

Quantitative data from Copenhagen showed that among those who selected one or more of the six options on the "Looking for" menu,[18] there were the following preferences: Dates (68.7%), "Right now" (i.e. sex) (64.2%), Friends (60.0%), Relationship (40.9%), Chat (38.3%), and Networking (33.2%). The most popular options—dating, immediate sex, and friendship—already show evidence of the socio-sexual character of Grindr.

---

[16]Grindr screens all profile photos (and prohibits those showing underwear or less) and the "seeking" menu only includes the suggestive "right now", but most users understand this to mean "sex" (often with "no strings," i.e. a "hook-up").

[17]Christian Grov et al., "Gay and Bisexual Men's Use of the Internet: Research from the 1990s through 2013," *Journal of Sex Research* 51, no. 4 (2014): 390–409.

[18]Quantitative data from 2016 to 2017 show that two-thirds of users select one or more items on the "looking for" menu. The data were based on five readings with an average of $N = 590$ based on a four-kilometer radius from a location by the Copenhagen University Southern Campus.

But additionally, Grindr profile texts reveal "off-label" uses of the platform.[19]

This following Grindr profile came from a recent immigrant from Asia who began his profile with "Looking for a cleaning job, if u need it, I would do my best" (Fig. 4.1). This profile is a paragon of the range of desired relationships for which one might advertise in a 50-word Grindr profile: the text begins as a work ad (i.e. "for a cleaning job"), and continues with a mix of other desired relationships (i.e. "friends... a date"), before appending a string of emojis that includes a wedding ring and two men holding hands, from which readers could infer that the user is interested in finding a serious partner. The user implies his status as a recent immigrant by saying that he speaks "*lidt [dansk]*" ("a little Danish") via an emoji of the Danish flag. This profile is archetypical of how a newcomer can use Grindr to make logistical, platonic, and romantic contacts in the host country.

Job-seeking Grindr ads fall into two categories: those seeking work in general (e.g. "looking for a job..."), and self-enterprising Grindr users seeking clients for their specific business (e.g. cleaners, hairdressers, language tutors); this second category also includes sex workers. Self-enterprising ads technically violate Grindr's terms of service:

> You will NOT use the Grindr Services for any commercial ... use, such as the sale or advertisement of ... services, and You understand that the Grindr Services are for ... non-commercial use only....[20]

Thus Grindr bans a variety of words that might assist sex workers or other self-enterprising individuals, including "pay," "massage," and "$." Nevertheless, these off-label uses of dating apps persist. This is partly because

[19] On "off-label" uses of social media, see, e.g., Stefanie Duguay, "Identity Modulation in Networked Publics: Queer Women's Participation and Representation on Tinder, Instagram, and Vine" (PhD diss., Queensland University of Technology, 2017), 61.

[20] Via § 8.3.3 of Grindr, "Grindr Terms and Conditions of Service," effective date: 30 March 2017, last accessed Fall 2017 via https://www.grindr.com/terms-of-service. See also § 8.3.6 in Grindr, "Terms and Conditions of Service": "You will NOT make unsolicited offers... to other Users of the Grindr Services. This includes unsolicited advertising, promotional materials or other solicitation material, bulk mailing of commercial advertising...".

Fig. 4.1 A paragon of socio-sexual networking (Grindr profile) (For a guide to reading these "skeleton profiles," see relevant pages in Chapter 3 [e.g. Fig. 3.5]. All profiles presented in Chapters 4–6 were gathered from various locations in the greater Copenhagen area, and Malmö, from 2015 to 2019. Originally, I sought to present these with the dates and locations of collection, but these data could be personally identifiable information [e.g. in the case of a visitor]. All texts are presented in English; if translated [by self], this is noted in the caption)

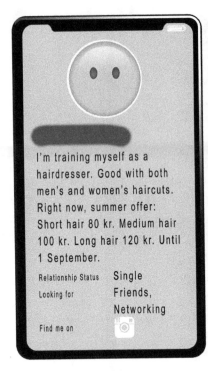 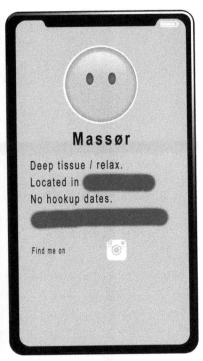

Fig. 4.2 Seeking clients (Left: originally in Danish; Right: originally in English with the Danish "massør" in place of the banned term "masseur")

not all languages set off red flags.[21] By writing in Danish or Swedish, self-enterprising individuals can slip through some cracks of Grindr's censorship, as long as other members of the Grindr community do not flag their profiles. The following two profiles—both of which were posted by Copenhagen area residents with immigration background—demonstrate Grindr's usefulness for self-enterprising individuals (Fig. 4.2). The first user had created a hair salon at his residence; his profile contained the name and slogan for the salon (redacted) and his business' Instagram page with images of

---

[21] But to my surprise, "*betale*" (to pay) flagged my profile! While at a concert in Jutland, I posted on Grindr asking if anyone was driving back to Copenhagen, adding, "*Jeg kan betale*"—I can pay [for the ride]—but an hour later, my profile text had been deleted! I was not banned for any period of time.

himself, his studio, and clients' haircuts. The masseur—whose previous name was "M/\SS/\GE"—also avoided censorship by writing in a Scandinavian language, and also linked to an Instagram profile with photographs of himself and his workspace. Despite Grindr's rules prohibiting commercial advertisements, most Grindr users in the greater Copenhagen appear to tolerate commercial ads like these, evidenced by the fact that the profiles persisted for years without being flagged as inappropriate.

Sex work, however, is *not* advertised publicly on Grindr in the greater Copenhagen area, even though the Grindr culture appears to tolerate other commercial profiles like those in Fig. 4.2; in reading thousands of profiles, I found none that explicitly offered transactional sex. Sex work's invisibility is particularly surprising in Denmark, where it is legal to both sell and purchase sexual services (as long as there is no middle-person, such as a brothel owner or pimp); and even in Sweden, one cannot be arrested for offering transactional sex (though purchasing sex is illegal) so one could attempt to offer services without fear of arrest. Yet sex workers *do* advertise through other methods on Grindr, namely by initiating private correspondence with Grindr users via copy-pasted messages. Some profile texts imply that transactional relationships, including sugar dating, might be commonplace "backstage": for example, a 55-year-old white Dane ended his profile text, "I [am] not a daddy, no money here ☺". This user sought to deter anyone who sought a relationship with monetary support.

Sex work can be ambiguous, especially in the context of the "blurred lines" of socio-sexual networking, when sex can elide with requests for jobs or housing. The aforementioned masseur claimed "no hook-up dates" in his profile, but it is no secret that some masseurs provide sexual services alongside their massages. Consider also the following ad posted in the greater Copenhagen area:

> Brazilian looking for a friend, husband... A job would also be very helpful... I want a nice, sweet, generous caring older man... who would like to have a boyfriend live with him...[22]

Embedded within this ad, the Brazilian also offered to "show off" his body for the friend, suggesting some type of sexual performance in exchange for a durable relationship with housing and thus financial support. In requesting

---

[22] Not posted on Grindr, but a related platform. Shield, "New in Town," 251; also cited in Brennan, 4 (below).

someone "generous," the Brazilian used one of the "commonly occurring codes used to communicate the exchange of sex for cash," according to Joseph Brennan in his study "Cruising for cash: Prostitution on Grindr."[23] Grindr was certainly not the first online platform where gay men advertised sex; in 2008, Light, Fletcher, and Adam suggested that Gaydar's parent company tolerated sex work profiles in order to increase the website's revenue.[24] Future research could explore the spectrum of requests that could be considered "transactional" posted by those who do not necessarily identify as sex workers (e.g. "sugardating").

Grindr can be a tool for finding accommodation, which can be particularly attractive to recent immigrants. However, some posts for housing are in Danish; and others, while in English, are explicitly for tourists, not immigrants. Consider the post of the "Nice Danish guy," age 61, whose profile text advertised: a "room for rent on a daily or weekly basis" in the center of Copenhagen "in the middle of the gayscene!!" The short-term nature of the room means that immigrants looking to settle in Copenhagen need not inquire. Consider also the following housing advertisements: a 45-year-old "Smiling guy in CPH" advertises a "vacant room for tourists," and a 70-year-old "rent[s] out a cheap room (tourist / Non smoking) situated in CPH."[25] These Danish users explicitly state that their vacant rooms are for (gay) tourists, not immigrants or others seeking longer-term accommodation. This is not to suggest that the men posting these advertisements are xenophobic, but more, to show that the gay tourist holds a different

---

[23] Joseph Brennan, "Cruising for Cash: Prostitution on Grindr," *Discourse, Context & Media* 17 (2017): 4. Brennan explores the "profit-seeking motivations" behind those who use Grindr for sex work. Brennan argues that many of those who offer transactional sex via Grindr view the act as an alternative to doing porn; in other words, they are combining sexuality and technology to make cash, without leaving the digital traces of more "traditional" pornographic endeavors like online videos.

[24] "While there is nothing that says that the developers of Gaydar explicitly condone escort activity, the design of the site greatly facilitates such activity and provides a source of profit for QSoft, therefore it is not unreasonable to claim that Gaydar represents a moral position that condones escort activity inscribed into its design." Ben Light et al., "Gay Men, Gaydar and the Commodification of Difference," *Information Technology and People* 21, no. 3 (2008): 307–308.

[25] Also a 72-year-old has a "ROOM FOR RENT IN THE CENTRE OF COPENHAGEN" at a price of 40 euro/day, which suggests that it is also for short-term visitors. The ads in this section come also from PlanetRomeo, a platform that better facilitates international contact (e.g. by potential tourists).

place within Grindr culture than the gay immigrant, even in non-sexual advertisements.

Friendship is the most common non-sexual relationship requested via Grindr profiles, and Grindr encourages users to seek out friendship by providing a drop-down menu with this option. But not all users think friend-seeking is an appropriate use of the app: Courtney Blackwell et al. reported that one of their interviewees "[did] not understand why people would use it [Grindr] to make friends or find dates," and compared this to "going to a [gay] bathhouse to meet friends."[26]

But as with all requests on Grindr, the desire for friendship often blurs with sexuality. Casual sex permeates Grindr culture, even though sex requests tend to hide behind the euphemisms "Fun," "Now," or "NSA." Because (casual) sex is an undercurrent of Grindr culture, requests for friends might blur with requests for sex, as the following newcomer profiles show (Fig. 4.3). The first newcomer's profile requests friends and a gym partner, but includes "fun" in the middle, suggesting that the friendship might elide with sex. The Italian's profile is replete with a logistical request for a tour guide ("show me the place!"), a platonic request for company over a drink ("coffee or beer with me"), a standard euphemism for sex ("fun"), with some parameters for the ideal match. In either ad, one cannot find a hard line between the explicit request for friendship and the implicit request for sex.

Other profiles are more explicitly sexual, such as the third tourist's profile who sought company in his hotel room. This profile shows some of the various ways people communicate desires in their Grindr profiles: by providing sexual identities ("top only"), turn-ons in a partner ("slimmer..."), and by hinting at "kinks" to lure in readers to initiate private messages. Although he ticked off that he was interested in "Chat, Friends," most would understand that the user foremost sought sex, at least while visiting Copenhagen.

Socio-sexual networking is not unique to foreign newcomers. Scandinavian students will sometimes post for housing at the start of the semester, especially those who recently moved for studies. And there are plenty of

---

[26]Courtney Blackwell et al., "Seeing and Being Seen: Co-situation and Impression Formation Using Grindr, a Location-Aware Gay Dating App," *New Media & Society* 17 (2015): 1128. Note that co-author Charles Abbott received his B.A. with a thesis titled, "'Going to a Bathhouse to Meet Friends': An Exploratory Study of Grindr, a Social Networking Application for Gay and Bisexual Men."

Fig. 4.3 Newcomers and "blurred lines" of socio-sexual networking (The redacted text in the third profile refers to specific hotel, and sexual desires)

users who express sexual, platonic, and/or logistical desires in their profiles, but who do not explicitly identify as a Scandinavian local, a tourist, or an immigrant: "Looking for friends, dates, work – if u could help me to find sth, I'd be thankful," is all that one user shares publicly. Thus in the following sections, we examine how tourists and immigrants identify as such in their public profiles, and identify some socio-sexual requests that are unique to tourists and to immigrants.

Identifying as Tourist

Being "new in town" can make one a hot commodity, and thus it behooves the plucky Grindr user to highlight this newcomer status to attract attention. Sometimes one merely needs to be a fresh face in order to get attention, as one U.S. American college student told Blackwell et al. about his experience visiting a small town:

> [It was] a pretty insulated gay world there. And so the minute I logged onto Grindr there it was like BAM! You know it was just everybody was just messaging me. And I got together with one guy at some point... and he was saying... 'you're like the new guy because we all know each other and we've all fucked each other 10 times. And all the sudden there's a new guy, you know, walking in.'

Newcomers' visibility on Grindr can be an asset to their experience on the platform. Thus many choose words like "Visiting" or "Hotel" in their profile name, as we saw in the previous figure.

Tourists and immigrants may identify their country of origin with words, language lists, or flag emojis. Some explicitly name the country of origin in words or emoji (e.g. "from Italy" or "from ❚❚"); others imply it with a nationality and/or ethnicity (e.g. "Italian visiting"). Sometimes the country of origin can be ascertained via the preferred languages (e.g. "EN, IT," or "❚❚✠"). Others avoid any reference to the country of origin, but imply a regional background (e.g. "Mediterranean traveler"). And yet others skip any reference to country of origin, such as the user who sought a gym buddy, while still identifying their "newcomer" status.

Tourist profiles in the greater Copenhagen area generally reify the image of the mobile "gay cosmopolitan tourist" as Western and white. But some profiles challenge this dominant conception of the gay cosmopolitan tourist, including those who identified as tourists from less typically wealthy countries (e.g. Vietnam, Thailand), and visitors from countries where homosexuality is illegal (e.g. Qatar, U.A.E.). One Emirati visitor presented a photo, with face, of himself in a white *thobe* (robe) with *agal* (headdress) tied on with a black cord, and the heartfelt text, "It took me 24 years to be comfortable with who I am, [so I'm] not looking for someone to get me back to where I started." As an Emirati man who presented himself as openly gay in a European city, he (likely) challenged some European readers to reflect on their assumptions about people from the Middle East. Via Grindr, these tourists might even create new queer networks that straddle the world.

One logistical request unique to tourists is the call for a "tour guide," or a local who can provide sightseeing tips, restaurant suggestions, or invitations to events. Not all tourists want to receive this local information face-to-face, so they conduct fact-finding missions on-app. As one U.S. American tourist shared with me about his experiences traveling Europe: "Everyone's like, 'Let's fuck!' But I'm like, 'I'm a tourist, I just want to know where the gay spots are.'"

But a request for a guide generally means that the tourist wants to meet in-person. As with other logistical requests on socio-sexual platforms, the desire for a tour guide can blur with sexual desire (Fig. 4.4). Each of these newcomers used Grindr for the logistical purpose of attempting to meet a local to show them around Copenhagen. The first is the most dry, and

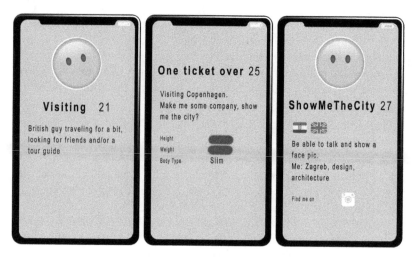

Fig. 4.4 Tourists seeking logistical connections

merely requests friends and a tour guide, but includes a face photo to help attract attention. The second profile is sexually suggestive with "make me some company," though the first and third users might also be open to flirtation.[27] The third user is the most vague with his identification as a tourist; but when one taps on his linked Instagram account, one can see he is identified as a "Croatian touring Europe" and has posted photos from his visits to Copenhagen's tourist-friendly sites (Nyhavn, Delfinsgade). In many ways, a tourist's request for a guide is analogous to the immigrant's request for friendship. In both cases, the newcomer seeks not just companionship, but also practical help navigating a city and learning insider tips, such as about LGBTQ events and spaces. Connecting with a local can cement feelings of connectedness to the new space.

[27]Two more examples of visitor profiles who might have sought a sexual relationship with their tour guide: in one profile, "Visiting," the user suggested meeting someone for "coffee/drinks/dates etc." but he also sought a fitness partner: "Anyone up for a run?" The "dates etc." implies that the user is interested in meeting for sex, but that platonic connections are also welcome, particularly if the Grindr user shares the visitor's interest in running. Similarly, a "Traveling photographer" writes in his profile text that he is "here 2 chat and kiss and take photos." Like the runner, the photographer would like to connect with locals intimately, but also appears open to chatting with those who share his interest in photography.

Identifying as an Immigrant

This chapter is scattered with dozens of examples of "immigrant ads," in which users identify with phrases like "new to Copenhagen," "expat in Malmö," or "foreigner in Denmark." Like tourists, some immigrants identify explicitly by city or country of origin with words or emojis; others imply their country of origin by saying their nationality, ethnicity, or preferred languages; and others eschew any specific country or regional label. The following profiles show some of these methods (Fig. 4.5).

Although the second user does not identify his region or country of origin, he does identify his "ethnicity" as Middle Eastern, though this does not necessarily mean he comes from this region of the world; most understand the menu to refer to "ethnic background" or "race," so this user could have moved from France. Similar to tourist profiles, my archive of unambiguous immigrant profiles is dominated by those from Europe, North America, and Australia: "From Belgium... living in København"; "Brit by birth, then CPH..."; "Spanish guy living in DK"; "[American flag] Just moved to Cph for work..."; "New Yorker living in Copenhagen"; "An

Fig. 4.5 Immigrant profiles (The flags on the third profile stand for Syria, Lebanon, UK, France, and finally Denmark. "*Vi hygger os!*" roughly translates to "Let's get cozy!")

Aussie living in Nørrebro… will be around for the next 2-3 years…"; and so forth.

Rarely do immigrants enter Scandinavia with knowledge of its languages, and thus immigrants in Scandinavia commiserate over the shared struggle of learning the language. If a Grindr user posts about knowing "a little Danish"—such as the Asian immigrant whose ad started this chapter—then it is safe to assume the user recently settled in Denmark and intends to remain long term.[28] Regarding the third profile in Fig. 4.5: this user lists his languages through flags: first Syria and Lebanon,[29] then UK, France, and finally (a bit of) Denmark. The flag choices and "ethnicity" section imply that he comes from Syria or Lebanon, but he could have moved to Denmark from anywhere. This user identified as an Arabic-speaking Danish learner, but kept his specific immigration background obscure.

By emphasizing that he speaks "a bit of" Danish, the author of the above profile communicates many things simultaneously. First, he shows that he is neither a tourist nor a Dane with immigration background, but an immigrant who relocated to Denmark (and hence is in the process of learning the language). Second, he shows that he is open to practicing Danish with Grindr users, whether in private chat messages, or in real life. Third, he ingratiates himself with Danish culture, and thus with Danes. By ending his profile with the quintessentially Danish phrase "*Vi hygger os!*"—meaning "We're enjoying ourselves," or "Let's get cozy!"—he presents himself as someone interested in his host's culture, and this could be a strategy for making connections with locals. With a more critical reading, one could view this as a performance of integration, and an effort to avoid being categorized as a "bad" immigrant.

"No, I Never Say I'm an Immigrant": Interviewee Experiences with Socio-Sexual Networking

"Most of my gay friends are from Grindr. And actually a couple of them are really good friends," said Ali (from Iraq, from the introduction of this chapter). He contrasted his experiences on Grindr with that of other dating platforms, like Tinder: "I haven't met a lot of people through Tinder, but

---

[28] Shield, "New in Town," 250–251.

[29] Likely to show familiarity with the Arabic dialects in both countries, and/or to clarify his immigration background.

those I met were for dates, and it didn't continue on to become friends." By contrasting the platforms, Ali suggested that the Grindr culture in the greater Copenhagen area included a mixture of social and sexual networking, whereas the Tinder culture fostered mainly dating.

"Sometimes the lines are not so clear," said Şenol (b. Turkey, immigrated 2010) when talking about finding friends versus sex on Grindr. "Maybe the first thing that comes to mind is sex or dating," he began; but these initial conversations or meet-ups might turn into friendships.

Daniel (b. Nigeria, immigrated 2016) expressed ambivalence about Grindr's central purpose; on the one hand, he insisted that Grindr should be used primarily to find sex partners:

> [If you're looking for friends] Well you have to look somewhere else. This [Grindr] is just for when you're horny. You come here, you pick someone, you have sex, and that's all. It's like a meat market.

Yet Daniel is one of this chapter's prime examples of someone who used Grindr to connect with the locals for logistical means: not only did he meet a Scandinavian man who offered to share his house—when Daniel was living in a refugee camp awaiting approval on his application for asylum—but also Daniel met a fellow Nigerian asylum seeker through Grindr, who became his (platonic) friend:

> I have a friend who is Igbo...We met on Grindr, wanted to have sex then, but ... when I found out he's from Nigeria we started talking, talking our pidgin, and the sex part left. Now we're friends.

Despite this positive connection, Daniel unfortunately had a negative experience with the aforementioned Scandinavian roommate, who eventually sought sex with Daniel (detailed later); perhaps for this reason, Daniel held the view that Grindr was mainly a sex app.

The sexual element of these apps is an important factor to consider when making practical or logistical connections. Asen (b. Bulgaria; immigrated to Denmark in 2014) was happy to post profiles on Grindr and Romeo that sought sex, friendship, and a flatmate, though he did *not seek to blur* the lines of sex/friendship with this flatmate. He complained that the few who responded to his housing request wrote "borderline sexual" messages, which turned him off from their housing offers.[30]

For similar reasons, Yusuf (from Egypt; immigrated 2013) said that Grindr would be his last resort for job-seeking, partly because he wondered whether a job found via Grindr would have sexual strings attached: "I don't want to have that weirdness of [a job found via] a sexual-perceived application. It feels a bit awkward to me." To Yusuf, a Grindr user who posted for a cleaning job (like the ad at the start of this chapter) risked getting hired for a sexual gig. That being said, Yusuf backtracked slightly: "However, I don't see these applications as hook-up-only applications."

Reflecting on his own use of Grindr and PlanetRomeo upon arrival in Denmark, Sami (b. Israel; immigrated to Denmark in 2015) exemplified an optimistic ethos of socio-sexual networking: he felt that these platforms "can really facilitate you to make positive things happen," like meeting a new network of friends or finding a job. Socio-sexual platforms were "not just to satisfy a physical need" but rather "can open doors" for their users, "and there will be possibilities through that. There will be things that benefit us, finding jobs, et cetera. It's good to remember that."

Finding Jobs and Housing

Despite Sami's optimism for finding friends and jobs via socio-sexual media, he also echoed Yusuf's skepticism about finding a job via Grindr: "If I'm seeking jobs, I consider that more private. I would be more looking the right ways." By contrasting job-seeking on Grindr with job-seeking "the right way" (as in LinkedIn, he suggested), Sami's statement suggests that socio-economic background can play a role in a migrant's expectations of socio-sexual networking. As a college-educated professional, Sami sought a technology job in Scandinavia; unlike the user posting for a cleaning job, Sami did not think Grindr could connect him to a useful network of potential employers.

Nevertheless, Sami befriended another immigrant (via Romeo) who tried to get him a job: "I met a guy who is Italian and had been here for four years, and as the conversation went on, I realized he's working in" the same field as Sami "at a Danish start-up company." So Sami offered his specific area of expertise, and the Italian friend spoke to his boss on Sami's behalf. In the end, "It didn't happen, but it could have—so that's nice."

[30]Shield, "New in Town," 249–250.

Sami continued to have faith that gay social networks—even those forged through socio-sexual media—could be a viable method of finding a job; yet at the time of our interview, he was seeking jobs through more traditional methods.

Pejman (b. Iran; immigrated 2013) arrived in Scandinavia with a green card, and was able to support himself during his first year. During that time, and via Grindr, he met another immigrant from Iran who had been living in the greater Copenhagen area for a few years. "We met and made friendship, and after a few weeks I asked him if he knew someone that I can rent a flat or a room from." Coincidentally the Iranian friend was looking to move out of his apartment and asked Pejman if he wanted to sublet his flat. Pejman did and he has lived there ever since.

"A few months later he introduced me to his boss," Pejman continued, "and I got a part-time job," where he worked for over a year. Yet while Grindr was the technology that introduced the two contacts, it did not play a direct role in matching Pejman to the apartment or job. Grindr merely facilitated the building of a more "traditional" social network, one that eventually assisted with these practical logistics.[31]

Other immigrants have had success finding long-term housing via Grindr. To start with two examples from informal conversations: a white, 21-year-old from the United States wrote on his profile that he sought "drinks, maybe some fun" in Copenhagen, then added, "Also looking for a room from September on, if you know of anything feel free to message me!" Via private message, I inquired about his luck in finding a room via Grindr: "It seems like it's working haha," he began. "I saw a room yesterday available from October on. I've had plenty of offers so far." Another user—a white, 27-year-old from Slovakia—had "Looking4room" as his display name. I wrote to enquire about his experiences, and he said that he was "very lucky" to have just found a great spot. I asked what inspired him to use Grindr to finding accommodation, and he said that he had first tried in Berlin for a short stay, and it worked there: "These were the first 2 attempts to use grindr too [to find housing], and it worked both times."

My interviewees, however, had less success finding housing via Grindr, despite their optimism. Asen (b. Bulgaria, immigrated 2015), like the Slovakian, found Berliners to be forthcoming with housing offers, and tried his luck on Grindr in Copenhagen: "But people use it here just for sex." Angelo

[31]Shield, "New in Town," 250.

(b. Greece; immigrated 2013) had been optimistic that PlanetRomeo could help him logistically upon arrival in Copenhagen. He remembered posting something like "I'm here looking for an apartment, or a job, part-time, because I'm a student," as he thought it was "a good idea to be part of the electronic community." He hoped he would meet someone with a room, or with a friend with a room, and he did receive sympathetic responses like "I will keep my eye out." But after two months living with a relative, he found housing through a more traditional housing website.

The most dramatic narrative about housing comes from Daniel (from Nigeria). Daniel arrived in Scandinavia as an asylum seeker in 2016, and was placed in a camp. He was openly gay, and one of the few people in his camp from sub-Saharan Africa, which made him feel alone and unsafe:

> Shield: How is being gay in the camp?
> Daniel: It's terrible! The same with racism as well. Because you're black and everything so they [the other asylum seekers] pick on you. I have complained to Migration many times that I feel unsafe in that camp, because a lot of people are trying to attack me.

In Scandinavia, he learned about Grindr from a gay acquaintance; through the app, he began to chat with Scandinavian men who lived in the area:

> I was staying at the camp, and I met this guy on Grindr and he asked me to move in with him... He said I don't have to pay, at the beginning. He said I could be cleaning, cooking, taking care of his cats. And I said, OK, because I wasn't working.

Daniel met with the older Scandinavian man, and despite their age difference—twenties versus sixties—they hit it off, and the man invited Daniel to live with him. Daniel was not interested in having sex with the man, but he agreed to share a bed with him. Within the first few weeks, however, Daniel found it difficult to keep his relationship entirely platonic. It started when the man began to flirt with Daniel by complimenting his body, and then touching him: "So that was when the whole problem's starting."

After Daniel refused sex with his roommate, the Scandinavian asked Daniel to contribute to rent. The amount was small compared to the price of the apartment—about 1000 kroner per month—but it consumed about 50% of Daniel's monthly allowance. Then the man asked Daniel to buy his own food; Daniel agreed. A few months later, the man began inviting guests to spend the night, and asked Daniel to stay with a friend. Daniel recalled telling him, "I am paying for this place! Even though the money is not much. You can't tell me just to stay outside—I don't have anywhere to go."

After a few fights, Daniel handed back his keys, and returned to living in the camp for asylum seekers. After relaying the aforementioned complaints about homophobia and racism at the camp, Daniel received a single-occupancy room. Despite continued complaints about the camp, Daniel preferred to live in his single room in an asylum camp rather than with a Grindr contact who blurred the lines between roommate and sexual partner.

Daniel's experience as an asylum seeker strapped for cash is not comparable to the experiences of Pejman or the Slovakian. Foremost, Daniel's legal and financial situations made him vulnerable to exploitation. Nevertheless, he confidently volunteered to leave the camp to live with a man he met via Grindr, and tolerated the living situation for several months. When he ended his relationship with the Scandinavian man, he faced no obstacle moving out or returning to the camp. Daniel's narrative shows that Grindr can be an important resource for an immigrant with no network of locals; but it is also a caveat about the difficulties in making truly platonic, logistical connections through socio-sexual platforms.

Finding Friendship

Among immigrants in Scandinavia, a common complaint concerns the "coldness" of Scandinavians; to provide just a few snippets from interviews: "It's very hard to make friends"; "You cannot make friends in Sweden" (or Denmark); "They don't want to open up to other people"; "They're just so cold and closed to themselves." For that reason, many interviewees felt that it was easier to initiate conversation on Grindr than approaching a Scandinavian at a gay bar. For interviewees who were self-conscious about their English (and Scandinavian) language abilities, digital communication can be a more relaxing way to communicate; even with real-time communications, a user can still pause to look up and translate unfamiliar words and phrases.

Matthew (b. China, immigrated 2015) had just arrived in Scandinavia for studies when he (via Grindr) met Karl, a (white, Scandinavian) fellow student, originally from a small town: "Nothing happened [sexually]. But we became friends." Three years later, they traveled to France together for a wedding: "He was my plus-one!" Nevertheless, Matthew felt that Scandinavians overall were more "cold" compared to other Europeans, based on his own personal experiences ("I used Grindr when I travel all around Europe"). But his friendship with Karl shows that some immigrants and Scandinavian locals form enduring relationships via Grindr.

When Abdul moved to Scandinavia (2014), he was in the closet, but sought to live relatively more openly as gay. Yet the surveillance of the small diasporic community from his country of origin prevented this. As he said, "If my family… knew, I could be in very serious trouble"; thus, he asked that his country of origin be identified only as a member of the Gulf Cooperation Council. Abdul has no face photo in his public profile, but did share photos when chatting with someone of interest. He was a heavy user of Grindr, paid for the upgraded app, and chatted with people in both Copenhagen and Malmö daily: "I just use it to socialize and make friends."

Abdul said he was too "anxious" to attend public LGBTQ events like Pride; and the few times he visited gay clubs, he would take his "hoodie on my head until I get in." But he identified as gay, and desired to make connections with other gay men. Thus, "One of the very few channels where I connect with guys is Grindr."

In contrast to his nervousness in physical LGBTQ spaces, Abdul felt relaxed chatting with men in online spaces primarily for gay men. Parvin (b. Iran, immigrated 2015) shared this sentiment, as he was not open about his sexuality to the relatives with whom he was living at the time of our interview. Azim (b. Egypt, immigrated 2014) was entirely in the closet at the time of our interview, except to the few contacts he met on socio-sexual apps and websites; for him, this small collection of sexual partners helped him come to terms with his sexual orientation and gay identity.

In sum, interviewees explained several reasons why they enjoyed, or even preferred, to chat with Scandinavian locals via apps: online communication alleviated their anxieties about approaching Scandinavians at bars, it reduced their self-consciousness around language abilities in English or Scandinavian, and it enabled users to disclose their identity in a controlled manner.

Finding Sex

Interviewees had a variety of experiences finding sex partners via the app. One complained that he had almost never matched with anyone and pondered if it related to his age, looks, race, or something else; but he had a feeling that his failures on Grindr related foremost to being closeted and unwilling to share clear face photos on the visual-centric platform. Another factor in a user's success finding sex partners relates to the user's level of engagement: those who were more persistent seemed to find matches. Luck is also a major factor. But what roles do migration background, nationality, and race play regarding an immigrant's attainment of sex via Grindr in Scandinavia?

Pavel (b. Russia; immigrated 2017) and Stepan (b. Russia; immigrated 2017) were seeking asylum on the grounds of sexual orientation at the time of our interview. They were in an open relationship and both had profiles on Grindr. While waiting for their decision, Pavel volunteered with a gay organization, attended a gym, and practiced photography; he also enjoyed cruising Grindr for casual sex, with apparently high success. Ultimately, he hoped to find a regular "fuck buddy" for repeated sessions. Pavel and Stepan both identified as Russian on their Grindr profiles, which prompted me to ask how people responded to this identification:

"Usually they just write, 'Mmmm, Russia! Hot boy!'" Pavel responded with a smile. For Pavel, who is white, his status as a foreigner was an erotic asset in the Grindr culture of Scandinavia.

Stepan also used Grindr foremost to find sex partners; like Pavel, he felt that he had never experienced rejection on the grounds of being Russian, or a foreigner. Stepan even broadcast that he was an asylum seeker: "Why not?" he responded to my inquiry. According to Stepan, Scandinavians tended to respond positively to this information: "They say: good, we listen about [are aware of] the problem in Russia for LGBT person." Yet not all interviewees experienced that Scandinavians were open to sex with an asylum seeker.

Daniel (from Nigeria) reflected on the allure of newcomers in Scandinavia. Like Blackwell et al.'s interviewee (mentioned earlier in the chapter) who felt that fresh faces were inundated with messages, Daniel felt that newcomers could use their status to their sexual advantage. Yet he clarified that this status worked better for tourists than for, say, asylum seekers:

They [the Grindr users] like tourists a lot. If you're a tourist in [redacted: Denmark/Sweden] or in Europe, then you're a piece of—you're a hot cake.... As soon as you say you're a tourist, they're very, very ready. They can drive all the way like 50 kilometers down to meet you.

Daniel's opinion on this matter related to his own autoethnographic work on Grindr, in which he observed that people did not want to meet him if he said he was an asylum seeker from Nigeria.

"No, I never say I'm an immigrant," Daniel reflected during our interview. Instead, he claimed to be a tourist: "I put that I'm visiting from Portugal." Daniel's strategic non-disclosure about his immigration status is central to this chapter's conclusion that not all newcomers are equally alluring.

CONCLUSIONS

Immigrants Are Optimistic About Socio-Sexual Networking

Foremost, the data presented in this chapter show that immigrants' behaviors on online platforms aimed primarily at gay men can best be described as *socio-sexual networking*. All interviewees used Grindr and related platforms for finding sexual partners or potential friends, and often both. Many also had sought logistical contacts who could help them with practical matters like finding housing or jobs, practicing the local language, or sharing other information. In forging networks of sexual partners, platonic friends, and logistical contacts, some interviewees felt that the lines might "blur"; in some cases, this blurring was stress-free (e.g. if a potential sexual partner became a platonic friend), but in other cases this blurring was problematic (e.g. when a roommate began to make unwanted sexual advances).

Almost all interviewees were open to finding platonic friends via Grindr, and several had successfully done so. Initiating conversation online was repeatedly described as less stressful than approaching someone at a gay bar, due to reasons such as the supposed taciturnity of Scandinavians, one's insecurity with one's own language abilities in English or Danish or Swedish, and—especially for those who were discreet about their sexual orientation—one's anxiety about being seen in physical LGBTQ spaces. For this last group, apps like Grindr became the primary mode for connecting with local gay men.

Social networks forged initially via Grindr and related apps helped Pejman find an apartment and a job, enabled Daniel to live semi-independently for several months instead of at a refugee camp, and connected Sami to a potential position at a technology company. Asen and Angelo were unsuccessful finding housing or jobs, but still tried their luck by advertising for these practical matters alongside their dating announcements. For brevity, not all anecdotes could be included. For example, Caleb (b. China; immigrated to Sweden in 2013) used a socio-sexual platform to find a summer sub-letter for a vacant room in his apartment, and Mehmet (b. Turkey, immigrated 2017) practiced his Scandinavian language abilities by chatting on Grindr and keeping lists of new vocabulary.

Even those who sought primarily sex via Grindr showed that cruising could also be social and even political: by coming out to potential sex partners as an asylum seeker from Russia, Stepan spread awareness about LGBTQ human rights abuses (e.g. in Chechnya), and provided a human face to the rights abuses that force LGBTQ people to flee to countries like Denmark and Sweden.

Immigrant-to-Immigrant Bonds Stronger Than Immigrant-to-Local Ones?

Although many immigrants are optimistic that socio-sexual platforms like Grindr can assist them in connecting to local Scandinavians, not all interviewees succeeded in doing so. Many found casual sex partners, but were unable to cement more durable relationships with local Scandinavians. Rather, the data in the chapter suggest that a recent immigrant is more likely to build enduring relationships via Grindr *with other immigrants* than with local Scandinavians.

Pejman (from Iran) is this chapter's biggest "success story" with regard to finding friendship, housing, and a job via Grindr; yet the fact that Pejman's chief contact was a fellow Iranian is not a coincidence. The two shared a strong bond that surpassed the mere commonality of sexual orientation: they had a common country of origin, language, and cultural background, as well as similar experiences adapting to life in Scandinavia. Parvin (also from Iran) felt that it was difficult to connect with locals, but found it easier to meet others who shared his ethnic background: "Iranians are in contact with each other. We meet together. We are really lonely here." For similar reasons, it is no coincidence that Daniel's best friend who he met via Grindr was a fellow Nigerian asylum seeker, especially as Daniel felt uncomfortable identifying as an immigrant when chatting with Scandinavian locals.

Immigrant-to-immigrant networks are not merely strongest among co-ethnics; immigrants appear to have an easier time connecting with other immigrants regardless of a shared language, cultural background, or country of origin. Abdul (from "an Arab country") described his best friend in Scandinavia as a local, but later clarified that the friend was a Kurdish refugee who had arrived in Scandinavia many years prior. Also, Şenol (from Turkey) emphasized how important it was to make his first gay friend in Scandinavia (whom he met via a socio-sexual platform); he later clarified that the friend was a Chinese student.

Also with casual sex, immigrant-to-immigrant bonds may be easier to build than immigrant-to-local bonds. An interviewee (in his mid-40s) expressed this sentiment most clearly when summarizing his experiences cruising for sex in Copenhagen's gay sauna: "I [have] had lots of encounters with non-Danes. Non-Danes are okay, even the young ones. But Danes— it's questionable for me." These examples show that Grindr is an instrumental tool for immigrants who want to connect to gay men in their surrounding area; but these examples also suggest that immigrants face limitations in their ability to form enduring bonds with Scandinavian locals.

Not All Newcomers Benefit Equally from the Allure of Newcomers

The chapter started with an outline of the socio-historic context surrounding conceptions of the Western "gay tourist"—as wealthy, mobile, and often white, male—versus the non-Western queer subject. This chapter's analysis of Grindr profile texts shows that gay tourists identify in a variety of ways, including with references to their country of origin, hotel name, and even travel itinerary. (It is not uncommon to see tourist profiles that state travel plans: "CPH 1-4 July, Stockholm 4-7 July, Oslo 7-10 July".) Immigrants present themselves in a variety of ways, including through countries of origin, nationalities, and languages, both in words and flag emojis. Yet some GBTQ immigrants keep their country of origin vague, such as the user who ingratiated himself in beginner's Danish ("*vi hygger os!*") after listing his "languages" with the flags of Syria and Lebanon; or to provide a new example, a (Turkish) user who identified only as an "expat" on his Grindr profile, but whose Turkish country of origin became clear upon examining his linked Instagram account.

Şenol (from Turkey) also remained vague about his immigration status on Grindr: "I don't write that I come from Turkey in my profile or anything." He made this statement when talking about his surprise in receiving a defamatory message from an anonymous user. Although Şenol did not provide a rationale for hiding his Turkish background on Grindr, the fact that he mentioned obfuscating his nationality in relation to aggressive messages suggests that some immigrants remain vague about their countries of origin so as to shield themselves from xenophobic messages. Anxieties about Islamophobia are indeed an important aspect of Grindr culture, as we explore in Chapter 5.

Non-disclosure of precise immigration status could be a strategy for maximizing one's sex appeal on Grindr, as Daniel (from Nigeria) suggested. As a black man with no Scandinavian language abilities, Daniel knew he had to identify as a foreigner. By choosing to identify as a Portuguese visitor rather than as an African asylum seeker, Daniel sought to benefit from the aforementioned stereotypes surrounding the "gay tourist": yes he was black, but he could still "pass" as a European Union citizen with the means to travel.

Daniel justified lying about his migration background on Grindr by asserting his belief that Scandinavians held prejudicial ideas about Africans, namely that they all wanted money. He referred to the scam emails that many Scandinavians receive from West Africa (e.g. by email, or on PlanetRomeo) telling them to send money, and feared that Scandinavians thought he was only interested in money too. By claiming to be a European tourist, Daniel showed that race and migration status *could* be decoupled: Daniel could align himself with wealth, mobility, and cosmopolitanism, despite also bearing the burdens of being a black foreigner. However, there were still stereotypes that Daniel could not avoid.

Immigration Status and Race Can Be Very Different Subject Positions

Race cannot be ignored in an analysis of immigrants in Europe. Remaining ambiguous about one's immigration status or country of origin could help some immigrants pass as cosmopolitan tourists or Western "expats" who are perceived by locals to be more desirable (for reasons embedded in historic and social practices). But the data in this chapter do not show that all immigrants can "pass" in these ways.

Blond-haired, blue-eyed Stepan did not need to lie about his immigration status in order to find local Scandinavians who were attracted to him. But Nigerian Daniel, even when pretending to be a jet-setting EU tourist, still faced obstacles on account of his race: blackness predetermined many of his experiences on Grindr. To include one final snippet from our interview:

People hate black people for no reason. They just judge you for no reason....
A [white] person will meet a black person who is looking for a relationship,
and they will say: a black person is all about money, and will use you...
because they think black people are looking for something.... They use your
skin color to determine what you're supposed be and do.

Later in the interview, he extended his argument to include sexual health:
they "see a black person and [think] he has HIV. That is the mentality."
Daniel believes that his skin color provoked users' prejudices about his
HIV status, his motives for connecting to Scandinavians on the site, and
his personality.

Daniel's narrative represents just a small part of what it feels like to
embody race—or Otherness—on Grindr. Fanon's *Black Skin, White Masks*
(1952) offers strikingly similar insights on the feelings of embodying race
(blackness) and the psychological consequences. He describes the "crushing objecthood" of being identified with a racial epithet, of being the object
of "Look a Negro!" shouted at him by a frightened boy.[32] Fanon analyzed
the psychological toll of embodying not just blackness, but sin and mon-
strosity, such as to that boy.[33] More generally, Fanon reflected, "When
[white] people like me, they tell me it is in spite of my color. When they
dislike me, they point out that it is not because of my color. Either way, I am
locked into the infernal circle."[34] Speaking sixty-five years later, Daniel's
experiences on Grindr continue to illustrate crushing objecthood in white
settings.

While this chapter presented some of the rosier sides socio-sexual networking—such as immigrants' successes in making new friends in a host
country—Chapter 5 centers on the various ways racism and xenophobia
hinder immigrants from connecting with local Scandinavians. Chapter 6

---

[32] Franz Fanon, *Black Skin, White Masks*, trans. Charles Lam Markmann (London: Pluto
Press, 1986 [1952]), 109.

[33] Fanon also analyzed the biography of a black woman married to a white man in Mar-
tinique; one evening at a dinner party, she remembered, "The [white] women kept watching
me with a condescension that I found unbearable. I felt that I was wearing too much makeup,
that I was not properly dressed, that I was not doing [my husband] André any credit, perhaps
simply because of the color of my skin...." Although Fanon was critical of the woman—
who he felt "dream[ed] of a form of salvation that consists of magically turning white" and of
"whiten[ing] the race"—he excused her racial paranoia due to the prevailing context of racism
and shame in the French colonies. Fanon, 44, 47; and Mayotte Capécia, *Je Suis Martiniquaise*,
1948, cited in Fanon, 43.

[34] Fanon, 117.

scrutinizes Grindr's "ethnicity" drop-down menu, and the weight that various labels carry when deployed by immigrants in the greater Copenhagen area. Migration status alone does not determine a newcomer's experience on Grindr in a new country; race, in tandem with the host society's dominant conceptions of racial difference, must also take center stage when examining the diversity of user experiences in socio-sexual online cultures.

BIBLIOGRAPHY

Aldrich, Robert. *Colonialism and Homosexuality*. London: Routledge, 2003.
Aldrich, Robert. *The Seduction of the Mediterranean: Writing, Art, and Homosexual Fantasy*. London: Routledge, 1993.
Blackwell, Courtney, Jeremy Birnholtz, and Charles Abbott. "Seeing and Being Seen: Co-situation and Impression Formation Using Grindr, a Location-Aware Gay Dating App." *New Media & Society* 17 (2015): 1117–1136.
Brennan, Joseph. "Cruising for Cash: Prostitution on Grindr." *Discourse, Context & Media* 17 (2017): 1–8.
Duguay, Stefanie. "Identity Modulation in Networked Publics: Queer Women's Participation and Representation on Tinder, Instagram, and Vine." PhD diss., Queensland University of Technology, 2017.
El-Tayeb, Fatima. "'Gays Who Cannot Properly Be Gay': Queer Muslims in the Neoliberal European City." *European Journal of Women's Studies* 19 (February 2012): 79–95.
Fanon, Franz. *Black Skin, White Masks*. Translated by Charles Lam Markmann. London: Pluto Press, 1986 [1952].
Grindr. "Grindr Terms and Conditions of Service." Terms of Service. Effective Date: 30 March 2017, accessed Fall 2017 via https://www.grindr.com/terms-of-service.
Grov, Christian, A. S. Breslow, M. E. Newcomb, J. G. Rosenberger, and J. A. Bauermeister. "Gay and Bisexual Men's Use of the Internet: Research from the 1990s through 2013." *Journal of Sex Research* 51, no. 4 (2014): 390–409.
Light, Ben, Gordon Fletcher, and Alison Adam. "Gay Men, Gaydar and the Commodification of Difference." *Information Technology and People* 21, no. 3 (2008): 300–314.
Luibhéid, Eithne, and Lionel Cantú. *Queer Migrations: Sexuality, U.S. Citizenship, and Border Crossings*. Minneapolis: University of Minnesota, 2005.
Massad, Joseph. *Desiring Arabs*. Chicago: University of Chicago Press, 2007.
Mitchell, Gregory. "TurboConsumers™ in Paradise: Tourism, Civil Rights, and Brazil's Gay Sex Industry." *American Ethnologist* 38, no. 4 (2011): 666–682.

Ong, Jonathan Corpus. "Queer Cosmopolitanism in the Disaster Zone: 'My Grindr Became the United Nations'." *International Communication Gazette* 79, nos. 6–7 (2017): 656–673.

Pérez, Hiram. *A Taste for Brown Bodies: Gay Modernity and Cosmopolitan Desire.* New York: New York University Press, 2015.

Puar, Jasbir. *Terrorist Assemblages: Homonationalism in Queer Times.* Durham, NC: Duke University Press, 2007.

Sedgwick, Eve Kosofsky. *Between Men: English Literature and Male Homosocial Desire.* New York: Columbia University Press, 1985.

Shield, Andrew DJ. "New in Town: Gay Immigrants and Geosocial Dating Apps." In *LGBTQs, Media, and Culture in Europe*, edited by Alexander Dhoest, Lukasz Szulc, and Bart Eeckhout, 244–261. London: Routledge, 2017.

CHAPTER 5

"Tend to prefer sane, masculine, caucasian (no offense to other flavours though)": Racial-Sexual Preferences, Entitlement, and Everyday Racism

Gay and queer immigrants are largely optimistic that socio-sexual platforms like Grindr can connect them not only to potential sexual partners, but also to friends and logistical contacts. Being "new in town" might attract a small flurry of attention from regulars, but not all immigrants experience the allure of newcomers equally, and many immigrants have better luck connecting with other newcomers than with locals. What are the hindrances that immigrants face when trying to connect with locals in a sexually charged setting like Grindr? How does the larger socio-political climate affect the online culture of this platform? When is xenophobia racialized? What is distinctive about the racism encountered on socio-sexual platforms?

The central aim of this chapter is to examine racism broadly and within the context of socio-sexual online cultures, using theories of everyday racism, entitlement racism, and sexual racism.[1] The chapter presents five recurring discourses about race within the Grindr culture of the greater

[1] Philomena Essed, *Everyday Racism: Reports from Women of Two Cultures* (Alameda, CA: Hunter House, 1990); Philomena Essed, *Understanding Everyday Racism: An Interdisciplinary Theory* (Newbury Park, CA: Sage, 1991); Philomena Essed, "Entitlement Racism: License to Humiliate," in *Recycling Hatred: Racism(s) in Europe Today*, ed. European Network Against Racism (Brussels: European Network Against Racism, 2013), 62–77.

© The Author(s) 2019
A. DJ Shield, *Immigrants on Grindr*,
https://doi.org/10.1007/978-3-030-30394-5_5

Copenhagen: persistent questions about the origins of people of color; racial-sexual exclusions; racial-sexual fetishes; conflation between (potential) immigrants and economic opportunism; and insults directed at immigrants based on race, nationality, or religion. By the end of the chapter, the reader should understand how race-related and racist private messages are part of the general, even daily, racial minority's experience on socio-sexual networking platforms.

Abdul (b. "an Arab country," immigrated 2014) experienced several incidents where Grindr users hurled insults at him because of his ethnic background and perceived religion. Reflecting on the online environment, Abdul made the interesting assertion that racism might be *more* visible on Grindr than in offline settings:

> On Grindr usually people just say whatever they want to. Because they don't know you, and there is a distance, and it's only chat. But in daily life [in Scandinavia], if there is someone who doesn't like me—like on a bus—he can't just say: "Go back to where you came from!"

On a bus, of course a stranger *could* shout a racist insult at Abdul; but the racist stranger would have to confront Abdul face-to-face and deal with any reactions directly, from Abdul or from others on the bus. On Grindr, however, a racist person can shout an insult directly at a user of color, and/or a user perceived to be Muslim, and then can make himself disappear by blocking Abdul; or he can send the insult anonymously from a blank profile. Culpability can be evaded on app.

This chapter begins with a discussion of *sexual racism*, that is, the notion that an individual's sexual "preferences" might exclude members of certain racial groups.[2] Those who defend racial-sexual preferences argue that they are ingrained and immutable (as in most gay men's preference for other men) and/or individual (as in someone's preference for someone taller or shorter). Those who criticize these preferences argue that an individual's sexual prejudices cannot be divided from that individual's general racist

[2] Jesus G. Smith, "Two-Faced Racism in Gay Online Sex: Preference in the Frontstage or Racism in the Backstage?" in *Sex in the Digital Age*, ed. Paul Nixon and Isabel Düsterhöft (New York: Routledge, 2018), 144.

attitudes.[3] Drawing from the latter argument, this chapter considers that an individual's racial-sexual preferences may relate to larger socio-political discourses about race, immigration, and Islam.

(Throughout this chapter, the reader might be wondering about the technological interface of Grindr: what exactly are the options on the "ethnicity" menu? Do all users really utilize the menu? Might this menu allow for race-selective searches? Questions about the interface and affordances of Grindr are reserved for Chapter 6.)

BACKGROUND: RACISM AS INDIVIDUAL, AS STRUCTURAL

Sexual Racism

Sexual racism has a long history in socio-sexual online cultures geared at gay men (see, e.g., discussion of Tsang's 1994 work, Chapter 2).[4] On message boards, in chat rooms, in profile texts, and through instant messages, queer people of color have experienced sexual stereotypes, racial fetishization, and outright exclusion. In and outside of academia, queer people of color have engaged LGBTQ people to be critical of these issues.[5] Many of these public and scholarly debates have taken place in North America, but some also in Europe.[6] In Denmark, for example, Sabaah brought attention to issues related to sexual racism online in a 2013 panel criticizing the web forum

---

[3]Denton Callander et al., "Is Sexual Racism *Really* Racism? Distinguishing Attitudes Toward Sexual Racism and Generic Racism Among Gay and Bisexual Men," *Archives of Sexual Behavior* 44 (2015): 1991–2000; Smith, "Two-Faced Racism," 135–136.

[4]Daniel Tsang, "Notes on Queer 'N Asian Virtual Sex," *Amerasia Journal* 20, no. 1 (1994): 117–128.

[5]In addition to the pieces cited in this chapter and in Chapter 2, see also Alexander Chee, "No Asians! Navigating the Pitfalls of Anti-Asian Sentiments in Online Hookup Sites," *Out Magazine*, 11 January 2012, https://www.out.com/news-commentary/2012/01/11/no-asians.

[6]E.g. Wim Peumans, "'No Asians, Please': Same-Sex Sexualities and Ethnic Minorities in Europe," in *Hand Picked: Stimulus Respond*, ed. Jack Boulton (London: Pavement Books, 2014), 128–139. But in France, however, the gay magazine *Miroir/miroirs* focused one recent issue on socio-sexual platforms, but paid no attention to race; and focused another attention on ethnic minorities in the gay scene, but paid no attention to sexual racism.

"I'm not turned on by Asians,"[7] and at public discussions at Copenhagen Pride,[8] as outlined in Chapter 1.

In 2015, a key scholarly text from Australia (henceforth Callander et al.) proclaimed it was the "first [study] to quantify attitudes relating to online sexual racism and the ways in which these attitudes relate to racism in general."[9] Earlier studies of race in gay men's digital culture hesitated to use the label "racist," even when they emphasized that "preferences for homogamy are sometimes structurally reinforced through lack of exposure to people of different cultures and xenophobia."[10] But the authors of the 2015 study—entitled "Is Sexual Racism *Really* Racism?"—aimed to show that white men's racial-sexual preferences tended to correspond to "generic racist attitudes" and "racist attitudes more broadly." The authors challenged the idea that racial-sexual attraction was "solely a matter of personal preference."

The phrase "sexual racism" has circulated increasingly in popular media as well, for example in a segment of *The Daily Show* (entitled "Sexual Racism: When Preferences Become Discrimination") which suggested that heterosexual African-American women's low response rates on OK Cupid corresponded to false information about black women's rates of sexually transmitted infections.[11]

Racial-sexual exclusions have not gone unchecked within Grindr culture. Since 2011 or perhaps even earlier, offended users have reacted to problematic profiles—those with racial-sexual exclusions and other problematic text—by posting screen-captures of these profiles with hashtags like #douchebagsofgrindr and #sexualracismsux. Others have taken to personal blogs, such as one Australian university student who posted the racist Grindr messages he received because of his Yolngu (indigenous) background; the story spread to news outlets across Australia and helped bring

[7] Sabaah, "[Debat:] Tænder ikke på asiater" [Debate: I'm Not Turned On by Asians], 19 February 2013, https://www.youtube.com/watch?v=qvSuHQPFWGw.

[8] E.g. "Grindr and Sex Culture," Panel at Copenhagen Pride with Kristian Møller, Fahad Saeed, Niels Jansen, and Andrew Shield, 16 August 2017, http://kanal-1.dk/14-grindr-sexkultur-lystfulde-politiske-hadefulde-perspektiver/; also Copenhagen Pride 2018 event, "Let's Talk About Race" with Saeed.

[9] Callander et al., 2015: 1999.

[10] Voon Chin Phua and Gayle Kaufman, "The Crossroads of Race and Sexuality: Date Selection Among Men in Internet 'Personal' Ads," *Journal of Family Issues* 8 (November 2003): 984.

[11] Jessica Williams and Ronny Chieng, "Sexual Racism: When Preferences Become Discrimination," *The Daily Show*, 12 April 2016.

mainstream attention to issues related to racism in Australian socio-sexual online cultures.[12] A 2015 British gay magazine focused its summer issue on the theme "Racism and the Gay Scene," and reported—among other findings—that one-quarter of its white readership had, in their survey, reported that they felt it was fine to list "No Blacks" or "No Asians" on dating profiles.[13] In 2017, a Dutch organization for queer Muslims called Maruf hosted a panel called "Sexual Racism," in which four members discussed their experiences with racial-sexual exclusions, and racism in the LGBTQ community more generally.[14] And in 2018, the British model Munroe Bergdorf brought attention to transphobia and racism on Grindr by posting screen-captures of conversations that her fans had shared with her.[15]

Critical race scholar Jesus G. Smith made an interesting hypothesis about the effect of "Douchebags of Grindr" and other efforts to shame users publicly for racist speech: the visibility of racist texts has decreased within gay men's online cultures, but the men who espouse these beliefs have not.[16] In his research on sexual racism in southern Texas, Smith observed relatively few profiles with explicitly racist speech, but he knew (from ethnographic work) that users of color faced racism and exclusion on Grindr via private messages or merely being ignored.[17] Smith theorized a "two-faced racism," borrowing from Erving Goffman's notion of the frontstage/backstage,

[12] E.g. as covered in Sophie Verass, "Racism on Grindr: Indigenous Gay Man Screenshots Racial Abuse Online," Special Broadcasting Service/National Indigenous Television, 14 April 2016, http://www.sbs.com.au/nitv/sexuality/article/2016/04/14/man-shares-experiences-of-racism-on-grinder.

[13] FS: The Gay Health and Life Mag (Special Issue: "Racism in the Gay Scene") 148 (June/July 2015). Last accessed June 2015 via http://issuu.com/gmfa/docs/fs148.

[14] Panel at the International Conference on Religion and Acceptance with Olave Basabose, Manju Reijmer, Timothy Aarons, and Amna Durrani, University of Amsterdam, 7 September 2017, http://www.maruf.eu/icra2017.html.

[15] Regarding "sexual racism" in the UK: Stephen Daw, "Munroe Bergdorf Calls on Grindr to Crack Down on Racist & Transphobic Users," Billboard (26 July 2018), https://www.billboard.com/articles/news/pride/8467230/munroe-bergdorf-grindr-racist-transphobic-users; FS, "Racism in the Gay Scene."

[16] Jesus G. Smith, "'No Fats, Fems, or Blacks': The Role of Sexual Racism in Online Stratification and Sexual Health for Gay Men" (PhD diss., Texas A&M University, 2017). See summary of this argument in Nico Lang, "In Trump's America, Racism on Gay Dating Apps Is Getting Worse," The Daily Dot, 23 June 2017, https://www.dailydot.com/irl/racism-gay-dating-apps/.

[17] Jesus G. Smith, personal correspondence, 13 July 2017.

wherein people are more likely to engage in racist speech "in the comfort of the backstage" while performing colorblindness in the frontstage.[18] In socio-sexual online cultures, however, Smith also noted "slippages" between the front and backstage, as users "disguise[d] racist desire in multiracial spaces" through the language of "preferences."[19]

This chapter documents the ways racial-sexual preferences are communicated on Grindr in the greater Copenhagen area, and foregrounds the experiences of immigrants of color in fielding and confronting sexual racism; doing so nuances the discussions of sexual racism with fresh perspectives from ethnic minority immigrants in Europe.

Racism and Intent

Chapter 1 overviewed some critical race perspectives that have emerged from Nordic scholars in the past decade, such as Lene Myong's and other scholars' critique of "colorblindness," that is, the white Scandinavian insistence on its own its supposed neutrality on race issues.[20] Myong also identified an "intentionality discourse" surrounding racism in Denmark: racism is generally understood with regard to (hurtful) intent. She dissected the complex relationship between intent and racism in an interaction between an Asian adoptee and her white mother. Myong introduced the reader to Sam, who relayed a story about her mother's use of an outdated racial epithet:

[18] Smith, "Two-Faced Racism in Gay Online Sex," 135–136.

[19] Smith, "Two-Faced Racism," 144.

[20] On the purported "colorblindness" of (white) Scandinavians, see, e.g., Lene Myong, "Adopteret: Fortællinger om transnational og racialiseret tilblivelse" [Adopted: Tales of Transnational and Racialised Origins] (PhD diss., Aarhus University, Copenhagen, 2009). For further reading: Tobias Hübinette and Carina Tigervall, "To Be Non-White in a Colorblind Society: Conversations with Adoptees and Adoptive Parents in Sweden on Everyday Racism," *Journal of Intercultural Studies* 30, no. 4 (2009): 335–353; Rikke Andreassen and Kathrine Vitus, eds., *Affectivity and Race: Studies from Nordic Contexts* (Farnham: Ashgate, 2015); Rikke Andreassen and Uzma Ahmed-Andresen, "I Can Never Be Normal: A Conversation About Race, Daily Life Practices, Food and Power," *European Journal of Women's Studies* 21, no. 1 (2014): 27–28; Stine H. Bang Svendsen, "Learning Racism in the Absence of 'Race'," *The European Journal of Women's Studies* 21, no. 1 (2014): 9–24.

Sam explains that the word... irritated her, even though she knows that her adoptive mother did not intend anything racist with the term. ... [When Sam confronts her mother, the mother] doesn't understand at all why Sam has raised the question.... A small division arises... on the one hand, [Sam] had to give her adoptive mother credit that there was no racist intent, and on the other hand, [Sam] experienced discomfort with the word...[21]

In this Danish context of understanding racism in terms of intentionality, Sam's adoptive mother could not comprehend Sam's criticisms.[22] Thus, Myong calls for reflection on discourses that are experienced as racism, but which remain unrecognized as such due to assumptions about intent: "It is important to reflect on which (speech) acts are recognized or dismissed as racism, and not least, which forms of power and powerlessness mark this recognition or dismissal...."[23] The same can be applied to a number of speech acts delivered as a mere "joke": a person who is offended by the racial joke has a right to experience the moment as racist, regardless of the intent of the joke-teller, or the insistence that no offense should be taken.[24] To Myong, the offended need not be chastised for her sensitivity, nor lectured about why her feelings are unnecessary.

Critical race scholars advise against the tempting compromise, wherein a person of color can experience something as racist, but the (white) offender is not necessarily a racist. That compromise would bring about the paradox of *racism without racists*, a concept critiqued by sociologists in the United States for decades.[25] For example, sociologist Eduardo Bonilla-Silva analyzes how whites' (non-sexual) "personal preferences" in the United States—such as preferring a certain neighborhood for its schools—relate to

[21] Myong, "Adopteret," 244. Myong notes that "Sam laughs a little while she retells the story." See also Lene Myong, "Bliv dansk, bliv inkluderet: transnational adoption i et in- og eksklusionsperspektiv" [Be Danish, Be Included: Transnational Adoption in an Inclusionary and Exclusionary Perspective], *Paedagogisk Psykologisk Tidsskrift* 48, no. 3 (2011).

[22] Myong, "Adopteret," 245.

[23] Ibid.

[24] See also Rachel E. Dubrofsky and Megan M. Wood, "Posting Racism and Sexism: Authenticity, Agency and Self-Reflexivity in Social Media," *Communication and Critical/Cultural Studies* 11, no. 3 (2014): 282–287.

[25] Grace Carroll Massey, Mona Vaughn Scott, and Sanford M. Dornbusch, "Racism Without Racists: Institutional Racism in Urban Schools," *The Black Scholar* 7, no. 3 (1975): 10–19; Eduardo Bonilla-Silva, *Racism Without Racists, Color-Blind Racism and the Persistence of Racial Inequality in America*, 4th ed. (Lanham, MD: Rowman & Littlefield, 2014).

larger racist structures, as talk about neighborhoods elides with prejudices about racial demographics.[26] Thus, one cannot remain blind to how societal structures and racial prejudice shape "personal preferences" and one must acknowledge that certain choices are direct results of racism, regardless of the individual's intent or self-awareness.[27] The race contexts in the United States and Denmark are different, of course, but not as different as many Danes think.

Scholars of race in Scandinavia have noted an historical amnesia about Danish colonialism and slave trade, Swedish race-hierarchy science,[28] and deportations and imprisonment of Roma. At least through 2008, Danish imperialism was absent from the mandatory public-school curriculum.[29] Public attention to Danish colonial and slavery history has begun to increase in recent years, however, with several exhibits on the Danish West Indies (e.g. at the Black Diamond Library, the Workers Museum), and the installment of a statue inspired by Mary Thomas who, along with two other black female leaders, led the largest labor (slave) revolt in Danish colonial history. There are parallel arguments about historical amnesia in the Netherlands, where Philomena Essed and Isabel Hoving have referred to Dutch "claims of innocence" with regard to culpability for constructing modern racism.[30]

[26] Bonilla-Silva.

[27] Related, look for forthcoming work related to the following peer-reviewed conference presentation: Nicholas Andrew Boston, "How Do I Put This Gently? Articulating the Links Between Race, Residence and Sexuality," Paper presented at the Annual Meeting of the American Sociological Association, Chicago, 22–25 August 2015.

[28] Bolette Blaagaard and Rikke Andreassen, "The Disappearing Act: The Forgotten History of Colonialism, Eugenics and Gendered Othering in Denmark," in *Teaching 'Race' with a Gendered Edge*, ed. Brigitte Hipfl and Kristín Loftsdóttir (Utrecht: ATGENDER, 2012), 91–103.

[29] Randi Marselis, "Descendants of Slaves: The Articulation of Mixed Racial Ancestry in a Danish Television Documentary Series," *European Journal of Cultural Studies* 11, no. 4 (2008): 447–469; Blaagaard and Andreassen.

[30] Philomena Essed and Isabel Hoving, eds., *Dutch Racism* (Amsterdam: Rodopi B.V., 2014); Gloria Wekker, *White Innocence: Paradoxes of Colonialism and Race* (Durham, NC: Duke University Press, 2016); Markus Balkenhol et al., "The Nativist Triangle: Sexuality, Race, and Religion in the Netherlands," in *The Culturalization of Citizenship: Autochthony and Belonging in a Globalizing World*, ed. Jan Willem Duyvendak et al. (Basingstoke: Palgrave Macmillan, 2016), 97–112.

Historical amnesia (or aphasia[31]) allows many Scandinavians to insist that cultural difference is "new" in Scandinavia, and thus some white Scandinavians feel entitled to denounce other cultures, religions or races as inferior. This relates to the concept of "entitlement racism," theorized by Essed via examples from both Scandinavia and the Netherlands. In defining entitlement racism, Essed underscored that "the core of racism is the humiliation of the 'other.'"[32] Essed observed that Europeans increasingly made "bold" statements directed at minority groups without the "I don't mean to sound racist, but..." disclaimer that she grew accustomed to hearing in the 1990s; and they defended their statements as "just telling it like it is."[33] But in tandem with a "European culture of entitlement",[34] certain speech acts quickly evolved from freedom of speech to the freedom "to offend and to humiliate."[35]

In Denmark, entitlement racism is prominent on the political right, and not just in the Danish People's Party (DF). Mattias Danbolt utilized this theory in relation to the Danish "racist gummy" debates in 2014.[36] The debates asked whether or not the racialized cartoon faces in a popular Haribo snack should be redesigned so that the African face, for example, did not resemble blackface minstrelsy. In response to a call to boycott the snacks, one prominent right-wing politician printed a letter in a local Jutland newspaper rallying Danes to "fight the political correctness that assaults freedom of expression and common sense in every way" by filling their shopping carts with this particular gummy snack, as well as any other products that might be deemed politically incorrect.[37] Danbolt argued this

---

[31] That is, the inability to see oneself as a colonial perpetrator, to see oneself as a racist, and to see the connection between the two. Ann Laura Stoler, "Colonial Aphasia: Race and Disabled Histories in France," *Public Culture* 23 (2011): 121–156.

[32] Essed, "Entitlement Racism: License to Humiliate," 74.

[33] Ibid., 62.

[34] Ibid., 74.

[35] Ibid., 62.

[36] Mathias Danbolt, "Retro Racism: Colonial Ignorance and Racialized Affective Consumption in Danish Public Culture," *Nordic Journal of Migration Research* 7, no. 2 (2017): 105–113.

[37] Esben Lunde Larsen, Member of Parliament for the Liberal Party and former Minister of Higher Education and Science in the Danish Government; cited in Pelle Dam, "Efter 'Haribo-racisme': Politiker vil sige neger om sorte" [After 'Haribo-Racism': Politician Wants to Say Negro About Blacks], *MetroXpress*, 22 January 2014, https://www.mx.dk/nyheder/danmark/story/15560966. Cited in Danbolt.

politician's call-to-action cannot be untied from ignorance of Denmark's colonial past and from popular discursive connections between anti-racism and the loss of freedom of speech, and thus represents entitlement racism.

Aside from providing an in-depth analysis of sexual racism on Grindr in the greater Copenhagen area, this chapter contributes to Scandinavian debates about racism and intent. By providing examples of entitlement racism on Grindr, this chapter also shows that socio-political rhetoric about immigrants (e.g. from the Danish or Swedish right) colors some of the communications within the Grindr culture of the greater Copenhagen area. Before exploring the first "type" of racism on Grindr, we overview one more theoretical concept useful for understanding racism in Scandinavia: everyday racism.

PERSISTENT QUESTIONS ABOUT ORIGINS

The first recurring pattern of speech that interviewees and others experienced as racism regards persistent questions about the "origin" of people of color. The person posing the question generally does not see the query as racist, but people of color in white-majority societies interpret the inquiry to mean that a person of color cannot be "really from" that white-majority society. However, immigrants in a new country do not always view the question as racist, since they *do* often identify as being "really" or "originally" from another country. Yet for people of color born in the white-majority country, the question is a constant reminder that whiteness and nationality (e.g. Danishness, Swedishness) are undyingly linked in the white majority's imagination.

Because white people rarely reflect on the racism undergirding questions of origin, people of color tend to field the question on a daily basis. Questions of origin are thus—to use a phrase from the United States—a "microaggression," or a tiny act that is experienced as hostile. In critical race theory, this is also known as "everyday racism." Published shortly after Philomena Essed received her Ph.D. from the University of Amsterdam, *Everyday Racism* (1990) and *Understanding Everyday Racism* (1991) emphasized that careful attention to everyday and subtle forms of racism are central to understanding systemic racism in a given culture.[38]

---

[38] Essed, *Everyday Racism*; Essed, *Understanding Everyday Racism*.

Everyday racism is a useful theory for understanding racism (and "intent") in Scandinavia. Paula Mulinari conducted interviews with waitresses of color in Malmö, Sweden, about their everyday interactions with their customers. Due to the culture of their service work—which requires friendliness and small talk in exchange for a possible tip—the women endured, though sometimes protested, "everyday racist practices" such as answering persistent questions about their ethnic and/or migration backgrounds, and responding to requests of having their hair (and sometimes skin) touched.[39] Mulinari defended her frame of everyday racism with the following:

> The frame of everyday racism is important, particularly in Sweden, where there is a tendency to recognise racism only in its extreme forms, rendering invisible those unremarkable and routine ways through which racism is reproduced. It expresses the current and systematic practices: those defined by hegemonic discourse as normal, natural and right (not the exceptional expressions of violent racism)...[40]

Mulinari acknowledged that customers' repetitive questions about origins could be seen—in the customers' minds—as mere curiosity or small talk. But in many cases, the waitresses felt pigeonholed by these questions: "I could be dying or got the Nobel Prize, and the only thing that they could have in their minds is to know where I come from."[41] Some of her interviewees resisted the questions by answering "my mother's belly" or that they had just come "from the kitchen"; and the Swedish-born women often answered with the hospital name in Sweden. But especially the Swedish-born women knew their answer could lead to the next question: but where are you *really* from? Mulinari identified white Scandinavians' repetitive questions about the origins of people of color as a "strategy of denial and displacement" of Swedishness from the bodies of people of color.[42]

---

[39] Paula Mulinari, "Racism as Intimacy—Looking, Questioning and Touching in the Service Encounter," *Social Identities* 2, no. 5 (2017): 600–613.

[40] Ibid., 602.

[41] Ibid., 8.

[42] Ibid.; Preliminary conversations with Danish-born Grindr users of color suggests that repetitive questions about "origins" persist in this online subculture, revealing assumptions between whiteness and Danishness that can be experienced as a form of racism. For many Danish people of color, the question does not relate to their origins, but to the origins of their parents or grandparents; thus the question underscores the poser's linkages between Scandinavian nationality, whiteness, and belonging.

Also on Grindr, certain behaviors that might seem like "small talk"—such as curiosity about the *real* origin of a person of color—can be experienced as racist.

In the greater Copenhagen area, one British immigrant (who identified his ethnic background as Asian) called on nearby users to reflect on why they might pose questions about origins to him and not others (Fig. 5.1).

Fig. 5.1 "No, you can't ask where I'm 'originally' from" (Redacted text about personal appearance. For a guide to reading "skeleton profiles," see relevant pages in Chapter 3 [e.g. Fig. 3.5]. All profiles presented in Chapters 4–6 were gathered from various locations in the greater Copenhagen area, and Malmö, from 2015 to 2019. All texts are presented in English; if translated [by self], this is noted in the caption)

The user explicitly asked Grindr users not to pose the question of where he was "originally" from. The fact that he put "originally" in quotation marks hints that he had heard this word in a number of questions before: "Where are you from?" "The UK." "Oh, but where are you *originally* from?" If a white person had said he was from the UK, would most Scandinavians accept that he was a Brit? By asking about his ancestral origins and not others, Grindr users revealed their prejudice that people of color could not be true Europeans.

Among the interviewees, Ali (b. Iraq, immigrated 2014) addressed this topic most explicitly, saying that although people did not ask him about his race explicitly (he is among those who reject the "ethnicity" drop-down menu), they often asked the question, "Where are you from?" Ali had grown sick of the origin question, and usually tried to avoid it: "I [just] say: 'Why is that relevant?'"[43] But because my interviewees were all immigrants, many felt that questions of national origins were merely small talk: "I don't mind at all," said Christina (b. Asia, immigrated 2010) on the topic.

But for Caleb (b. China, immigrated 2013), questions about origins could not be separated from other racial stereotypes. Caleb was originally from China, but had lived in several "Western" countries before moving to Scandinavia. Despite having lived abroad since his teenage years, Caleb observed that Scandinavians saw him as "just" Chinese, mainly because of race. The fact that they always saw him as Chinese meant they held other stereotypes about him. Reflecting on the numerous conversations he had had with gay men in Copenhagen and Malmö, Caleb said:

> I feel the need to prove myself, that I'm not necessarily a stereotype.... I need to show that I may be good at math, but that doesn't mean that's who I am. Or I am not necessarily a geek, a nerd—well I have nothing against that—but I don't want someone to have a fixed impression of me.... I have [had] so many cases of people getting to know me and saying, "I thought you were a different person," and I don't know why.... You shouldn't need that, to prove yourself to people.

---

[43] Once he chatted with a Grindr user who mixed up Iran and Iraq, and when Ali corrected him, he said "What's the difference?" and Ali "didn't even continue with him... But that's more ignorance than racism," he said.

People's fixed impression of Caleb relates to Fanon's "fixing" of race onto a body (Chapter 4): Caleb embodies Asianness, whatever that means to Scandinavians, in various settings including Grindr. The fact that he has lived in numerous Western countries is irrelevant: Caleb is indisputably Asian. The stereotypes that Caleb faces are not necessarily negative, but that is not the point; what frustrates Caleb is how these stereotypes persist with every new encounter. In a sexually charged setting like Grindr, racial stereotypes take on a sexual element as well, such as the idea that Asian men are submissive and/or bottoms[44]; or that black men are hypersexual and/or dominant tops (also known as the "Mandingo" figure[45]). Drawing also from notions of everyday racism, the next section on "sexual racism" homes in specifically on sexualized race-related communications, and racialized sex-related communications.

Racial-Sexual Exclusions

Immigrant Experiences

It would be an exaggeration to say that racial-sexual exclusions—e.g. "No Asians"—run rampant on public Grindr profile texts in the greater Copenhagen area, as some critics imply. Even after reading through thousands of profiles tests, a Grindr user in Copenhagen might "only" come across ten profiles with racial-sexual exclusions. However, among interviewees, it was clear that these exclusions reared their head in one-on-one messages; or the interviewees felt the brunt of these exclusions by merely being ignored (i.e. Smith's "two-faced racism"). As discussed before, Daniel (b. Nigeria, immigrated 2016)—like academics Daniel Tsang, Andil Gosine and Russel Robinson—made a fake profile of a white user to test his hypothesis that people disproportionately ignored him because of race, and Daniel concluded that he was not unfoundedly paranoid: his white profile received a higher response rate.

We will begin with a few examples of profile texts with explicit racial-sexual exclusions in order to get an understanding of how and when Grindr

---

[44] David Eng, *Racial Castration: Managing Masculinity in Asian America* (Durham: Duke University Press, 2001).

[45] Andil Gosine, "Brown to Blonde at Gay.com: Passing White in Queer Cyberspace," in *Queer Online: Media Technology and Sexuality*, ed. K. O'Riordan and D. Phillips (New York: Peter Lang, 2007), 148; Shaka McGlotten, *Virtual Intimacies: Media, Affect, and Queer Sociality* (Albany: SUNY Press, 2013), 68 and 74.

users communicate unambiguously on this topic (Fig. 5.2). Both of the white-identified users in Fig. 5.2 excluded people of color from contacting them; the first "only" rejected Asians, while the latter (who wrote, ironically, in English) rejected anyone without Nordic ancestry. Both users had explicitly sexual profiles, and thus their race-related exclusions contribute to a Grindr culture in which people with certain ethnic backgrounds (e.g. Asian) are portrayed as less sexually desirable, and people with other ethnic backgrounds (e.g. Scandinavian) are seen as more sexually desirable.

Many interviewees identified racial-sexual exclusions as the most visible form of racism on Grindr. Şenol (b. Turkey, immigrated 2010) faulted Grindr cultures for allowing these exclusionary discourses to persist: "[Grindr culture] kind of reproduces all the racism in a disguised form, under the name of preferences, and 'what I like.'" To Şenol, racial-sexual

Fig. 5.2 Racial-sexual exclusions (including white homogamy)

preferences were not merely innocent individual preferences, but related to larger issues about racism in Scandinavia.

Interviewees who identified as East Asian or black tended to have the strongest opinions about sexual racism in Denmark and Sweden. Caleb (originally from China) explicitly stated in his profile, "Dating based on racial preferences is racist"; and on another gay platform, Caleb linked to a blog post on sexual racism. In his profile text, Caleb's position aligned most closely with the arguments about sexual racism made by Callander et al. as well as on *The Daily Show* and in other popular media: that those who have race-related sexual preferences tend to hold racist opinions in non-sexual spheres as well. But in our interview, he toned down his position: "It's not so much that people are racist, but people are not very open to different things, or they're not familiar with things outside of their country." This position aligned more with Phua and Kaufman's argument that preference for homogamy might relate foremost to lack of exposure to other cultures.

Daniel was confident that many Grindr users rejected him because of his race. At the end of Chapter 4, we touched briefly on the racialized sexual stereotype that blackness might be equated with HIV: "[T]hey see a black person and he has HIV. That is the mentality they have." Daniel noticed a difference when he experimented with offers for bareback sex (BB) on both profiles:

> Chatting on my fake [white] account that's where I found out. [I write:] "I just like BB." And they say, "No problem, if you're healthy. Let's do it." But on my real account, I say "I like BB" and they say, "NO, I don't fuck without a condom, let's use a condom."

Similar to the African-American woman on *The Daily Show* who realized that at least one potential match ignored her because of his prejudice that black women had herpes, so too did Daniel experience more paranoia about HIV directed at his black profile than his white profile. Medication that effectively prevents the transmission of HIV—pre-exposure prophylaxis (PrEP)—was not commonly used in Scandinavia until 2018, just after the interview with Daniel.

But aside from association with STIs, sexual racism also relates to notions of attractiveness, which may tie directly to media representations (or lack thereof) of people of color in white-majority cultures. In Shaka McGlotten's research on black men's experiences on the hook-up website Manhunt, he interviewed one gay man who confronted racial exclusions directly in his Manhunt profile by writing, "I challenge you to imagine how this might be a form of racism, racial attractions ingrained in us through media images." "Might your racialized desires be different if you grew up in a different society or time period?"[46] The informant had only made three matches in over a year on Manhunt—two of whom were Asian—and added that the one that became an enduring friendship started with bonding over anti-racist statements in profile texts.

Nir (b. Indonesia, immigrated 2014) said that some of the most offensive messages he received since moving to Scandinavia related to aesthetics. One white Scandinavian on Grindr, he mentioned, was "basically getting disgusted over seeing my face and body pics, claiming I shouldn't even be on Grindr for looking so unattractive." To Nir, the user's attacks related directly to Nir's race and the Scandinavian user's narrow views about men's attractiveness.

Christina voiced a similar comment about the racialized connotations of being called "ugly." When asked about experiences with racism on Grindr, Christina said that on a weekly basis someone would write, "You're ugly." I asked Christina to home in on explicitly race-related comments: "It's all racist—if they say I'm ugly or they don't like my clothes," she responded. Christina then tied these comments directly to those who wrote that they were not attracted to Asians more generally, suggesting that many Grindr users connected notions about race, looks, and attractiveness. "Before, I would cry," she said, regarding how these comments made her feel, "but it makes me stronger."

Racial-sexual exclusions are not limited to the Grindr culture of Scandinavia of course. One Asian interviewee noticed racial exclusionary profiles across Europe and the United States, though with some differences:

In the [United] States, there are a lot more comments, "No blacks, no Latinos, no Asians." But in Europe it's specifically, "No Asians." That's something I've noticed. To me that's interesting because it affects me personally.

Another interviewee observed racist profiles "all around Europe: Amsterdam, Paris, Rome, Prague. They don't always write 'No Asians,' but they might say something like 'Only whites.'" Yusuf (b. Egypt, immigrated 2013) concurred: "Story of my life: 'No Asians, no blacks,'" but then added that this was not unique to the greater Copenhagen area. "And that

[46] McGlotten, 72.

was happening even before I came to Europe. That was happening from Egypt even [also]."

Several interviewees vacillated over the connections between being ignored or rejected on Grindr, and their race. To Abdul, being ignored on Grindr was just a fact of the app:

> I get rejected on Grindr. I text and almost 95-98% do not respond, but I wouldn't call it racism. I think it's "not my type." If I say hi, they just say: picture. [Abdul does not include a profile photo.] And I send a photo and they say nothing.... I guess I'm just not they're type, or he's just horny and looking for someone else. It's a very hard hypothesis [to call it racism].

In this scenario, the user of color (Abdul) is left in the dark about a particular dismissal: perhaps it was race-related, perhaps it wasn't.

But Daniel was certain that he gets ignored because of race. He explored the "hypothesis" on his fake (white) profile and his other (black) profile:

> Sometimes the black guy chats and they just block. It has happened to me, like three different people... They don't even chat with you before they block you. As soon as they see the black, they just block.... Then they chat with the white person, and they prefer to meet the white person.... That is... racism.

Daniel was unaware that his "fake profile" method had scholarly precedence, from research dating back to 1994. Indeed, this method continues to be attractive: a recent article spoke with an informant who "change[d] his profile picture to a male friend's photo. The friend is cute and clean-cut, but most importantly, he's white. Hammond gets 50 messages in less than a half hour." According to the 30-year-old interviewee, this was more than he had received in the two months on his personal (person-of-color) profile.[47] The prevalence of this method shows that the paranoia of being ignored or rejected because of race is common in white-majority contexts, and the (often anecdotal) data show that the paranoia is not unwarranted.

[47] Lang.

"Racism" or "Preference"? Debates Among Grindr Users in Scandinavia

Among Grindr users in the greater Copenhagen area—whether white Scandinavians, immigrants of color, Scandinavians of color, etc.,—there is no consensus about whether or not racial-sexual exclusionary preferences are racist, or about how users can best express these preferences. During an informal chat with a white Danish man in his fifties, the Dane insisted that racism on Grindr was "no problem at all," and that I had to "be careful that ordinary rudeness of certain people doesn't get interpreted as racism, because some of it [is] just the way certain people [behave]... in this kind of forum."

Another white Dane—Viktor—chatted with my researcher profile with a similar viewpoint: "Isn't Grindr about sex mostly? Is it racism to follow one's sexual preference?" He shared with me that he was not "into Asians and black people," but mentioned that he had diverse tastes otherwise. As our conversation continued, however, he clarified something that was not immediately obvious: he "would never write something like that, never," on his public profile: "I find it offensive." Later he specifically referred to profiles that said "no Asians" or "no Blacks" as "racist" profiles (again, supporting Smith's "two-faced" theory). Viktor held ambivalent views about racial exclusion on Grindr: on the one hand, he felt that having any racial preference was "just about sex mostly" and not racist; but on the other hand, he felt that public statements about these preferences were indisputably racist.

Several interviewees also shared ambivalence over sexual racism. When I asked Ali (from Iraq) about racism on Grindr in general, his immediate association was racial exclusion: "For sure; the first thing I think of is 'No Asians, no Indians.'" This suggests Ali felt that public declarations of racial-sexual exclusions were the dominant racist discourse on Grindr. But when further reflecting on the concept of racial-sexual exclusions more generally, he shared that having these preferences were not necessarily problematic: "I don't think this is racism," he said confidently. Another Middle Eastern interviewee shared a similar opinion:

> There's a big difference between racism and "you're not my type." You know? It's just the way people express it. I find it very offensive if someone's writing, "no Asians".... When it comes to ethnicity I find it very offensive to write that.... If someone who is not your preference is texting you, you can just ignore them, or say "Sorry, it's not a match."

Later in our interview, he reiterated the point that one should avoid targeting people with racial exclusions, partly because it would offend them personally: "The way to avoid that [offense] is just not to write it." Yet this proposed strategy—not disclosing racial exclusionary preferences, and then merely ignoring someone who is not one's "type"—could also be experienced as racist (as Daniel and others attest).

Several interviewees urged something along the lines of "Don't say what you're *not* interested in, say what you *are* interested in," but there are flaws with this optimism that phrasing preferences positively would be less offensive. Profile texts explicitly requesting white homogamy are certainly not counter-hegemonic (and along intersectional lines, nor are requests for "masculine," "sane," or "clean"/"disease-free" men). And while most interviewees agreed that sexual-racial preferences could not be untied from sexual stereotypes—e.g. of the submissive Asian, the Mandingo—there was also debate about whether *positive* interracial-sexual preferences (or racial fetishes) constituted racist speech within Grindr culture (the section after next).

Social Desirability Bias

Jesus G. Smith's theory that sexual racism is becoming *less visible* on gay socio-sexual media as (white) users move their sexual-racial preferences from the "front stage" to the "back stage" is supported by the narratives of Viktor, Ali, and arguably Abdul.[48] Indeed, I encountered fewer profiles in the greater Copenhagen area than I expected to find with blatant racial exclusions. This could relate to the aforementioned Scandinavian claims of "colorblindness" and unwillingness to discuss racial (but rather, cultural) differences altogether.[49] But it is worth considering Smith's hypothesis as the reason for the relative invisibility of "front stage" racial exclusions. His hypothesis parallels discussions of social desirability bias, that is, that people change their public behaviors (e.g. when filling out a survey) because of what they think they are supposed to answer. Consider the following example of a user who updated his racial-sexual preferences several times during the course of this research (Fig. 5.3).

[48] Smith, "Two-Faced Racism," 144.
[49] Smith.

Fig. 5.3 Social desirability bias? Self-censoring racial-sexual preferences (Four profiles belonging to the same user, listed chronologically: June 2015, December 2015, March 2016, and December 2016)

Over a period of eighteen months, the user updated his profile text at least three times, while his profile photo, personal description and drop-down menu selections (except age) remained the same. The first change occurred some time in late 2015, when he adjusted his preference for "Caucasian" men to add that he hoped he would **not offend "other flavours"**—meaning men of color—with this preference for white homogamy. Doing so suggests that he did not want to appear racist, as he (somewhat) apologized for his (still public) preference for white homogamy.

The user's next revision occurred a few months later, when he switched out his preference for "Caucasian" men to "Western" men (and removed his half-apology). The change from "Caucasian" (a racial label) to "Western" (an ethno-cultural label) can be read in a Danish socio-political climate whereby race-related conversations are eschewed in place of "colorblind" discussions of immigrants' cultural differences. Finally, by the end of 2016, the Dane decided to remove any reference to white homogamy altogether.

Without interviewing this white Dane, it is impossible to tell his motivations for updating his profile. It is possible that his "preferences" widened, and he no longer desired a white lover. But it is also possible that his preference for white homogamy moved from the "front stage" to the "back stage." In that case, it would be interesting to know what precipitated the "self-censorship": could a fellow Grindr user have written to him that he was racist? By removing the text from the profile, did he hope to make the Grindr culture more welcoming to people of color? Or, more cynically, did he hope to make himself more attractive to white Grindr users (because, after all, appearing as racist was passé)?[50]

Social desirability bias—or Smith's "two-faced racism"—means that sexual racism in the greater Copenhagen area is obfuscated. Some racial groups are more explicitly targeted front stage—such as Asians—but others might be targeted backstage. In response to a question about whether he had ever seen a Swedish user declare "No Arabs," "No Turks," or "No immigrants," one interviewee in Sweden responded: "They don't say it. They don't write it on their profile. But they will write it in messages. That has happened to me, twice, directly saying that." The fact that so few profiles explicitly request white homogamy—despite interviewees' experiences with this rhetoric elsewhere—suggests that explicit racial-sexual exclusions are not socially desirable in the Grindr culture of the greater Copenhagen area.

"Talking to You in Plural": On Racial-Sexual Fetishes

Historians of sexuality have theorized the "sexotic" as the locus between (white) Orientalism and sexualized depictions of people of color.[51] Tropes of the exotic and erotic person of color have historical roots in European imperialism, related also to the European tradition of longing for the "unspoiled" within the "uncivilized" cultures. Erotic depictions of men of color have entertained white gay fantasies in Europe for decades, and have also affected the experiences of men of color in gay subcultures.[52]

Scholarly ruminations on the "fetish" from Marx to Freud have defined the term in various ways. In traditional, heteronormative sexology, a fetish was anything that a person desired sexually that was not the sexual organ of the opposite sex: the fetish could be hair, gloves, lace, boots, any material object that had become imbibed with (sexual) value beyond its "original"

[50] For brief reflections on social desirability bias in dating profiles, i.e. putting one's best self forward, "strategic authenticity": Giulia Ranzini and Christoph Lutz, "Love at First Swipe? Explaining Tinder Self-Presentation and Motives," *Mobile Media and Communication* 5, no. 1 (2017): 84 and 92.

[51] Ulrike Schaper et al., "Sexotic: The Interplay Between Sexualization and Exoticization," *Sexualities* (published online November 2018; full citation forthcoming).

[52] Andrew DJ Shield, "'A Southern Man Can Have a Harem of Up to Twenty Danish Women': Sexotic Politics and Immigration in Denmark, 1965–1979," *Sexualities* (published online November 2018; full citation forthcoming).

meaning. Thus, when a person fetishizes another person's race, the result can resemble dehumanization.

Like racial-sexual exclusions, racial-sexual fetishes can relate to misinformation or stereotypes, and can show a lack of familiarity with another racial or ethnic group. To return to the discussion of intent: users who state positive racial-sexual preferences likely do not intend to offend, but this can be the result. For example, there are many white men who have a sexual preference (or fetish) for Asian men, and identify themselves as "rice queens." To many of these white men, this label is lighthearted; but to some Asian-identified Grindr users, that term is offensive:

"BTW [by the way] rice queens scare the shit outta me, so pls stay away," wrote one Copenhagen-based user (not an interviewee) in his profile text. There is also popular and personal literature on the topic.[53]

In socio-sexual media, there is a larger (white) trope of referring to people of color as foods: not just rice, but also chocolate, spice, curry (matzah?), and so forth. Food metaphors and (heterosexual) interracial desire were analyzed in 2006 by two researchers who read through the texts of (United States) dating ads and addressed the problematic pattern of white users interested in "dark chocolate" and "brown sugar."[54] In their article "Eating the Black Body," Erica Owens and Bronwyn Beistle argued that these terms dehumanized and fetishized black and brown bodies, and thus did not give the intended effect of playfulness.

These discourses found a new platform on Grindr, prompting Canadian author Jamie Woo in 2013 to write an "Open Letter to Grindr Users: I Am Not Rice, He Is Not Curry."[55] In it, Woo asked users who referred to East Asians as "Rice" or South Asians as "Curry" to reflect on how these terms related to racial representations of people of color in the gay

[53] E.g. Alexander Chee, "My First (and Last) Time Dating a Rice Queen," The Strangler, 21 June 2017, https://www.thestranger.com/queer-issue-2017/2017/06/21/25227046/my-first-and-last-time-dating-a-rice-queen.

[54] Erica Owens and Bronwyn Beistle, "Eating the Black Body: Interracial Desire, Food Metaphor and White Fear," in *Body/Embodiment: Symbolic Interactions and the Sociology of the Body*, ed. Dennis Waskul and Phillip Vannini (Hampshire and Burlington: Ashgate, 2006), 201–212.

[55] Jamie Woo, "Open Letter to Grindr Users: I Am Not Rice, He Is Not Curry," *The Huffington Post*, 28 June 2013, https://www.huffingtonpost.com/jaime-woo/open-letter-to-grindr-users_b_3506180.html.

community more generally, adding, "Do you ever wonder why only certain ethnicities get treated this way? I mean, have you ever seen anyone write 'no croissants' or 'no pasta'?"[56] Food metaphors were not just a joke; they often target people of color for exclusion or fetish. Similarly in Denmark, Myong's discussion of intent helped explain why so many racist comments get brushed off as "just a joke."

Scholarship on interracial desire has also nuanced the position that racial desire should be thought about foremost in terms of racism: media and race scholar Nicholas Boston has asked if it is possible to view racial-sexual preferences from the perspective of openness to difference, and not narrow-mindedness. Boston does build from literature on sexual racism: he finds Callander et al.'s research valid, and acknowledges that those who espouse identities such as "rice queens" and "chocolate queens" often pursue inter-racial desire in problematic ways. But his research focuses also on those who examine their racial positions, question the sources of their desires, and pursue interracial sex with a range of motivations including a rejection of hegemonic norms (e.g. about masculinity, about prohibitive sex), or from the perspective of "shared or parallel oppression, and political allegiance" (for example, between Eastern European immigrants and black locals in Western Europe).[57]

Among my interviewees, there was some disagreement about the racism undergirding positive racial-sexual preferences. Christina, for example, had not differentiated between those who fetishized Asians, and those who were merely open to dating Asians and people of other races too. This topic arose when Christina estimated that "half of the guys on Grindr" in the greater Copenhagen area "like Asians." I mentioned that some Asians found it offensive to read terms like "rice queen," to which she responded, "Those people are just making drama."

Similarly, when I asked an Arab interviewee what he thought about comments like "I prefer Asians," he responded: "This is not discrimination,

---

[56] Ibid.

[57] Nicholas Boston, "Libidinal Cosmopolitanism: The Case of Digital Sexual Encounters in Post-enlargement Europe," in *Postcolonial Transitions in Europe: Contexts, Practices and Politics*, ed. Sandra Ponzanesi and Gianmaria Colpani (London: Rowman & Littlefield, 2016), 306–308; Andrew DJ Shield, "New in Town: Gay Immigrants and Geosocial Dating Apps," in *LGBTQs, Media, and Culture in Europe*, ed. Alexander Dhoest et al. (London: Routledge, 2017), 300.

this is a preference. It does not exclude others; well, it might, but it's more politically correct."

But Caleb (who identifies as Asian) and Yusuf (who identifies as black) felt that positive preferences were as problematic as negative ones. Caleb reacted to messages from guys who were "into Asians" with discomfort:

> I never respond to those requests, I feel a bit offended, honestly. Whenever I meet someone, I prefer that they also date other races. I don't really want to be with someone who dates just one race. Even though a lot of my friends say I'm crazy.

Although Caleb's friends had challenged him to think that (white) men who were "into Asians" were harmless, Caleb linked their sexual preference to stereotypes they had about Asians more generally.

Yusuf (from Egypt, who identifies as black) addressed food metaphors directly, and described the problematic speech with the phrase "talking to you in plural":

> There is another sugar-coated racism: exotification. When people contact you just because you're black, or just because you're Middle Eastern. Because you are the fantasy they have and nothing more than that. And I also have [encountered] this a lot: people are talking to me and addressing me as a piece of chocolate. Or "I've never been with a black guy." "Black guys are so hot." **Talking to you in plural**, I'm like, "I'm not that plural."

To Yusuf, positive sexual-racial preferences for black men related to stereotypes about black men. Assumptions about dominance, hyper-masculinity, and large penis size are among the most common stereotypes fixed to black men.[58]

Fahad Saeed from Sabaah also spoke about this at Copenhagen Pride 2017, when he mentioned that racism in the gay community went on a spectrum, where being "exoticized for your ethnicity" was on the lighter side of the spectrum. But it was still racism: "Racism that is masked as curiosity—hidden insults, hidden racism, like a well known pick up line: 'I

---

[58] An interviewee for a 2004 article about gay men's online cultures concurred: "If they suspect or find out you are black MANY immediately go to the penis size thing." John Edward Campbell, *Getting It on Online: Cyberspace, Gay Male Sexuality, and Embodied Identity* (London: Harrington Park Press, 2004), 79; cited in Gosine, 148.

Fig. 5.4 White men convey preferences for non-white men

usually don't go for—*insert ethnicity*—but you specifically, you are some-body who do[es] something for me, in spite of me not usually being turned on by people like you.'"

Figure 5.4 presents four examples of (white) users' profiles with racial-sexual preferences. Racial stereotypes peek through each of these four texts. As with the "no offense to other flavours" text, one cannot make conclusions about any of these Grindr users' motivations for writing racial-sexual preferences into their profile texts. But I include them here—with relatively little discussion—partly to archive them for future considerations on this question: how can one decide when a desire for interracial sex is conveyed in an open-minded versus a prejudicial manner?

The first user seeks "hot bottom guys" and "especially Asians," drawing a discursive link to the trope of submissive and passive Asians. Similarly, the second profile links Asians with "shorter and younger bottoms," while the fourth links Asians with "smooth" (hairless) guys. Additionally, the third and fourth profiles show that positive preferences can go hand-in-hand with racial-sexual exclusions: in seeking "Arab and Middle Eastern" men, the third profile explicitly excluded Asians; and in seeking Asian men among others, the fourth profile implicitly excluded black men. All of these examples could support the general argument in Callander et al.'s 2015 sexual racism study: that an individual's racial-sexual preferences cannot be untied from that individual's general racial prejudices.

"No Ghana Guys": Conflation of Nationality and Economic Opportunism

Immigration is so closely connected to the topic of economics that it should not be surprising that Scandinavian conceptions of the immigrant (and racial) Other relate not only to topics like culture and religion, but also to notions of socio-economic background (i.e. social class, employment, education). This next section explores white Grindr users' associations between immigrants and their economic opportunism, such as assumptions that immigrant users are seeking money and/or documents via marriage, or related, that they are sex workers or drug dealers. Some of the more brazen attacks on immigrants can be best understood through the lens of *entitlement racism*.

Over the past few years, Philomena Essed has theorized entitlement racism as racism that takes the form of offensive statements in which the attackers defend their statements as merely "speaking their mind" about immigrants, ethnic minorities, or minority cultures.[59] Entitlement racism must be understood in relation to a backlash against anti-racism (i.e. as overly "politically correct") and in a European political climate that is increasingly hostile to Islam and Muslims in Europe.

At the start of this research (2015) I was particularly interested in how this type of entitlement racism circulated on a web-based platform, PlanetRomeo. Though this platform dwindled in popularity in subsequent years (and became less relevant for this research), I could not depart with one pattern of speech I observed and archived on that website: what I called the "No Ghana Guys" pattern of racist exclusion. Thus I include this discussion briefly, as the pattern is part and parcel of the discourses about immigrants and economic opportunism in gay men's digital cultures in Scandinavia.

The "No Ghana Guys" exclusion was found on a web-based platform (rather than a geo-locative app) because the website facilitated communication regardless of users' physical location.[60] The racist pattern differs from racial-sexual exclusions because the dismissal related foremost to global inequality: the dismissal was directed at international users for (perceived)

---

[59] Essed, "Entitlement Racism: License to Humiliate," 62; Philomena Essed, "Entitlement Racism: A Public Lecture with Professor Philomena Essed & Professor Martin Parker," Copenhagen Business School, 19 April 2016.

[60] See, for example, Boston's discussion of "speculators" on Romeo: Boston, "Libidinal Cosmopolitanism," 306.

economic reasons (and not directed at racial minorities in relation to aesthetics, sexual health, or individual "preferences").

International messages with requests for assistance immigrating to Europe, often sent via profiles of men with locations in sub-Saharan Africa or southeast Asia, frequently arrived into Europe-based users' PlanetRomeo inboxes. Angelo and Sami, two interviewees who used PlanetRomeo in 2015, received (and usually ignored) these messages monthly, but were unsure whether these messages came from real people who were desperate to leave their countries of origin, or from robot profiles made to trick naïve users into divulging bank account or other personal information.

Whether or not these profiles belong to real GBTQ people is irrelevant when considering the aggressive responses they prompted from many Danes, dozens of whom had become so enraged with messages from the developing world that they tried to prohibit people from specific countries from contacting them. I noticed this first with several profiles about "Guys from Ghana," so I keyword-searched "Ghana" among PlanetRomeo profiles in Denmark (note: Grindr does not afford this search method). Over two-dozen profiles with exclusionary messages appeared, such as the following three:

...GUYS FROM GHANA I'M NOT SENDING YOU ANY MONEY, SO DON'T BOTHER WRITING ME!!...
...And people from Ghana who want to marry me: I wish you all the best, but I am NOT going to pay for your fares or visa to Europe, and I don't want your eternal and faithful love...
...no Ghana guys!...
...All of you people from Africa (Ghana), who only wants to beg for my money in ANY way: STAY AWAY!!!...[61]

In the culture of PlanetRomeo in Denmark, "Ghana" had become a metonym for the developing world and for the source of economically opportunistic migrants.

With Essed's theory of entitlement racism in mind, one can re-read the previous profile texts—all of which tied international correspondence and specific nationalities to economic opportunism—as speech acts that might

---

[61] All collected in 2015 from PlanetRomeo. In another profile, a user forbade correspondence from users in "Ghana, Togo and likely 'exotic' countries"; his use of an Orientalist and sexualized word ("exotic") provides insight into his imagining of the developing world.

be defended as mere "truth telling." And though *intention* is not necessary for identifying these speech patterns as racist, one can see that a handful of related profiles were more deliberately hurtful:

> ...Ghana, Benin, everybody from Africa, Philippines, Romania, Bulgaria and Russian guys, who is only looking for money and an easy lifestyle: ALL OF YOU STAY OUT!!! Send no messages cause I am not interested in supporting you and your family. Gold diggers, twinks and transvestites the same.

> ...If you're messaging me from Ghana, Russia, The Philippines (or some other godforsaken country), chances are you've got something ridiculous to say and I WON'T be remotely interested...

The flippancy with which these profile texts prohibited communication from users based in the developing world (also/including Eastern Europe and Russia) helped me identify this as a pattern of entitlement racism.

These speech patterns have real effects for those who are, or who are perceived to be, immigrants or potential immigrants from these countries. Daniel tied some of his negative experiences on Grindr directly to Scandinavians' experiences with Africans on other platforms such as Romeo, as was mentioned in Chapter 4: "Because of what people from Africa have asked of them over here in Europe, like 'Send Money,' or 'Do this.'"

Daniel said that these messages (these "lies") were detrimental to the image of Africans in Europe: "A [Scandinavian] person will meet a black person in [Scandinavia] who is looking for a relationship, but they will say: oh, but a black person is all about money, they will use them [the Scandinavian]."[62] To Daniel, being associated with economic opportunism recurs in both online and offline socio-sexual cultures.

Related, a (white) Scandinavian's stereotype that a black or immigrant man is "all about the money" might translate to other assumptions, such as that the person is a drug dealer or sex worker. Yusuf (who identifies as black) made a related point when he mentioned experiences with gay men asking him for drugs, whether at a gay club or on Grindr:

> Being approached, even on Grindr, asking about drugs... I would assume that the person chose to talk to me because of the way I look. Not because he's randomly asking for drugs.... The problem is some of them don't see

---

[62] Redacted: "Scandinavian" replaces Swedish or Danish; "Scandinavia" replaced Sweden or Denmark.

offense in that. When a guy in a packed club chooses a black one, out of everyone else, to ask for hash and drugs—they don't see it as offensive.

While there are niches of gay men who brazenly post about "chemsex"—or sex on drugs, often amphetamines, and often with multiple partners[63]— Yusuf does not accept that Grindr users randomly contact him regarding drugs; rather, they write to the black user with the hope, or assumption, that he uses and has connections to drugs.

Christina (who is Asian) expressed that her race predetermined some Grindr users' ideas about her economic motives for being on Grindr: "This guy wrote, 'You're Asian. You're just a fucking hooker.'" Scandinavians, she said, associated countries like Thailand and Cambodia with prostitution, so an immigrant perceived to be from these countries must be a sex worker. (One male-identified interviewee also remarked that a stranger on Grindr called him a "Turkish prostitute" before blocking him entirely.[64]) The stereotypes Christina faces are exacerbated by her gender: as a trans woman, she also has to deal with issues of sexism and transphobia, which underscores that racisms in Grindr cultures are intersectional.[65]

INSULTS ABOUT RACE, RELIGION, NATIONALITY

This chapter began by asserting that racism does not always go hand-in-hand with intent; many aspects of the racist patterns described thus far had nuance: even those who had experienced these communicative acts firsthand hesitated to call them "racist." Not everyone who asks "Where are you from?" or says "I'm into Asians" intends to offend the person of color, but these discourses can be experienced as racism depending on their contexts, repetitions, and (Othering) effects. The previous pattern ("No Ghana guys") focused on communicative acts that reflected entitlement racism, that is, whereby the white Dane was merely "speaking

---

[63] Kane Race, *The Gay Science: Intimate Experiments with the Problem of HIV* (London: Routledge, 2018), Chapter 7 (page numbers not yet available).

[64] Shield, "New in Town," 244.

[65] These areas intersect also in the ways that she received offensive messages: for example, she loathes being called a "lady boy," partly for its dismissal of her gender identity (as a woman), and partly for the term's discursive connections to sex work. I will add, however, that another feminine Asian Grindr user in the greater Copenhagen area does use the display name "lady boy," so opinions on this term are personal.

his mind" about potential migrants on socio-sexual platforms. In some of these posts, the PlanetRomeo user's "intention" to offend is unequivocal. This final section focuses on other incidents that interviewees described as indisputably racist, unambiguously hurtful, and directed at them because of their race, ethnicity, nationality, or perceived religion.

"Fuck [your Arab country], fuck Islam, and fuck you!" This was a private message that Abdul received on Grindr during his first year living in the greater Copenhagen area, shortly after opening up about his migration status and country of origin. Abdul also spoke generally about other offensive messages that locals had written him: some spewed "brainwashed media things" about religion and terrorism, for example, in ways he found to be offensive. Another made a comment associating Abdul "with ISIS" (a.k.a. ISIL, *Daesh*) terrorism, as the opening of this book foreshadowed.

Nir (from Indonesia) received similar Islamophobic messages, even though his country of origin was quite far from Abdul's: "Twice on Gay-Romeo and once on Grindr.... [someone wrote] messages with seemingly mass-generated bullet-point lists of offensive, stereotypical claims, allegations, of what being Asian and Muslim entail[s]."

"Go and fuck kids in your country!" one user wrote to a Danish-born Grindr user with Iraqi roots. The Dane wrote to my researcher profile to share this, and emphasized that he was born in Denmark and had never stepped foot in Iraq. The other user's statement also reflects a sexual racism in which the commenter stereotyped Middle Eastern men as engaging in homosexual sex only when it is age-structured.

Yusuf (from Egypt) was called an "idiot" and a "taxi driver", and received a strange "slave joke," all via Grindr since he moved to the greater Copenhagen area in 2014. All of these examples are just some of a number of intentionally hurtful insults that interviewees shared. But perhaps most surprisingly, interviewees tended to downplay these experiences with racism by categorizing the culprits as bad apples. For example, Abdul shrugged off the tirades he relayed to me with the following:

Well, that [only] happened a couple of times. I can't say that people are racist here [on Grindr in Scandinavia] because that [only] happened two or three times in two years.

Although I added the key words "only" for emphasis, the tone with which Abdul relayed this point conveyed the idea that that the extreme experiences were not to be taken as emblematic of Grindr culture. In other words, Abdul could stomach a few online insults per year in exchange for the positive benefits of using Grindr. Yet as this analysis has shown, these seemingly isolated incidents repeat and repeat; when looked at with a broader lens, these recurring patterns add a gloomier cloud over the everyday communications on socio-sexual networking platforms.

There are common threads between the various patterns of racism described in this chapter: those who exclude or ignore racial groups from their communications, those who try to prohibit correspondence from men in the developing world, those who spew indisputably insulting private messages, all seek to create borders in a virtual world. These borders can be national or racial, and have consequences for, for example, gay-identified immigrants in Copenhagen. As scholar Sara Ahmed wrote on queerness and exclusion:

> ...[Q]ueer bodies have different access to public forms of culture, which affect how they can inhabit those publics. ... I have felt discomfort in some queer spaces, again, as a feeling of being out of place. ...[T]he discomfort is itself a sign that queer spaces may extend some bodies more than others... At times, I feel uncomfortable about inhabiting the word 'queer,' worrying that I am not queer enough... or am just not the right kind of queer.[66]

Queer subcultures like bars, organizations, or social circles might amplify the visibility of certain groups more than others—i.e. white, middle-class young Europeans vs. immigrants and people of color—but further and related, queer identities and feelings of belonging might also attach to certain groups more than others. Racism on Grindr and related platforms foments discomfort in yet another queer subculture, albeit a digital one. By Ahmed's logic, unease within Grindr Culture could translate to immigrants' and people of color's unwillingness to engage and identify with other LGBTQ subcultures.

---

[66] Sara Ahmed, *The Cultural Politics of Emotion* (New York: Routledge, 2004), 151.

Anti-racist Texts

There are also anti-racist speech acts on Grindr, and these are also part of the discourses that comprise Grindr culture. As I humbly joked to the audience of the "Grindr and Sex Cultures" panel at Copenhagen Pride 2017: "More people will read your Grindr profile text than will read my article about your profile. So write something good."

Some Grindr users transform their dating profiles into soapboxes from which to broadcast messages of tolerance that could influence future users' communiqués on these platforms. Anti-racist texts can counter hegemonic understandings of "preference" circulated by other users on the shared interface, and demonstrate how gay profiles can be spaces for activism online.

This chapter has already showcased a few profile texts that address sexual racism, such as Caleb's ("Dating based on racial preferences is racist"). There is also Abdul's: "If ur profile includes stuff like 'no Asians, no blacks...' or any stupid sh*t... DON'T talk to me." I stumbled across another text posted by a Middle-Eastern-identified man, written in imperfect Danish: "Foreigner... seeks chemistry. No racist guys pls! We are one big society. Everyone deserves to be happy :-)" he shared.

A few interviewees mentioned Scandinavian friends who had anti-racist profile texts. Şenol (from Turkey) recounted that a friend announced in his profile, "Do not contact me unless you are an anti-racist feminist." And Ali (from Iraq) had a few friends who wrote anti-racist messages, but he added that these were not common among the general Scandinavian population: "Those who write something inclusive, either they have experienced that [racism] firsthand, or they work with it," meaning that only those (white) people who studied race-related topics, or worked for migration-related organizations, would write anti-racist profile texts.

Indeed that was true of one person whom I met "in the field," whose profile stated "Ageism, fat shaming, racism and discrimination against feminine boys = go away!" (Figure 5.5). Interestingly, he was not an immediate target for any of these forms of discrimination (as he self-described through drop-down menus as a 27-year-old "toned" "jock," and via private message as "white"). Indeed, this user was a student working in cultural studies.

Then I came across the profile of a 25-year-old, white-identified Dane whose profile headline was, "Relaxed, funny, smart. Feminism, anti-racism,

Fig. 5.5 Two paragons of intersectional anti-racism

love" (Fig. 5.5). I sent a private message to him, and after an initial compliment of his profile text, asked: "Is it safe to bet that you are a student of sociology or cultural studies?"

"Not at all," he responded. "I'm a tour guide ☺."

We chatted about the hypothesis that only those with personal, academic, or work-related connections to racism and xenophobia would challenge systems of power within the platform, and he asserted that he was evidence that these discourses circulated also in other Danish circles. He hoped his text would have a ripple effect on Grindr, as he ruminated, "I do hope I'm setting an example" for others to self-reflect on their assumptions about race or sex.[67] (Several months later, I spotted his profile again, this time with the message "Internalized homophobia is not hot. Neither is racism. Feminism [is] a plus.") Caleb voiced something similar regarding his motive for posting about racism on his socio-sexual profiles: "I want people to think about it [racism]."

One (cynical) critique—drawing from scholarly analysis of performative rage in other queer online forums—is that anti-racist Grindr texts could be public performances of progressive politics (similar to the social desirability bias, mentioned earlier).[68]

When writing with the authors behind the "Racism and discrimination = go away" and "Feminism, anti-racism, love" profiles about their motives for including these texts, neither mentioned getting any pushback from their fellow Grindr users. Granted we did not have in-depth interviews, but my other interviews do suggest that users of color receive more negative feedback about their choice to discuss racism on Grindr. When I asked Daniel (from Nigeria) if he had ever written anti-racist messages on his Grindr profile, he responded with the following:

> I've done it before, when I first came. And a lot of people attacked me. ... A lot of people started writing to me: Why do I write *white people* [are racist]? Black people are racist too, not just white people. So I change my writing.

Daniel expressed his feelings about racism in Scandinavian society, but in doing so exposed himself to attacks from defensive (white) locals.

Similarly, Yusuf received pushback when trying to engage Scandinavians on the problematic aspects of fetishizing his blackness (e.g. "addressing me as a piece of chocolate"): "And when you comment on that, you get accused of over-sensitivity. 'No, you're over-sensitive! It was a compliment!' This happens also on Grindr." And Abdul—whose profile text asked users not to contact him if they wrote things like "No Asians"—received a message from someone who wrote, "I find your profile text weird, because it's every

---

[67] See also Andrew DJ Shield, "Grindr Culture: Intersectional and Socio-Sexual," *Ephemera: Theory & Politics in Organization* 18, no. 1 (2018): 149–161.

[68] E.g. Jakob Svensson, "Gay the Correct Way: Mundane Queer Flaming Practices in Online Discussions of Politics," in *LGBTQs, Media, and Culture in Europe*, ed. Alexander Dhoest et al. (London: Routledge, 2017), 192–207; Adi Kuntsman, "Belonging Through Violence: Flaming, Erasure, and Performativity in Queer Migrant Community," in *Queer Online: Media, Technology and Sexuality*, ed. Kate O'Riordan and David J. Phillips (New York: Peter Lang, 2007).

person's right to write whatever they want, because when it comes to sex, you want the right person." Of course this user was welcome to write this message to Abdul. But reading these pushback experiences together—from Daniel, Yusuf, and Abdul—one might wonder if white Grindr users feel more compelled to challenge anti-racist announcements posted by Grindr users of color (rather than by fellow white Grindr users).

CONCLUSIONS

Race-Related Communication Is Part of the Day-to-Day Experiences on Socio-Sexual Media, Especially for People of Color

On socio-sexual platforms aimed primarily at gay men, such as Grindr, race-related communication occurs in public profile texts and in one-on-one messages, and also via the absence of communication (being ignored). People of color are attuned to "everyday" othering practices. Paranoia about being excluded or ignored because of race pushes some users of color to experiment with secondary profiles wherein they "tour" the online culture under a fake profile of a white-identified man. Scholar Andil Gosine underscored this identity tourism does *not* mean that the user wants to *be* white, but rather that the user wants to experience the online community *without race*.[69] In many white-majority settings—Scandinavia no least—white people tend not to reflect on their own racial position, or how their speech acts might fix race only onto people of color.

In an erotically charged environment, race-related communications take on a sexual bent. When asked about "racism on Grindr," the majority of informants immediately gravitated to racial-sexual exclusions, rehashing the profiles they had seen with "no Asians," "no blacks," "no Indians," and so forth. Many then turned to the flip side of the coin: being fetishized for one's skin color, physiognomy, or assumed (racial-)sexual personality. Yusuf described his discomfort when white users talked to him "in plural" (that they were into "black guys") a speech pattern that made him feel more like a specimen from a racial group rather than an individual. Fahad Saeed (foreperson of Sabaah) critiqued the common remark that someone is attractive *in spite of* their race. All of the above comments go hand-in-hand with the (often white) user's expectations about members of a

---

[69] Gosine, "Brown to Blonde," 150.

certain race. These assumptions might be communicated explicitly, or they can remain implicit.

The interviewees in this chapter shared no consensus about if and when racial-sexual preferences were acceptable. Some interviewees decried these preferences as racist, while also espousing their own racial-sexual preferences. Nevertheless, in scholarly literature, mainstream media, and Grindr culture, many are brazenly calling out "sexual racism." Some do so on personal blogs, via hash tags, or even in their socio-sexual profile texts: "Dating based on racial preferences is racist." Period. But drawing from the hypothesis of Jesus Smith, this chapter pondered whether attention to sexual racism can actually change users' behaviors, or if counter-hegemonic discourses serve to push sexual racism "back stage."

Interviewees experienced communications as racialized, even in the absence of any mention of race: comments about being "ugly" may reveal a user's prejudice about (racial) aesthetics, inquiries about buying drugs may suggest the user associates people of color with criminal activity; these communications contribute to the paranoia that Shaka McGlotten theorized as part and parcel of queer men of color's online experiences in socio-sexual cultures.

Racial-Sexual Exclusions Cannot Be Separated from Other Racist Speech Acts

Racism on socio-sexual platforms is broader than "just" racial-sexual exclusion. Racial-sexual exclusions are part of a Grindr culture in which (often white) users' prejudices reveal themselves through "everyday racist" speech acts, and in which some users take advantage of the technology to hurl anonymous insults. Especially those who have been unfortunate to receive "intentionally" racist messages—including insults that have nothing to do with sexuality—know that Grindr racism extends beyond the "No [ethnicity]" exclusion. Looking broadly at Grindr communication as a whole, one cannot neatly separate these "types" of racism. Discrete texts are written by individuals, but reveal a broader pattern about the culture in which these individuals are based.

Callander et al.'s 2015 study on sexual racism argued, using quantitative data gathered from surveys, that (Australian) white men's exclusionary racial-sexual preferences corresponded to general racist attitudes more broadly. The narratives and data in this chapter suggest that Callander et al.'s argument could apply to the Grindr culture of the greater Copenhagen area, as online discourses about race, migration status, or perceived religion mirror some dominant socio-political discourses.

Race-Related Communications "on App" Reflect the Socio-Political Context of the Geography of the App

Continuing on this point, one cannot separate the racist speech patterns on Grindr in the greater Copenhagen area from dominant discourses about race and immigration in the greater Copenhagen area (outlined in Chapter 1). In 2016, Denmark's right-wing government upheld the controversial border control with Sweden and Germany in order to stop an alleged "uncontrolled flow" of refugees and migrants, while also introducing new demands for immigrants' "integration into Danish society." New nationalist and anti-immigrant parties gained supporters in Denmark and Sweden. Anti-immigrant rhetoric and pro-"integration" policies have increasing support across the spectrum. Media outlets focus on stories about cultural clashes between immigrants and Danes or Swedes, such as on topics related to sexuality. Within this context, it is no surprise that an Arab Grindr user like Abdul would field accusations about ties to ISIS. This socio-political climate cannot be separated from online environments in the greater Copenhagen area; particularly with geo-locative apps, the culture of a physical geography will influence the subculture of the online platform.

Political and journalistic rhetoric fixes many Muslim people and people of color as constant "immigrants." In this socio-political climate, it is also no surprise that a Danish-born Arab user would be told to return to "your country." Xenophobia, Islamophobia, and racism blur on socio-sexual platforms, just immigration, race, and Islam elide in the Scandinavian public sphere.

Attention to Race on Socio-Sexual Media Extends Beyond Users' Speech Patterns

This chapter established that race-related and racist speech permeates the communicative culture of Grindr in the greater Copenhagen area, and acknowledged that although individuals are ultimately responsible for each discrete racist encounter, these individuals (and their biases, prejudices, racism) are also products of their socio-political context.

But what is the organization's (Grindr's) role in all of this? In what ways does the technology itself—including its interface, drop-down menus, search functions, pop-up ads—exacerbate race-related communications? What is going on with that "ethnicity" drop-down menu? Chapter 6 examines users' modes of racial self-identification on Grindr and simultaneously considers the role of the technology in promoting racial identifications and racial-sexual preferences as central to the socio-sexual culture.

BIBLIOGRAPHY

Ahmed, Sara. *The Cultural Politics of Emotion*. New York: Routledge, 2004.

Balkenhol, Markus, Paul Mepschen, and Jan Willem Duyvendak. "The Nativist Triangle: Sexuality, Race, and Religion in the Netherlands." In *The Culturalization of Citizenship: Autochthony and Belonging in a Globalizing World*, eds. Jan Willem Duyvendak, Peter Geschiere, and Evelien Tonkens, 97–112. Basingstoke: Palgrave Macmillan, 2016.

Basabose, Olave, Manju Reijmer, Timothy Aarons, and Amna Durrani. "Sexual Racism: On Racism Within LGBTQI Spaces." Panel at the International Conference on Religion and Acceptance, University of Amsterdam, 7 September 2017. http://www.maruf.eu/icra2017.html.

Blaagaard, Bolette, and Rikke Andreassen. "The Disappearing Act: The Forgotten History of Colonialism, Eugenics and Gendered Othering in Denmark.' In *Teaching 'Race' with a Gendered Edge*, edited by Brigitte Hipfl and Kristín Loftsdóttir, 91–103. Utrecht: ATGENDER, 2012.

Bonilla-Silva, Eduardo. *Racism Without Racists, Color-Blind Racism and the Persistence of Racial Inequality in America*, 4th ed. Lanham, MD: Rowman & Littlefield, 2014 [2006].

Boston, Nicholas. "Libidinal Cosmopolitanism: The Case of Digital Sexual Encounters in Post-enlargement Europe." In *Postcolonial Transitions in Europe: Contexts, Practices and Politics*, edited by Sandra Ponzanesi and Gianmaria Colpani, 291–312. London: Rowman & Littlefield, 2015.

Boston, Nicholas Andrew. "How Do I Put This Gently? Articulating the Links Between Race, Residence and Sexuality." Paper presented at the Annual Meeting of the American Sociological Association, Chicago, 22–25 August 2015.

Callander, Denton, Christy E. Newman, and Martin Holt. "Is Sexual Racism *Really* Racism? Distinguishing Attitudes Toward Sexual Racism and Generic Racism Among Gay and Bisexual Men." *Archives of Sexual Behavior* 44 (2015): 1991–2000.

Campbell, John Edward. *Getting It on Online: Cyberspace, Gay Male Sexuality, and Embodied Identity*. London: Harrington Park Press, 2004.

Chee, Alexander. "My First (and Last) Time Dating a Rice Queen," The Strangler, 21 June 2017. https://www.thestranger.com/queer-issue-2017/2017/06/21/25227046/my-first-and-last-time-dating-a-rice-queen.

Chee, Alexander. "No Asians! Navigating the Pitfalls of Anti-Asian Sentiments in Online Hookup Sites," Out Magazine, 11 January 2012. https://www.out.com/news-commentary/2012/01/11/no-asians.

Dam, Pell. "Efter 'Haribo-racisme': Politiker vil sige neger om sorte" [After 'Haribo-Racism': Politician Wants to Say Negro About Blacks]. MetroXpress, 22 January 2014. https://www.mx.dk/nyheder/danmark/story/15560966.

Danbolt, Mathias. "Retro Racism: Colonial Ignorance and Racialized Affective Consumption in Danish Public Culture." Nordic Journal of Migration Research 7, no. 2 (2017): 105–113.

Daw, Stephen. "Munroe Bergdorf Calls on Grindr to Crack Down on Racist & Transphobic Users," Billboard, 26 July 2018, last accessed Autumn 2019 via https://www.billboard.com/articles/news/pride/8467230/munroe-bergdorf-grindr-racist-transphobic-users.

Eng, David. Racial Castration: Managing Masculinity in Asian America. Durham: Duke University Press, 2001.

Essed, Philomena. "Entitlement Racism: A Public Lecture with Professor Philomena Essed & Professor Martin Parker," Copenhagen Business School, 19 April 2016.

Essed, Philomena. "Entitlement Racism: License to Humiliate." In Recycling Hatred: Racism(s) in Europe Today, edited by European Network Against Racism, 62–77. Brussels: European Network Against Racism, 2013.

Essed, Philomena. Everyday Racism: Reports From Women of Two Cultures. Alameda, CA: Hunter House, 1990.

Essed, Philomena. Understanding Everyday Racism: An Interdisciplinary Theory. Newbury Park, CA: Sage, 1991.

Essed, Philomena, and Isabel Hoving, eds. Dutch Racism. Amsterdam: Rodopi B.V., 2014.

FS: The Gay Health and Life Mag (Special issue: "Racism in the Gay Scene") 148 (June/July 2015). Last accessed June 2015 via http://issuu.com/gmfa/docs/fs148.

Gosine, Andil. "Brown to Blonde at Gay.com: Passing White in Queer Cyberspace." In Queer Online: Media Technology and Sexuality, edited by Kate O'Riordan & David J. Phillips, 139–154. New York: Peter Lang, 2007.

"Grindr and Sex Culture." Panel at Copenhagen Pride with Kristian Møller, Fahad Saeed, Niels Jansen, and Andrew Shield, 16 August 2017. Archived and last accessed Autumn 2017 via http://kanal-1.dk/14-grindr-sexkultur-lystfulde-politiske-hadefulde-perspektiver/.

Kuntsman, Adi. "Belonging Through Violence: Flaming, Erasure, and Performativity in Queer Migrant Community." In Queer Online: Media, Technology and

Sexuality, edited by Kate O'Riordan and David J. Phillips. New York: Peter Lang, 2007.

Lang, Nico. "In Trump's America, Racism on Gay Dating Apps Is Getting Worse," *The Daily Dot*, 23 June 2017. https://www.dailydot.com/irl/racism-gay-dating-apps/.

Marselis, Randi. "Descendants of Slaves: The Articulation of Mixed Racial Ancestry in a Danish Television Documentary Series." *European Journal of Cultural Studies* 11, no. 4 (2008): 447–469.

Massey, Grace Carroll, Mona Vaughn Scott, and Sanford M. Dornbusch. "Racism Without Racists: Institutional Racism in Urban Schools." *The Black Scholar* 7, no. 3 (1975): 10–19.

McGlotten, Shaka. *Virtual Intimacies: Media, Affect, and Queer Sociality*. Albany, NY: State University of New York Press, 2014.

Mulinari, Paula. "Racism as Intimacy—Looking, Questioning and Touching in the Service Encounter." *Social Identities* 2, no. 5 (2017): 600–613.

Myong, Lene. "Adopteret: Fortællinger om transnational og racialiseret tilblivelse" [Adopted: Tales of Transnational and Racialised Origins]. PhD diss., Aarhus University, Copenhagen, 2009.

Myong, Lene. "Bliv dansk, bliv inkluderet: transnational adoption i et in- og eksklusionsperspektiv" [Be Danish, Be Included: Transnational Adoption in an Inclusionary and Exclusionary Perspective]. *Paedagogisk Psykologisk Tidsskrift* 48, no. 3 (2011): 268–276.

Owens, Erica, and Bronwyn Beistle. "Eating the Black Body: Interracial Desire, Food Metaphor and White Fear." In *Body/Embodiment: Symbolic Interactions and the Sociology of the Body*, edited by Dennis Waskul and Phillip Vannini, 201–212. Hampshire and Burlington: Ashgate, 2006.

Peumans, Wim. "'No Asians, Please': Same-Sex Sexualities and Ethnic Minorities in Europe." In *Hand Picked: Stimulus Respond*, edited by Jack Boulton, 128–139. London: Pavement Books, 2014.

Phua, Voon Chin, and Gayle Kaufman. "The Crossroads of Race and Sexuality: Date Selection Among Men in Internet 'Personal' Ads." *Journal of Family Issues* 8 (November 2003): 981–995.

Race, Kane. *The Gay Science: Intimate Experiments with the Problem of HIV*. London: Routledge, 2018.

Rachel E. Dubrofsky and Megan M. Wood, "Posting Racism and Sexism: Authenticity, Agency and Self-Reflexivity in Social Media," *Communication and Critical/Cultural Studies* 11, no. 3 (2014): 282–287.

Ranzini, Giulia, and Christoph Lutz. "Love at First Swipe? Explaining Tinder Self-Presentation and Motives." *Mobile Media and Communication* 5, no. 1 (2017): 80–101.

Sabaah. "Debat: Tænder ikke på asiater" [Debate: I'm Not Turned On by Asians], 19 February 2013, https://www.youtube.com/watch?v=qvSuHQPFWGw.

Schaper, Ulrike, Magdalena Beljan, Pascal Eitler, Christopher Ewing, and Benno Gammerl, "Sexotic: The Interplay Between Sexualization and Exoticization." *Sexualities* (published online November 2018; full citation forthcoming).

Shield, Andrew DJ. "'A Southern Man Can Have a Harem of Up to Twenty Danish Women': Sexotic Politics and Immigration in Denmark, 1965–1979." *Sexualities* (published online November 2018; full citation forthcoming).

Shield, Andrew DJ. "Grindr Culture: Intersectional and Socio-Sexual." *Ephemera: Theory & Politics in Organization* 18, no. 1 (2018): 149–161.

Smith, Jesus G. "'No Fats, Fems, or Blacks': The Role of Sexual Racism in Online Stratification and Sexual Health for Gay Men." PhD diss., Texas A&M University, 2017.

Smith, Jesus G. "Two-Faced Racism in Gay Online Sex: Preference in the Frontstage or Racism in the Backstage?" In *Sex in the Digital Age*, edited by Paul Nixon and Isabel Düsterhöft, 134–145. New York: Routledge, 2018.

Stoler, Ann Laura. "Colonial Aphasia: Race and Disabled Histories in France." *Public Culture* 23 (2011): 121–156.

Svensson, Jakob. "Gay the Correct Way: Mundane Queer Flaming Practices in Online Discussions of Politics." In *LGBTQs, Media, and Culture in Europe*, edited by in Alexander Dhoest, Lukasz Szulc, and Bart Eeckhout, 192–207. London: Routledge, 2017.

Tsang, Daniel. "Notes on Queer 'N Asian Virtual Sex." *Amerasia Journal* 20, no. 1 (1994): 117–128.

Verass, Sophie. "Racism on Grindr: Indigenous Gay Man Screenshots Racial Abuse Online," Special Broadcasting Service/National Indigenous Television, 14 April 2016. http://www.sbs.com.au/nitv/sexuality/article/2016/04/14/man-shares-experiences-of-racism-on-grinder.

Williams, Jessica, and Ronny Chieng. "Sexual Racism: When Preferences Become Discrimination." *The Daily Show*, 12 April 2016.

Woo, Jamie. "Open Letter to Grindr Users: I Am Not Rice, He Is Not Curry." *The Huffington Post*, 28 June 2013. https://www.huffingtonpost.com/jaime-woo/open-letter-to-grindr-users_b_3506180.html.

CHAPTER 6

"White is a color, Middle Eastern is not a color": Drop-Down Menus, Racial Identification, and the Weight of Labels

Race is central to the communicative culture of socio-sexual platforms like Grindr, due partly to users' own conceptions and biases around racial difference; but how does the *technology* of a platform affect the way users conceive of race? How can an interface, for example, impart notions of racial difference? The last chapter established that many gay men espouse racial-sexual preferences; how can a platform justify or challenge the notion of racial-sexual preferences? Across various socio-sexual platforms aimed at gay men, how are racial categories conceived, and what can we learn from scrutinizing the ways these categories expand, collapse, and bend across platforms? How do individual users—e.g. coming from areas of the world where these race categories do not always align with their own understandings of race and racial difference—negotiate (utilize and challenge) these race categories? A seemingly innocent interface can transform users' understandings of racial categories, identities, and boundaries.[1]

This chapter begins by overviewing the "ethnicity" drop-down menu on Grindr and how (quantitatively) it is used in the greater Copenhagen area. We then turn to two concepts that are central to the arguments in this chapter: the notion that interface-design can be culturally biased;

---

[1] On critical analyses of human "categorization" see Geoffrey C. Bowker and Susan Leigh Star, *Sorting Things Out: Classification and Its Consequences* (Cambridge, MA: MIT Press, 1999).

A. DJ Shield, *Immigrants on Grindr*,
https://doi.org/10.1007/978-3-030-30394-5_6

and the "weight" (or burden) associated with different racial categories and identities. We then scrutinize Grindr's "ethnicity" menu for evidence of (U.S. American) cultural bias in its interface design. As users around the world make Grindr profiles, Grindr "exports" its racial logic internationally, and some Grindr users find the menu options insufficient or unnecessary. We thus look *qualitatively* at how Grindr users in the greater Copenhagen use and nuance the "ethnicity" menu and its preprogrammed options. In doing so, we observe also that counter-hegemonic discourses disrupt the dominant notions of race propagated by the "ethnicity" menu. But by bending or rejecting the "ethnicity" menu, is a Grindr user challenging notions about racial hierarchies within Grindr culture, or maintaining the status quo?

"Ethnicity" on the Grindr Interface

There are nine options listed on Grindr's "ethnicity" menu: Asian, Black, Latino, Middle Eastern, Mixed, Native American, White, South Asian, and Other. The options are listed alphabetically (though "South Asian" is inexplicably misplaced), followed by "Other." Based on quantitative data (Chapter 3), I found 57% of Grindr users in Copenhagen city center, and 58% of Grindr users in the greater Copenhagen area, utilized this menu.[2] (Incidentally, two Italian researchers also found that 57% of respondents in Rome and Milan utilized the ethnicity menu.[3]) Of those who selected a label from the "ethncitity" menu, 16% in Copenhagen city center and 18% in the greater Copenhagen area selected something other than "White."

The total number of active users who identified as something other than "White" in the greater Copenhagen area averaged 176 at a given reading, with the highest reading at 222 individuals. Their responses to the menu broke down as the following: Mixed (29%), Asian (23%), Latino (20%), Middle Eastern (14%), Other (8%), Black (4%), South Asian (2%), and Native American (1%) (Fig. 6.1).

---

[2]Based on fifteen readings from December 2016, March 2017, and September 2017, and based on 4- and 36-km radii from a point by the Copenhagen University Humanities Campus. For 4 km, $N = 586$ average.

[3]Based on just 206 profiles in Rome and Milan (also in 2016). The Italian researchers did not specify the likelihood that someone responded with "White" or another label from the menu. Lorenza Parisi and Francesca Comunello, "Exploring Networked Interactions through

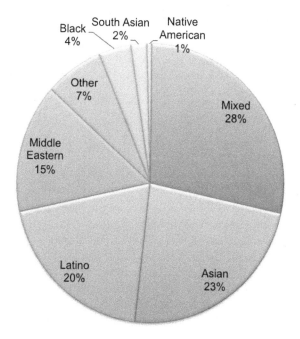

Fig. 6.1   "Ethnicity" selections among non-"White" responders (i.e. about 18% of Grindr users) in the greater Copenhagen area and Malmö (based on fifteen readings in 2016–2017, with average of $N = 176$ per reading, using the 36-km radius from my point in Copenhagen South)

At first glance, one might assume that the above pie chart represents the demographics of the population of Grindr users of color in the greater Copenhagen area. But these quantitative data do not take into consideration various points of discussion: what are the demographics of those who do not use the menu altogether? How do users choose one "ethnicity" label when they might identify with multiple? Why might someone choose one label, despite feeling that another label is more "accurate"?

To start with the first question—what are the demographics of those who do not use the menu altogether—one can scrutinize each profile individually and manually count the results. Based on one quick tally, I could

Table 6.1 Usage of drop-down menus (in Copenhagen)

Height	86.8%
Weight	72.0%
Age	68.0%
Relationship status	63.5%
Looking for	63.1%
Ethnicity	57.0%
Body Type	55.9%
[Sexual] Position	23.5%
Tribe	17.5%

see that the 39% of users who did not identify with an "ethnicity" label also remained ambiguous about most aspects of their appearance or identity: most had no profile photo and nothing about race/ethnicity in their profile text, and a few had photos that relayed no racial information (e.g. their legs in jeans). Of the remaining profiles, most included hints about "race" through profile photos, and a few clarified their ethnic background in profile texts (i.e. "Half Filipino"). This chapter focuses solely on the profiles of those who utilized the "ethnicity" menu or discussed race or ethnicity in their profile texts, and on interviews with users about racial and ethnic identification on socio-sexual media.

Usage of "Ethnicity" vs. Other Menus

The likelihood that a Grindr user in Copenhagen would identify with *any* of the drop-down menus is shown in Table 6.1. Not surprisingly, the most commonly used menus are for height and weight, followed by age. Height, weight, and age are the straightforward categories: when it comes to giving a response, one can either tell the truth, lie, or omit a response. The next two commonly used menus are "relationship status" and "looking for." When given a wide range of possible relationship statuses, most users felt enough affinity with the drop-down menu options to choose one.[4]

---

[4]The data was based five readings with an average of $N = 590$. Additionally, 89.5% of users displayed a profile photo, but as mentioned in Chapter 3, a researcher would have to scrutinize these profiles individually to see how many were face photos, how many were unrelated landscape photos, and so forth. Age can still be ascertained via filter even when invisible; data on percentage who display age must be tallied individually. The vast majority of those who clarified their relationship status were single (85%). Though 14% of users specified being in relationships by selecting "Married," "Partnered," or "Open Relationship." The final

It is no coincidence that user response rates begin to drop with "ethnicity" and "body type" (followed by sexual "position"[5] and one's so-called "tribe"[6]); as the drop-down-menu options become increasingly subjective. With body type, the options seem to reflect moral judgment on the part of Grindr's creators.[7] Who has the "average" body, from which all others are judged as larger or slimmer? At what point is a "slim" body "toned," or a "toned" body "muscular"? When does a "stocky" body become "large," or perhaps *too* large? Which of these labels attract responses from Grindr users, and which labels are less desirable? How often do users skip this menu because they feel their response would make them less attractive? Similarly to the "body type" menu, the "ethnicity" menu also reflects cultural bias on the part of the app's programmers.

Scholar Russel Robinson argued that by making "ethnicity" menus central to the profile creation process, socio-sexual platforms forced users to "provide information that others may then use to discriminate against

---

1% identified with one of Grindr's more ambiguous drop-down menu options: "Committed," "Dating," "Engaged," and "Exclusive."

[5] The "position" menu also received very low response rates, which could relate to the menu options' focus on penetrative anal sex (with options Top, Vers Top, Versatile, Vers Bottom, and Bottom), with no options for those preferring oral or non-penetrative sex. Users' unwillingness to engage with this menu could also reflect that sexuality is still a "big deal" and that users are hesitant to declare personal sexual identities openly on their profiles. See, e.g., Stefanie Duguay, "Three Flawed Assumptions the Daily Beast Made About Dating Apps," Social Media Collective Research Blog, 16 August 2016, https://socialmediacollective.org/2016/08/16/three-assumptions-the-daily-beast-made-about-dating-apps/.

[6] Tribes are listed alphabetically. Grindr's unpaid users can select one option, while Grindr Xtra users can select three options. The most underutilized menu is Grindr's "Tribe" menu, which I argue is a result of the vast majority of Grindr users (at least in Copenhagen) feeling discord with the concept of a "tribe" and with the limited options. Some of these options include physical-related labels common in (especially U.S. American) gay cultures, such as "twink" (e.g. for young, often smooth/hairless guys), "bear" (e.g. for husky, hairy, often older men), and "otter" (e.g. for slim, hairy men). Other tribes focus on personal adjectives (clean-cut, discreet, geek, rugged), object fetishes (leather), or other typically masculine identities (daddy, jock). Some labels might correspond to leisure activities, meaning that "geeks" might like computer games, or "jocks" like sports. The remaining tribes are "poz" (for HIV positive people) and "trans" (e.g. for those who identify as transgender), perhaps the most immutable of the tribes.

[7] The fact that "Toned" falls out of alphabetical order appears to be a mistake, but I can recall that it was changed from "Athletic."

them."[8] When enough users of a socio-sexual platform identify with an "ethnicity" or race, the platform then *affords* users the possibility of *race filtering*, or the restricting of people with specific racial identities from appearing in one's grid of possible matches.

Race Filtering

Affordances are the range of possibilities understood from a technology.[9] A well-designed door handle conveys to its users to push the lever down and to pull the door open; the door handle is the technology, and the act of opening the door becomes the affordance.[10] Grindr enables users to tap buttons that send messages to nearby users, and cruising for sex is a key affordance of these platforms. The geo-locative platform's messaging feature is the *technology* that *affords* its users the possibility of sex; the user must figure out how to harness that technology in order to take full advantage of it. Grindr also provides users with an advanced search feature (i.e. a technology) that users can harness for race filtering.

Grindr appears ambivalent on the topic of race filtering. On the one hand, they condone race filtering by allowing users to conduct advanced searches based on "ethnicity." (Grindr does *not* allow users to conduct advanced searches based on HIV status, which suggests Grindr has taken a stand *against* sero-sorting.) Grindr has taken no clear stand against race filtering.

On the other hand, Grindr does not explicitly promote race filtering in its promotional materials, as it does with almost all of its other filters. If users on the free version attempt to use most filters, Grindr redirects the

[8] Russell Robinson, "Structural Dimensions of Romantic Preferences," *Fordham Law Review* 76 (2008): 2792. See also McGlotten, 147 fn40.

[9] For more on affordances specifically within a digital culture framework: Gina Neff et al., "Affordances, Technical Agency, and the Politics of Technologies of Cultural Production: A Dialogue," Culture Digitally, 23 January 2012, http://culturedigitally.org/2012/01/affordances-technical-agency-and-the-politics-of-technologies-of-cultural-production-2/; Peter Nagy and Gina Neff, "Imagined Affordance: Reconstructing a Keyword for Communication Theory," *Social Media + Society* 1, no. 2 (2015): 1–9.

[10] Victor Kaptelinin, "Affordance," in *The Encyclopedia of Human-Computer Interaction*, ed. Mads Soegaard et al., 2nd ed. (Interactive Design Foundation, 2011).

users to screens advertising an "Upgrade to Xtra."[11] Each filter brings a different advertisement related to that filter; for example, if one tries to filter by relationship status (e.g. for single users), Grindr redirects the user to, "Find a keeper: Filter guys by relationship status." Or if one tries to filter users by height, Grindr's advertisement reads, "Make sure he measures up: Filter guys by height."[12] But something interesting happens when a user tries to filter by ethnicity: the user is told that on Grindr Xtra, the user can "Find Your Type" (Fig. 6.2).

It is only with the "ethnicity" filter that Grindr redirects to this "generic" ad; this reveals that Grindr does not want to (appear to) condone race filtering by explicitly promoting, "Filter guys by ethnicity!" In the geneic ad, one sees a Grindr welcome screen with "Filters off," and there are several prominent men of color in on the grid (though unfortunately I could not get permission to reprint the original screen capture). The ad does not mention the ethnicity filter—which would have made it parallel to the other redirect ads—but one can infer from the diverse, unfiltered grid and references to "type" that race-based searching is the offer.

It is telling that a free user's attempt to race-filter brings about an advertisement to "Find Your Type" with Grindr Xtra. This "type" is presumably not a specific person, but a group of people with whom the user might hope to match. And as one reviewer of this book noted: the phrase "you're not my type" is often a "polite" euphemism for "I'm not into..." people with particular physical traits, including entire races. In this ad, Grindr avoids specifically saying that one's "type" is racial, even though this ad is only attached to the "ethnicity" menu. Nevertheless, the Grindr advertisement draws an immediate link between the technology of the "ethnicity" search option, the affordance of race-selective filtering, and the end-goal of finding one's "type" of person.

---

[11] For analysis of the commercial agency at work in an online gay business: Ben Light et al., "Gay Men, Gaydar and the Commodification of Difference," *Information Technology and People* 21, no. 3 (2008).

[12] The other three possible ads are the following: when attempting to filer by weight: "Your size is in stock"; by body type, "Shape up your search"; or by sexual position, "Top or bottom bunk?" One cannot search by gender identity as of 2019, except via the 'Trans' tribe. Age and tribe filters are free to all users, as is "looking for."

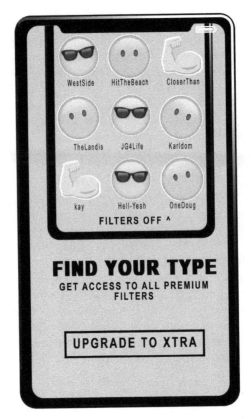

Fig. 6.2 "Find Your Type": Grindr pop-up ad in response to a free user's attempt at race filtering (This is a mock-up of how Grindr's 2018 redirect ad appeared on a user's phone; the emojis represent real faces, many of whom were men of color)

Before continuing with our analysis of race labels in the Grindr culture of the greater Copenhagen area, we move to scholarly literature on cultural bias in interface design, in order to build the argument that Grindr users of color might feel discord with the "ethnicity" drop-down menus, resulting in their refusal to use the menu, or even their rejection of Grindr altogether.

Cultural Bias in Technology Design

As the previous section on affordances argued, a platform's interface directs a user's action, and thus can influence a user's understanding of the possibilities of action on that platform.[13] Information studies scholar Johanna Drucker has explained that user interaction with an interface is often directed via "visual cues"[14]; visual cues on Grindr like speech bubbles and back arrows allowed a new user to interact with the platform almost intuitively. But the user can only understand visual cues in relation to "situated knowledge, cultural conditions, and training, the whole gamut of individually inflected and socially conditioned skills and attitudes."[15] For example, tapping a flame icon on someone's Grindr profile sends that user a notification of interest: "Hot!" But this flame button might only be intuitive for a user accustomed to using the words "hot" and "sexy" interchangeably. Visual cues help users make sense of the information within an interface, but can include bias from the creators: in other words, value systems can be expressed in web/app design.[16]

Interfaces can reflect the designers' bias with regard to gender and sexuality, as Danish communication scholar Anne-Mette Albrechtslund argued in a paper about the popular early 2000s computer game, The Sims 2. As a user oversees a microcosm of computer people (Sims), she can encourage her Sims to talk to or tickle one another, but the outcome is not always predictable. Sometimes a Sim grows annoyed with another's flirtation;

---

[13]As Erwin Goffman theorized with regard to more traditional media, "frames" modify a subject's perception of information, expanding or contracting certain features so that the subject (e.g. a reader, an audience) can make sense of the information. The frame guides the audience to interpret and interact with the media in specific ways. This is parallel in some ways to the interface, with its visual cues. Erving Goffman, *Frame Analysis: An Essay on the Organization of Experience* (London: Harper & Row, 1974).

[14]Johanna Drucker, "Humanities Approaches to Interface Theory," *Culture Machine* 12 (2011): 4. To Drucker, an interface is a "zone of affordances organized to support and provoke activities and behaviors probabilistically." Drucker observed a dearth in academic inquiries about technological interfaces. Rather, the discourses that dominated discussions of interfaces—words like "user feedback" and "design"—came from the software industry. Consequently, Drucker outlined a humanities-based theory of discussing interfaces, drawing from three main fields: graphical reading practices (especially from literature on comic books), frame analysis (especially from Goffman), and the understanding of "the subject" as something fundamentally tied to environment and human psychology. See also Drucker, 7; Goffman, *Frame Analysis*.

[15]Drucker, 6.

[16]See discussion of sociologist Geert Hofstede's work in Drucker, 11.

but other times the Sims fall in love and mimic sex. Sex could happen between two members of the same or opposite sex, and could even occur between a member of the Sim household and a visiting maid. But sex could not happen between two teenagers (even though they could kiss), and no romantic activity could occur between teenagers and adults. Moreover, if one partner in a Sim couple flirted with another Sim, the other partner would get angry; thus the game (arguably) presupposed monogamy. The Sims' interface guides users to interact with the game in certain ways—to tickle, to flirt, heterosexually or homosexually—but the design includes biases about (age-appropriate, non-polyamorous) sex.

One could also purchase a "Nightlife expansion pack" that allowed players to fine-tune the sexual chemistry between their Sims with "turn-ons" and "turn-offs" including options related to hair color, clothing, and odor.[17] There are some parallels with Grindr, namely in the designers' assumptions about the types of sexual turn-ons and turn-offs that users might espouse (i.e. filtering by ethnicity or body type).

The Sims' creators also demonstrated gendered assumptions about bodies: users could change Sims bodies, but all males' bodies were "broad-shouldered and tall," and all females' were "voluptuous."[18] Although Grindr's body types are arguably gender-neutral (e.g. slim, toned, muscular), it is worth considering how Grindr presupposes that its users will not identify with more typically "feminine" adjectives like "curvy" or "petit(e)." Similarly, Grindr's tribe options are implicitly masculine (e.g. jock, rugged) or explicitly masculine (e.g. daddy), leaving little room for people to identify with "feminine" adjectives (except under gender identity, since 2018).

These gendered assumptions in the drop-down menu not only affect trans and non-binary users, but they also reinforce cultural biases about gender roles for all Grindr users. Or as Ben Light, Gordon Fletcher, and Alison Adam wrote in their 2008 study of Gaydar, a technological design "may reinforce a stereotype that is defined with reference to a collective cultural norm of what being a gay man means" and in that way "constrains expressions of difference."[19] Drop-down menus, tick boxes, and advanced

---

[17] Anne-Mette Albrechtslund, "Gender Values in Simulation Games: Sex and the Sims," *Proceedings of Computer Ethics Philosophical Enquiries* (2007): 3.

[18] Ibid., 4.

[19] Light et al.

searches "preclude[d] variations... or even resistance to" identification with a platform's pre-defined selections.[20] Returning to Grindr's interface: what cultural biases are included in the platform with regard to "ethnicity"? How does Grindr limit variation in racial and ethnic identifications, or even resistance to racial and ethnic identification? How might bias in interface design affect a user's willingness to engage with the platform?

The "Burdens" of Race Labels

As with biases about gender and sexuality, biases about race and ethnicity also saturate technologies, such as in racial drop-down menus. Media scholars have long noted that racial drop-down menus reduce individuals' complex racial identities, stir anxiety, and promote discrimination in digital cultures. In 2002, Lisa Nakamura devoted Chapter Five of her influential text *Cybertypes: Race, Ethnicity and Identity on the Internet* to the topic of online racial drop-down menus. Entitled "Menu-Driven Identities: Making Race Happen Online," the chapter focused on the ethnicity menus of a few web portals and early social media platforms.[21] To Nakamura, this "clickable box" for race and/or ethnicity was reductive and limiting, as users were "given no means to define or modify the terms or categories available to them"; thus "identities that d[id] not appear on the menu are essentially foreclosed on and erased."[22] Ultimately, she used her analysis to theorize that "interface design features... [can] force reductive, often archaic means of defining race upon the user."[23]

Yet despite these critiques, drop-down menus for race and/or ethnicity have persisted on social media platforms. Queer media scholars have explored the consequences of these menus in online subcultures for men who have sex with men. For example, Andil Gosine extended Nakamura's argument about reductive categories in his 2008 anthology chapter,

---

[20] Ibid., 307.

[21] Lisa Nakamura, *Cybertypes: Race, Ethnicity, and Identity on the Internet* (New York and London: Routledge, 2002). Nakamura looks at early social media geared at people of color—such as AsianAvenue.com and BlackPlanet.com—and how "mestiza or other culturally ambiguous identities—such as those belonging to hyphenated Americans—are rendered unintelligible, inexpressible, and invisible, since they can't be (or rather, aren't) given a 'box' of their own"; Nakamura, 120.

[22] Nakamura, *Cybertypes*, 101–102.

[23] Ibid.

"Brown to Blonde at Gay.com: Passing White in Queer Cyberspace."[24] Although the chapter focused mainly on the privileges extended to some users (e.g. white gay men) over others (e.g. gay men of color), Gosine also included this poignant parenthetical self-reflection about his own selection(s) from racial drop-down menus on a gay platform:

> Having been born in the Caribbean to parents descended from Indian indentures, which category do I now pick in the gay.com chat rooms: am I "Asian," "Black," "Latin," or "Other"? Each category carries **a different set of burdens**, and each will position me differently in the chat rooms.[25]

The gay platform on which Gosine conducted his research—and also participated recreationally—"oblige[d] users to declare essentialist identities" via the racial drop-down menu (among other methods for "ensuring racial identification").[26] Gosine expressed a feeling of dissonance between his own racial identity and the simplified options provided on the interface of (especially gay) social media and/or dating platforms.

Further, by noting that each category "carries a different set of burdens," Gosine touched on the anxiety of embodying race or ethnicity in gay men's digital cultures. Beyond "the burden of not being white," people of color bear unique burdens in gay men's digital cultures.[27] Specific characteristics, aesthetics, and behaviors "fix" to racial categories, such as the stereotypes of the submissive Asian man, and the dominant and hypersexual Black man (i.e. Mandingo).[28] This topic is explored also outside of academia, where journalists and other writers[29] have shared extensive anecdotal evidence about being pigeonholed with racial-sexual stereotypes.

[24] Andil Gosine, "Brown to Blonde at Gay.com: Passing White in Queer Cyberspace," in *Queer Online: Media Technology and Sexuality*, ed. K. O'Riordan and D. Phillips (New York: Peter Lang, 2007): 139–153.

[25] Gosine, 145. Emphasis added.

[26] Ibid.; On the four strategies "employed to encourage, if not ensure, racial identification" in Gay.com chat rooms, see Ibid., 143.

[27] Gosine, 150 and 148.

[28] E.g. Shaka McGlotten, *Virtual Intimacies: Media, Affect, and Queer Sociality* (Albany: SUNY Press, 2013), 68 and 74; Gosine, 148.

[29] Some of this literature is cited in Gosine and McGlotten; see also, e.g., Alexander Chee, "My First (and Last) Time Dating a Rice Queen," The Stranger, 21 June 2017, https://www.thestranger.com/queer-issue-2017/2017/06/21/25227046/my-first-and-last-time-dating-a-rice-queen.

Certain racial labels carry different weights. A user like Gosine—who feels he has the option to identify with at least four labels on a certain platform, and who is aware of the weight of each label—can tailor his racial identification to "fit" with the online culture, or to avoid certain burdens, like feelings of anxiety, depression, or rejection. This was a topic further explored by Shaka McGlotten in *Virtual Intimacies: Media, Affect, and Queer Sociality* (2013), which paid some attention to drop-down menus. In a chapter titled "Feeling Black and Blue," McGlotten began by observing how drop-down menus elevated the status of race to an "essential element of the profile creation process... like age, weight, and height...."[30] Then through interviews and online ethnography, he showed various ways that racism persisted in gay online subcultures, which prompted the gay person of color to "become more anxiously attuned to... his own position within a racist economy of desires."[31]

McGlotten also used autoethnographic methods, and reflected on how fears of racial stereotyping affected his own behaviors with race-identification online: "Increasingly, I tended not to select a definitive racial category that would disclose my political or physiognomic affinities to blackness," McGlotten wrote. "So rather than select Black/African-American, I would typically select Mixed or Other."[32] Fanon's notion of "crushing objecthood"—in which race gets fixed onto people of color—is still relevant to today's socio-sexual online cultures.[33] Gosine's articulation of the "burdens" associated with embodying race, and McGlotten's point about (white) assumptions regarding the "political or physiognomic affinities" of certain labels provide insights for this chapter's analysis of how Grindr users of color utilize the "ethnicity" menu in the greater Copenhagen area. (Those eager to hear from interviewees can skip to the section, "Am I Middle Eastern?")

---

[30] McGlotten, 67.

[31] Ibid., 69.

[32] Ibid., 70.

[33] See final paragraphs of Chapter 4, via Franz Fanon, *Black Skin, White Masks*, trans. Charles Lam Markmann (London: Pluto Press, 1986 [1952]).

The U.S. Hegemony of Grindr's "Ethnicity" Menu

Grindr's nine options under the "ethnicity" drop-down menu—Asian, Black, Latino, Middle Eastern, Mixed, Native American, White, South Asian, and Other—are embedded largely in dominant U.S. American notions of race and ethnicity, such as those of the decennial census. The six racial categories in the 2010 decennial census were the following: "White," "Black or African-American," "American Indian or Alaska Native," "Asian," "Native Hawaiian or Other Pacific Islander," and "Some Other Race."[34] Since 2000, respondents have been allowed to identify with more than one of the options. The 2010 Census justified these labels with the following:

> The race categories included in the census questionnaire generally reflect a social definition of race recognized in this country [the U.S.A.] and are not an attempt to define race biologically, anthropologically, or genetically. In addition, it is recognized that the categories of the race question include race and national origin or sociocultural groups.[35]

In other words, the Bureau of the Census understands race as fluid and culturally specific: race is a social construction without a genetic component, and understandings of racial borders change across cultures and across time.

But the Bureau also asserts that race data are a valuable tool for understanding the demographics of the United States, and hence race cannot be ignored. Scholarship on classification schemes underscores that official attempts to categorize people often become sites of political and social struggle.[36] South African apartheid, for example, relied on confused theories of eugenics and race to classify millions of people into rigid categories (over 100,000 of whom made formal appeals regarding their categorization).[37] Yet despite acknowledging the social constructions of racial

---

[34]Karen R. Humes et al., "Overview of Race and Hispanic Origin: 2010" (U.S. Census Bureau 2010 Census Briefs, March 2011), 2–3, https://www.census.gov/2010census/data/.

[35]Ibid., 2 fn7. Also, Elizabeth M. Hoeffel et al., "The Asian Population: 2010" (U.S. Census Bureau 2010 Census Briefs, March 2012), 3 fn9, https://www.census.gov/2010census/data/.

[36]Bowker and Star, 196.

[37]Ibid., Chapter 6, which underscores the government's brute force with regard to classification, and its distain for ambiguity. Under apartheid, South Africans were classified by

borders, many also advocate for collecting data about race; this can be "strategic essentialism," whereby a group reifies a category (e.g. African-Americans) to achieve empowerment.[38] With regard to the understanding of "race" both as a social construction and as something that shapes the lived experiences of individuals, this book aligns with the U.S. Census's general understanding of race.

Separate from "race," the U.S. Census asks about "ethnicity," which is defined solely as "Hispanic/Latino" or not Hispanic/Latino. These labels (Hispanic, Latino) have never appeared as "race" options, as they have been relegated to a separate "ethnicity" question since 1970. The 2010 Census states this clearly: "[R]ace and Hispanic origin (ethnicity) are separate and distinct concepts," and must be asked in two separate questions.[39] The two questions were presented next to each other with the following instructions: "Please answer BOTH Question 8 about Hispanic origin and Question 9 about race. For this census, Hispanic origins are not races."[40] Despite this clarification, 37% of Hispanic/Latino-identified respondents still selected "Some Other Race" and tended to write in responses like "Mexican" or "Hispanic" as their racial identity, which in itself is a critique of the Census and its categories.[41] (A recent survey of Hispanic-identified Americans found that two-thirds of respondents considered "Hispanic" part of their racial background, so the U.S. Census is considering merging the two questions for the 2020 Census.[42])

On both the U.S. Census and the Grindr interface, the question of race is presented as a basic and natural way for an individual to identify, similar to age or location. In fact, the decennial census—at every interval since 1790—has collected data about age, location, and race among their first

race according to characteristics such as complexion, hair, earlobe softness, facial profile, and reportedly even social behaviors, from club affiliations to eating and sleeping habits.

[38] Ibid., 224. Defined by critical race theorists as the "pragmatic junction between that which is perceived as real, and the consequences of that" category.

[39] Humes et al., 2.

[40] Bureau of the Census, "United States Census 2010," Department of Commerce, last accessed via https://www.census.gov/history/.

[41] Ana Gonzalez-Barrera and Mark Hugo Lopez, "Is Being Hispanic a Matter of Race, Ethnicity or Both?" Pew Research Center, 15 June 2015, http://www.pewresearch.org/fact-tank/2015/06/15/is-being-hispanic-a-matter-of-race-ethnicity-or-both/.

[42] Ibid.

questions, just as Grindr has elevated the status of age, location, and race in every interface design since its inception in 2009.

The U.S. Census and Grindr's "Ethnicity" Options

The label "**White**" has appeared on every U.S. census as the first option for racial identification. The second option is "**Black** or African-American," a category which has also appeared on every U.S. Census, though often with different terms (e.g. Negro, which was included as a possible identity through 2000). Aside from white and black, the U.S. Census has catego-rized other groups in various ways, the most simple of which was the 1940 Census, which only provided three options: "White", "Negro", and "All other."[43] Since the 1970s, "Black" was clarified with regard to regional origin—that is, African-American—but white was not. In fact, no cen-sus has provided an alternative label for white-identified people, such as "European-American," "person of European descent," or "Caucasian."

On both Grindr and the U.S. Census, "White" and "Black" are the only labels that refer to colors; the other options refer to ancestral regional origin, such as Asian or Native American. But one major difference: Grindr alphabetizes its options, whereas the U.S. Census has always listed "White" first. The fact that white is always first on the U.S. Census reflects an idea that the United States is majority white, historically white, and geared for whites. By listing the options alphabetically, Grindr actually removes some of the association between whiteness and hierarchy.

As mentioned in the introduction, the U.S. Census asks anyone who identifies as "**Latino**" to choose a race (e.g. White, Black, Native Amer-ican), but many Latino-identified Americans consider "Latino" as central to their racial identity. Thus by including "Latino" alongside racial labels (e.g. White, Black), Grindr's menu differs from the census' definition of race/ethnicity, but still reflects the U.S. Census' discourses (with the words "Latino" and "ethnicity").

The decennial U.S. Census has never included one box for "**Asian**" citizens and residents, and in 2010 provided an extensive list of nationalities and ethnicities under the umbrella of "Asian." As early as 1870, the Census included an option for Chinese residents; by 1950, the options included separate boxes for Japanese, Chinese, and Filipino residents; by 1980, there

---

[43] Bureau of the Census, "Sixteenth Census of the United States: 1940—Housing," Depart-ment of Commerce, last accessed via https://www.census.gov/prod/www/decennial.html.

were many more options, including one for "Asian Indians" (a group that corresponds to **"South Asians"** on Grindr). Note that the terms Asian and South Asian—unlike White, Black, or African-American—treat the subject as perpetually foreign from U.S. American culture.

Indigenous Americans (or on Grindr, **"Native Americans"**) were recognized on the 1870 U.S. Census as "Indians"; the group was omitted from the U.S. Census for several decades, and returned in 1950 as "American Indians," which is the term that has been used through the last census (along with "Alaskan Native"[44]). Since 1970, members of this group have been asked to specify their tribe(s).[45]

The 1960 Census also introduced the option "Hawaiian," and the 2010 Census considered "Native Hawaiian or Other Pacific Islander" as one of the five distinct race groups. Grindr conspicuously omits "Pacific Islander," though its competitor Scruff includes it.

"Other" has appeared consistently on the U.S. Census since 1940, always with the request that respondents specify their race in their own words. Grindr also offers the "Other" menu (last on the list), but without an explicit space for users to define this "Other" in their own words.

Multiracial individuals have been permitted to identify with two or more races on the U.S. Census since 2000.[46] On Grindr, however, there is only one general category for **"Mixed"**-identified individuals, and users are unable to select multiple options. The reason for this restriction is unfathomable, since it would be so easy to allow users to select two options. This technological limitation relates to what Nakamura argued in *Cybertypes* regarding "the repression of interracial" and "the denial of mixed identities" in drop-down menu design.[47]

A major difference between the U.S. Census and Grindr regards the separation of **"Middle Eastern"** from **"White."** The U.S. Census has never included people with Middle Eastern origins as a separate race; rather,

[44]The 1960 census also provided options for "Aleut" and "Eskimo," two groups that were later integrated under the umbrella "American Indian *or Alaska Native*."

[45]Bureau of the Census, "Untitled [1970 Census Questionnaire]," Department of Commerce, last accessed via https://www.census.gov/prod/www/decennial.html.

[46]See, e.g., Kimberly McClain DaCosta, *Making Multiracials: State, Family, and Market in the Redrawing of the Color Line* (Stanford, CA: Stanford University Press, 2007); Debra Elizabeth Thompson, "Seeing Like a Racial State: The Census and the Politics of Race in the United States, Great Britain and Canada" (PhD diss., University of Toronto, 2012).

[47]Nakamura, *Cybertypes*, 119–121.

the majority of people of Middle Eastern and North African origin have
been included in the Census' definition of "White": a white person is "a
person having origins in any of the original peoples of Europe, the Middle East, or North Africa," including those who otherwise/also identify
as "...Lebanese, Arab, Moroccan..." among other random suggestions.[48]
Of all the Grindr drop-down menu options, "Middle Eastern" differs the
furthest from the U.S. Census' categorical distinctions of race.[49] Though
in practice, many U.S. American Arabs are racialized as non-white and
Othered.

Internalizing Race Menu Options

In his research on immigrants in the UK and their uses of a socio-sexual platform primarily for gay men, Nicholas Boston made an interesting observation about the internalization of racial taxonomies. One Polish interviewee
told Boston, "Online, I'm usually looking for South Asian..., Arab, black,
and mixed-race" men, and Boston could not help but notice how these
terms corresponded to the "preprogrammed options in the drop-down
menu" on the platform.[50] Thus, drop-down menus on popular platforms
can also serve the purpose of "exporting" racial logics (again: categories,
identities, differences, and boundaries) from one culture to another.

[48]Humes et al., 3. This definition does not acknowledge ethnic minorities in North Africa
and the Middle East, such as Egyptian Nubians, nor does it acknowledge the long histories
of ethnic mixing and fluidity between definitions.

[49]One possible explanation for the separation of "White" from "Middle Eastern" is the
fact the Grindr's founder—Joel Simkhai, who was born in Israel and raised in the United
States—has identified as "Middle Eastern" on all of the Grindr profiles he has shared with the
media since 2010. In interviews, he has never clarified his rationale for separating "Middle
Eastern" from "White" on Grindr's drop-down menu. Having grown up in the United States,
Simkhai would have been accustomed to identifying as "White" on official documents like the
U.S. Census; see, e.g., Elliot, "Ten Money Questions: Grindr CEO Joel Simkhai," Queercents, 14 December 2010, http://queercents.com/2010/12/14/grindr-ceo-joel-simkhai-
interview/; Olivia Goldhill, "People Really Are Finding Love on Dating Apps Like Grindr
and Tinder," *Business Insider*, 2 July 2013, http://www.businessinsider.com/we-found-love-
on-grindr-2013-7?r=US&IR=T&IR=T.

[50]Nicholas Boston, "Libidinal Cosmopolitanism: The Case of Digital Sexual Encounters
in Post-enlargement Europe," in *Postcolonial Transitions in Europe: Contexts, Practices and
Politics*, ed. Sandra Ponzanesi and Gianmaria Colpani (London: Rowman & Littlefield, 2016),
304–305; also Andrew DJ Shield, "New in Town: Gay Immigrants and Geosocial Dating
Apps," in *LGBTQs, Media, and Culture in Europe*, ed. Alexander Dhoest et al. (London:
Routledge, 2017), 254.

Grindr's drop-down menu is embedded in U.S. culture and history, but users around the world employ the menu and its categories in various contexts and languages. During their encounters with the foreign interface, these users learn to adopt and repeat the platform's racial discourses. As international users internalize Grindr's notions of race—notions that are embedded in U.S. American culture and history—Grindr can be seen as part and parcel of U.S. American cultural imperialism.

Translating Race Categories

Grindr's Spanish "ethnicity" options are almost identical to the English terms (i.e. *Asiático, Negro, Latino, Medio Oriente, Mixto, Nativo Americano, Blanco, Sudasiático, Otro*) with color labels for Black and White, regional labels for Asian and South Asian among others, and a general category for Mixed individuals.[51] In Portuguese, however, Middle Eastern becomes the equivalent of "Arab" (*Árabe*), which suggests an ethnolinguistic understanding of the Middle East that might exclude certain groups (e.g. Turks, Kurds, Persians). Also in Portuguese, South Asian becomes the equivalent of "Indian" (*Indiano*, similar to the "Asian Indian" on the U.S. Census), which potentially excludes Pakistanis, Bangladeshis, and Sri Lankans.

In Portuguese, Grindr also uses the word "*Mestiço*" for Mixed. This Portuguese racial label has a long colonial history, much like "mulatto" in the United States: the term has referred to mixed-race people, many of whom were born out of forced marriages or rape between European men and native women. (The Spanish equivalent in colonial history is "*mestizo*," and although this term is not used on Grindr, one does find it on the Spanish version of PlanetRomeo.) In 2018, Grindr became available in even more languages, including Russian. A Russian interviewee explained that Grindr's equivalent of "White" in Russian is "European."

Racializing Southern Europe

Broadening the scope from Grindr to other socio-sexual networking platforms for gay men, the argument remains that racial drop-down menus

---

[51]A Grindr user cannot change the app's language via Grindr's settings. But if the user's smartphone is programmed for Spanish or Portuguese, for example, then Grindr will automatically translate to these languages.

reflect a specific context, culture, and history and can reify (arbitrary) racial borders. PlanetRomeo, for example, was founded in Germany in 2002, and its eight racial/ethnic categories (see Table 6.2) reflect that, namely in the way it divides people of European descent between "Caucasian" and "Mediterranean." Further, the "Mediterranean" group is divided between those who are European, and those who live in (the Arabic-speaking areas of) the Middle East and North Africa, as Romeo offers a separate category for "Arab" users. (Further still, "Mediterranean" may or may not include Europeans from Spain, who—at least according to the U.S. Census definition—could select Romeo's "Latin" option.) When one sets Romeo to German, the terms "Caucasian" and "Mediterranean" respectively become *"Europäer"* (European) and *"Südländer"* (Southerner). Similarly, the Swedish translation of "Mediterranean" was *"Sydländsk"* (Southerner).

Romeo's distinction between "Caucasian" and "Mediterranean" in English—or between "Europeans" and "Southerners" in German—has some historical precedent in discourses about migration to Germany in the 1960s and 1970s (also to Austria, Belgium, Denmark, the Netherlands, Sweden, and Switzerland) from Greece, Italy, Portugal, Spain, Turkey, and the former Yugoslavia. During and after this "guest-worker" labor boom, sources sometimes referred to members of this group collectively as "Mediterraneans" or "Southerners."[52]

There are other aspects of this menu that could be explored further, such as why "Black" becomes "African" in French (on Romeo); or why (on the Swedish LGBTQ platform Qruiser) Europeans are divided into five ethno-phenotypic categories (Table 6.2). While beyond the scope of this book, my research has identified these phenomena for future further exploration. In sum: Grindr's race categories are problematic in the United States, and arguably irrelevant in other geographies, yet have been adopted globally.

---

[52] E.g. (on "Mediterraneans") Frank Bovenkerk, "The Netherlands," in *International Labor Migration in Europe*, ed. Ronald E. Krane (New York: Praeger Publishers, 1979); (on the Scandinavian equivalent of "Southerners") J. W. Sørensen, "Der kom fremmede: Migration, Højkonjunktur, Kultursammenstød, Foreign Workers in Denmark up to 1970" [There Were Strangers Who Came: Migration, High-Conjuncture and Culture Clash], Aarhus University, Working paper for the Center for Culture Research, 1988.

Table 6.2 Ethnic/racial drop-down menus on English-language versions of four platforms used by GBTQ (and LGBTQ for Qruiser) Europeans

Platform	Grindr	Scruff	PlanetRomeo	Qruiser
Origin	U.S.A., 2009	U.S.A., 2010	Germany, 2002	Sweden, 2000
Category	"Ethnicity"	"Ethnicity"	"Ethnicity"	"Looks and origin"
Options (listed in order as presented on platform)	• Asian • Black • Latino • Middle Eastern • Mixed • Native American • White • South Asian • Other	• Asian • Black • Hispanic/Latino • South Asian (*formerly Indian*) • Middle Eastern • Pacific Islander • White • Native American • Multi-Racial	*On website:* • Caucasian • Asian • Latin • Mediterranean • Black • Mixed • Arab • Indian *On app:* Alphabetical	• north european • western european • central european • mediteranean [sic] european • eastern european • asian • indian • african • middle eastern • south american • other
Languages offered	3	14	22 (→ 6 in 2017)	6

We turn now to the qualitative inquiry into how immigrants adopt, nego-tiate, or customize Grindr's race labels in the greater Copenhagen area.

"AM I MIDDLE EASTERN?": RACIAL AMBIGUITIES, AND NEGOTIATING THE "ETHNICITY" MENU

Foregrounding the words of the interviewees, this empirical section exam-ines racial ambiguity on Grindr, and returns to concepts like the desirability or burdens attached to certain labels, and categorization schemes as sites of political and social struggle. The following sections serve two purposes: to understand how users negotiate their "ethnicity" label, and to consider why people use or eschew certain labels.

Internalizing the Concept of a "Middle Eastern" Iranian (Parvin)

Understandings of the definition of "Middle East" change across time and cultures, as the examples in this section show. Among my interviewees, some internalized and identified with terms about which they were initially critical, such as Parvin (b. Iran, immigrated 2015), who recalled feeling discord with the label "Middle Eastern," though ultimately included it on his Grindr profile. As he said during our interview, he remembered thinking as he filled out his first Grindr profile, "What do I say? Asian? What's East? Who says that it's East?" In Iran, he was accustomed to identifying himself and his neighbors with labels like Iranian, Afghani, or Azerbaijani. "It's not like when you're in the Middle East it's one race. But now [here in Denmark], I'm 'Middle Eastern,'" he said while gesturing quotation marks around the label.[53]

I also engaged with a Grindr user with Iranian background who identi-fied with the menu-label "Other." I asked him, "Out of curiosity, is there a reason you selected 'Other' instead of 'Middle Eastern'?" He responded flatly, "Because I'm not Arab." This Iranian Grindr user espoused the ethno-linguistic understanding of the term "Middle Eastern" that we saw with Grindr's Portuguese label *Árabe*. This example also shows that there is no uniform acceptance or rejection among immigrants from a particular region or even country.

---

[53] See also Shield, "New in Town," 254.

Considering "Middle Eastern" but Choosing Black (Yusuf)

But Yusuf (b. Egypt, immigrated 2013) discarded the "Middle Eastern" label, even as he identified in his profile by nationality (i.e. from Egypt) and by language (i.e. as an Arabic speaker). Yusuf is part of an ethnic minority group from southern Egypt—Nubians—and identifies as black. But choosing Grindr's "Black" option negated the possibility for him to identify with Grindr's drop-down menu option "Middle Eastern":

> The one I identify with is "black"—although I might have different ethnicities: I might be North African, I might be Middle Eastern, I might be Arab. Because I come from a place where there is a mixture between ethnicities. So you can't put it as simple as—It annoys me, because why should I even put it [an "ethnicity" selection]? I have my picture: if someone likes me, he likes me.

Yusuf's interview provided further evidence to the argument that racial taxonomies are culturally specific: "[The majority of] Egyptians would never think of themselves as African or blacks... [instead] they see themselves as whites or Egyptians," he explained. This statement shows that even though Grindr's labels are from a U.S. context, they carry weight in multiple contexts: the label "black" bears certain burdens in Egypt. Thus Yusuf is hyper-aware and even anxious about the weight of this label.

Yusuf felt that the label "Middle Eastern" reduced the cultural complexity of the diverse country from which he emigrated, and said (in a statement that echoes Parvin's):

> This category in itself is a problem to me. What do they mean by "Middle Eastern"? Persian? Western Asian? Arab peninsula? North African? Turkey? I mean, it's problematic enough to me that I don't choose it. And I identify more as a black person.

In the end, Yusuf *did* utilize the menu, but remained critical of its assumption that labels like "Middle Eastern" and "Black" were mutually exclusive. More generally, Yusuf's anecdote also shows that racial labels (e.g. black) carry different meanings in different local contexts.

"White Is a Color, Middle Eastern Is Not a Color; So I'm Not Sure What the Difference Is": Negotiating "White" and "Middle Eastern," and Rejecting Both

In the last chapter's discussion of sexual racism, we learned that Şenol (b. Turkey, immigrated 2010) felt that Grindr's racial drop-down menu normalized statements like "No Asians" within the Grindr culture. Şenol claimed that in order to combat sexual racism, he rejected the menu entirely:

> No, I don't believe in that [choosing an "ethnicity" on Grindr]. It doesn't make any sense to me. Why would anyone need to know my race? I think it has to do with this—racism in the gay community is quite visible, and it gets away because people say it's a preference, which I disagree. So I don't want to be a part of that in any way. I guess it's a political kind of decision. So I don't put my race.

Rejecting the ethnicity menu was a "political kind of decision," as he believed the menu was characteristic of racism in the gay community (and perhaps also constitutive of it).[54] In rejecting the menu, he dampened the racial discourses on Grindr altogether.

But "Middle Eastern" was not the only label Şenol considered applicable to him; he—like the following interviewee—also considered the ambiguities between "Middle Eastern" and "White." When Ali (b. Iraq, immigrated 2014) was asked if he utilized the "ethnicity" menu on Grindr (or Scruff), he responded immediately in the negative:

> No, because for me, when the options are "White" and "Middle Eastern"— **White is a color, Middle Eastern is not a color.** So I'm not sure what the difference is [supposed to be]. For example, I'm white compared to some Iraqis, and I'm not white compared to other Iraqis.

Ali did not see the labels "White" and "Middle Eastern" as mutually exclusive, and he acknowledged the phenotypic diversity among those in Iraq. In Scandinavia, some might expect Ali to identify as Middle Eastern, he said, since he emigrated from the Middle East; but Ali implied that the label

---

[54] Angelo (from Greece) echoed this sentiment: "I don't even like these categorizations that they have. And if you're mixture, or have a lot of everything somehow—I don't know. And it could be racist, too," he ended, referring to racial filtering.

"White" might also apply to him. Reflecting on the act of choosing his ethnicity from Grindr's menu—whether White, Middle Eastern, or something else—Ali proclaimed that the act of choosing any of these options was "a very political power dynamic that I really don't want to support."

Identifying as "Middle Eastern" but Clarifying Ethnicity

One way users contribute to alternative discourses about race and ethnicity is to choose one of Grindr's drop-down menu options, and to clarify its meaning through country names, nationalities, flags, languages, or other ethnic labels. Doing so brings attention to the diversity attached to the generic labels in Grindr's menu. Figure 6.3 shows a few of those who

Fig. 6.3 Clarifying one's "Middle Eastern" identity (Original languages retained. Redacted text on left about neighborhood, on right about sexual proclivities)

chose "Middle Eastern" and then clarified their specific relationship to that word in their profile text.

The first user highlighted his Kurdish ethnicity twice in his profile: first in his display name, and then again in his text; an earlier version of his profile (from 2016) included the word "Kurdish" as well as a Turkish flag. Taken together, one understands that the Grindr user identifies with his Kurdish background, his Turkish background, the "Middle Eastern" label, as well as his Danish culture (as he lists his interests, "swimming, fitness, politics," in Danish). The second user also selected "Middle Eastern" and clarified his ethno-national background through both his profile text (i.e. as "Turkish boy") and his profile name (i.e. *İstanbul* with the Turkish spelling).

Other users who clarified their "Middle Eastern" selection include one man with the display name "Persian, 27," and a "Furry cub" in Copenhagen who identified with the flags of Denmark and Iran.[55] There are numerous other examples, but I chose these four users to demonstrate that participants shape the meaning of Grindr's racial (and/or regional) labels through ethnic and national terms. In doing so, these users contest the meanings and borders of the menu and its racial categories within Grindr culture.

CHALLENGING THE "ETHNICITY" MENU: A POLITICAL ACT? OR MAINTAINING THE STATUS QUO?

Both Şenol and Ali described their rejection of the menu as disruptive to the status quo, since it was a refusal of the norm that one must identify by race on socio-sexual platforms:

> Şenol: No, I don't believe in that. It doesn't make any sense to me. Why would anyone need to know my race?
> [and]
> Ali: When people ask me: *where are you from?* I say: *why is that relevant?* This is cliché but I don't identify as a certain nationality... Maybe that's why I don't get these [racist] messages, at least not directly.

---

[55] "Kurdish guy, 30" also highlighted his Kurdish background, which clarified his "Middle Eastern" selection from the Grindr menu and "Türk, 22" puts a Turkish flag at the end of his display name, but wrote in his profile that he (only or also) spoke English and Danish.

With this (optimistic) view about the potential to effect activist change on Grindr, we turn now to examples of profiles that introduce alternative discourses about race to the Grindr culture of the greater Copenhagen area.

"Brown" as a Political Identity

The use of the racial identity "brown" has taken an empowering turn among scholars and activists of color in recent decades, despite the historical use of the word "brown" in European racial taxonomies and in racist texts throughout the nineteenth and early twentieth centuries.[56] In her 1988 essay "Can the Subaltern speak?," Gayatri Chakravorty Spivak famously used the term when she critiqued the white (post)colonial impulse to "save brown women from brown men," for example in South Asia.[57] In his 2006 essay "Feeling Brown, Feeling Down," queer theorist José Esteban Muñoz used the label "brown" not only as a racial and ethnic position in the Latinx[58] community, but also as an affective position (i.e. "feeling brown") to describe "the frequencies on which certain subalterns speak and are heard or, more importantly, felt…. How does the Subaltern feel?"[59] Hiram Pérez referred to the racial classification "brown" as "a kind of constitutive ambiguity" that destabilizes racial logics, for example in the United States, beyond "white/black or white/Asian binaries."[60] Pérez himself identifies with the term, and calls for more research on usages of the word, for example in "cosmopolitan gay male" subcultures.

[56] E.g. George Orwell's text cited and analyzed in Edward W. Said, *Orientalism* (New York: Vintage Books and Random House, 1979), 251–252; original text: "It is always difficult to believe that you are walking among human beings… Are they really the same flesh as yourself? Do they even have names? Or are they merely a kind of undifferentiated brown stuff, about as individual as bees or coral insects?".

[57] Gayatri Chakravorty Spivak, "Can the Subaltern Speak?" in *Marxism and the Interpretation of Culture*, ed. Cary Nelson and Lawrence Grossberg (Urbana: University of Illinois Press, 1988).

[58] Latinx is a gender-neutral term for the binary Latino/Latina, beyond the neutral but binary term Latin@.

[59] José Esteban Muñoz, "Feeling Brown, Feeling Down: Latina Affect, the Performativity of Race, and the Depressive Position," *Signs* 31, no. 3 (Spring 2006).

[60] Hiram Pérez, *A Taste for Brown Bodies: Gay Modernity and Cosmopolitan Desire* (New York: New York University Press, 2015), 104.

In Denmark, people with various ethnic backgrounds have used "brown" as an empowering identity.[61] In a dialogue about race, jazz, and identity in Scandinavia, saxophonist John Tchicai (b. 1936, Copenhagen) spoke about his race: "[A]lthough our father was so-called black, I and my brothers and sisters were not black but brown"; and later, "[B]eing brown in Denmark made it easier for me to feel at ease with black musicians."[62] In this same conversation, musician Marilyn Mazur (who describes her father as African-American and her mother as Polish-American), who also grew up in Denmark, echoed the racial identity.[63] Activist Uzma Ahmed (born in Denmark to Pakistani parents) identifies as a *brun feminist* (brown feminist), and promotes the term in a Facebook group by that name: "We choose to define ourselves today as brown feminists because it describes the intersection at which we stand, between the glass ceiling [for women] and

---

[61] In my previous research collecting oral histories about the 1960s–1980s, I interviewed a gay man (b. 1947) living in Jutland who identified as half-black, half-white, and preferred the word "colored" in Danish (*farvede*), but added that he knew that the term was outdated. Younger generations, he said, might prefer "mixed" (*miksede*); but he did not mention that people might identify with the term "brown." See Andrew DJ Shield, *Immigrants in the Sexual Revolution: Perceptions and Participation in Northwest Europe* (Cham, Switzerland: Palgrave Macmillan, 2017), 227–228, and especially 240 fn1.

For a recent example of the Danish word for "brown" being used in regard to a racial minority with no other reference to ethnic background, see for example a passage in a teaching manual about race in the classroom where a comment is directed at "the classroom's only brown student": Mette Lindegren Helde, *Du har et valg! Lærervejledning: En undervisningspakke om emnet social kontrol* [You Have a Choice! Teacher Guidance: A Teaching Pamphlet on the Subject of Social Control] (Denmark: Danish Ministry of Immigration and Integration, April 2017).

[62] Cecil Brown et al., "The Midnight Sun Never Sets: An Email Conversation About Jazz, Race and National Identity in Denmark, Norway and Sweden," in *Afro-Nordic Landscapes: Equality and Race in Northern Europe*, ed. Michael McEachrane (London: Routledge, 2014), 65, 75–76. Later, he contradicted himself slightly by saying, "I've never really seen myself as black, brown or white," but although Tchicai expresses some hesitation in identifying with the label "brown," it seems that this was a label toward which he frequently gravitated.

[63] Mazur: "I can relate to what John [Tchicai] wrote about growing up as a 'brown' kid in Denmark. During my childhood in Denmark there were very few people of color around, which sometimes brought out some curiosity in people, but few negative reactions." Ibid. [Brown et al.], 81.

white power structures."[64] In Denmark, the term is also used in relation to the Latinx community.[65]

Within Grindr profile texts, the term "brown" becomes an alternative racial discourse, a way for the individual to identify as a member of the community of people of color without (necessarily) relying on any of the hegemonic race labels of Grindr's drop-down menu. Consider the profiles (the first in English, the second originally in both Danish and English) in Fig. 6.4. In the first profile, the user did not select an "ethnicity" at all, but identified solely as "brown." In the second profile, the user chose "Mixed" from Grindr's drop-down menu, but clarified "brown" in his profile text. Another user whose display name was "BrownHero" also identified with the "Middle Eastern" drop-down option. As the word "brown" circulates within activist circles in Denmark and internationally, the term resonates as empowering on Grindr; thus, these "brown" Grindr users contribute to alternative discourses about racial categories and identities on Grindr.

Selecting "Other" and Clarifying

Selecting the label "Other" also challenges Grindr's "ethnicity" options, as it conveys the sentiment that someone has decided that the available racial labels are insufficient. In one informal chat, I asked a user—an immigrant from a European country—why he chose the label "Other"; he responded:

> Simply because there's no option for sino-indo-afro-caucasian-native-american, and when you write mixed people often assume something far from my ethnic reality.... Other feels as the far less confusing option.

---

[64]Translated from Danish. Uzma Ahmed, "About: Brown Feminists," Facebook.com, last accessed December 2017 via https://www.facebook.com/pg/brunefeminister/. See also personal website http://uzma.dk/om-uzma/. Uzma also uses the term "brown" when describing the darker of her two mixed-race daughters: Andreassen and Ahmed-Andresen, 35.

[65]Anne Middelboe Christensen, "Ung, brun, og søgende" [Young, Brown, and Searching], *Information*, 28 August 2016, https://www.information.dk/kultur/anmeldelse/2016/08/ung-brun-soegende. See description of Ernesto Piga Carbone's role (as a gay man) in the Copenhagen play "Vinger" about "brown" Danes.

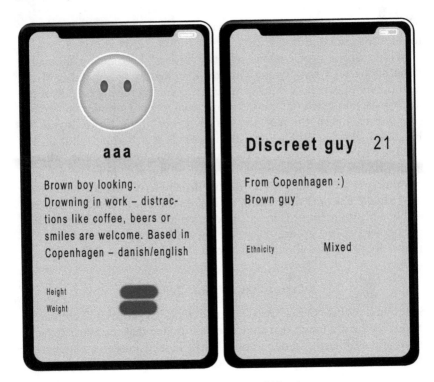

Fig. 6.4 "Brown" as a counter-hegemonic racial identity

And while some—like this user—merely select "Other" and leave their background ambiguous, others clarify the meaning of "Other" in their profile text, such as those in Fig. 6.5.

Many in the greater Copenhagen area would recognize the Greenlandic flag in Kunuk's profile, as Greenland—with its centuries-long colonial connections to Denmark—remains a semi-autonomous overseas territory in the Kingdom of Denmark. Kunuk, who included a smiling face photo, identified with Denmark's small Greenlandic diasporic community, though he did not say this explicitly: he merely used the flag of Greenland and

Fig. 6.5 Clarifying one's "Other" ethnic/racial identity ("Kunuk" changed from another Greenlandic name)

his Greenlandic name to clarify his "Other" ethnicity.[66] (Though another Greenlandic-identified Grindr user selected "Native American.")

The second user above selected "Other" and clarified his ethnic/racial identity as "PacIslander" (Pacific Islander), which—as mentioned before—is the one major race category from the U.S. Census that Grindr omitted from its drop-down menu. The user brought some attention to Grindr's oversight by using this label in conjunction with the "Other" menu

---

[66] Another user identifies as "Mixed" and included the flags for Denmark and Greenland.

option.[67] As with the aforementioned examples of Grindr users who identified as Kurdish or Nubian on their public profiles, these Greenlandic- and Pacific Islander-identified Grindr users bring nuance the "ethnicity" menu, and bring attention to the menu's insufficiency or inapplicability for many Grindr users.

"You Shouldn't Put That...": Maintaining the Status Quo?

Some Grindr users who withheld their ethnic identification on their Grindr profiles—such as Şenol and Ali—claimed it to be a political decision, something that might combat racism in the LGBTQ community. Others shrouded their ethnic identity with vague terms like "brown" and might hearken to subaltern and postcolonial scholarship and activism. But there could be other reasons that users withhold or shroud their racial/ethnic identities, reasons that are embedded in hegemonic conceptions about about racial hierarchies within Grindr cultures.

Fahad Saeed, the spokesperson for Sabaah (Denmark's organization for LGBTQ+ ethnic minorities), took part in a panel at Copenhagen Pride 2017 about Grindr and Sex Culture. When asked a question about racism on Grindr, Saeed began by referring to Grindr as "an economy" where "some things have more value, and some have less." With this meat-market metaphor in mind, Saeed continued:

> You see a lot of our [Sabaah's] members—and the people I know—who hide specific aspects of their identity because it has less value. Hiding the fact that you're South Asian, for example. Hiding the fact that you're this or that ethnicity, or this or that body type, or this or that in any ways. This creates a hierarchy that some things have more value than others. Obviously we all have preferences, but we're perpetuating this [hierarchy of valuable traits] in many ways [with our practices online].[68]

A month later, Fahad and I spoke again on the topic, but this time to the members of Sabaah who came to participate in an evening meeting

[67] On Scruff, he would be able to select Pacific Islander from the "ethnicity" drop-down menu; and I would wager he has a profile on Scruff, a platform that caters to "bears," since he identifies with this niche.

[68] Fahad Saeed, via "Grindr and Sex Culture," Panel at Copenhagen Pride with Kristian Møller, Fahad Saeed, Niels Jansen, and Andrew Shield, 16 August 2017, http://kanal-1.dk/14-grindr-sexkultur-lystfulde-politiske-hadefulde-perspektiver/.

about Grindr and race. The dozen or so members were diverse with regard to ethnic background, though many shared some subject positions: most were ethnic minorities in the Danish LGBTQ community, cisgender male, under 25 years old, and fluent in Danish (the language of the discussion). During the conversation, one member shared the following anecdote:

> I remember when I was filling out my Grindr profile, I put "South Asian" [because I'm Pakistani]. But then my friend said to me, "No, you shouldn't put that, because people don't like Asians. You should put that you're Middle Eastern." [Laughs.] So that's why I put "Middle Eastern."[69]

While the young man chuckled as he considered how to maximize his "sexual capital"[70] on Grindr, Saeed would see it as representative of larger problems in the community, as he shared at Copenhagen Pride. Saeed suggested a vicious cycle perpetuated both by Grindr users' racist preferences—which serve to cast certain groups (e.g. Asians) as less "valuable" within Grindr culture—and the self-censoring of some users of color (e.g. some Asians), which reinforces these hierarchies on Grindr.

The Sabaah member's ability to identify ambiguously as either South Asian or Middle Eastern suggests some fluidity between these categories. But more, the anecdote illustrates what Gosine wrote about identifying his race on Gay.com ten years before (that "each category carries a different set of burdens, and each will position [the user] differently").[71] The Sabaah member's decision to avoid the label "South Asian" suggests that "Asian" and by extension "South Asian" are low in this Grindr culture's racial hierarchy, whereas Middle Eastern ranks higher. (Presumably "White" would be the top of the hierarchy; indeed, the Sabaah discussion that day also centered on the overrepresentation of white people in erotic depictions of homosexuality.)

When McGlotten considered his own racial position on Grindr, he mentioned that he observed that "increasingly" he would avoid the label

---

[69] Sabaah meeting, November 2017. This quotation is a rough approximation of what the young man said (in Danish), as I did not record the meeting, but instead took notes immediately following it.

[70] Adam Isaiah Green, "Sexual Capital and Social Inequality: The Study of Sexual Fields," in *Introducing the New Sexuality Studies*, ed. Nancy L. Fischer and Steven Seidman (New York: Routledge, 2016); also Catherine Hakim, "Erotic Capital," *European Sociological Review* 26, no. 5 (2010): 499–518.

[71] Gosine, 145. Emphasis added.

"Black," which might imply something about his body or his politics, and would choose instead the labels "Mixed" or "Other." Although none of my interviewees mentioned identifying as "Mixed" as a strategy for avoiding the weight of other labels, it is likely that there are some in the greater Copenhagen area who do so. Similarly, we might critique the usage of "brown" or other vague terms—such as "dark"—as strategic, vague labels that users of color utilize to distance themselves from race- and ethnicity-related prejudice. This avoidance strategy could explain why "Mixed" was the most common "ethnicity" label selected by those who do not identify as white in the greater Copenhagen area.

Conclusions

Racial Categories Are Insufficient for Many

First and foremost, this chapter has shown that many immigrant Grindr users in the greater Copenhagen area find Grindr's "ethnicity" drop-down menu to be insufficient for their own identities. In the greater Copenhagen area, 42% of users do not bother with the "ethnicity" menu; this chapter shows that some of those 42% skip the menu because they feel the options are insufficient, or more, that they contribute to racism within Grindr culture.

Among users of color who *do* select a label, many do so reluctantly; and others bend their racial identities, or choose seemingly arbitrary labels. As one observes how the boundaries between racial groups collapse and bend across socio-sexual platforms (as well as across geographies), one should better understand that there are no "true" racial categories.

However—and this argument was not presented thus far in this chapter—not all interviewees felt that Grindr's categories were insufficient. Interviewees from East Asia or Russia, who are absent from this chapter, identified unequivocally as Asian or White, respectively. Daniel (b. Nigeria, immigrated 2016), who identified unequivocally as "Black," even felt that it was pragmatic and imperative for people of color to identify with Grindr's "ethnicity" menu:

> Definitely, you have to put in your profile where you're from—like Middle Eastern or black—in case the person doesn't want to talk to you. If you don't put anything about your nationality [then many are]... expecting this person to be white. ...Then you look stupid. It's better to just put it immediately.

The person wants to chat with you, fine, and if the person don't want to chat with you, then "Go fuck yourself!"

Despite Daniel's numerous critiques about racism on Grindr, and despite the fact that Daniel toyed with his migrant identity in other ways, Daniel asserted that people of color in Scandinavia should openly declare their racial identities so as to weed out those who inevitably hold racial-sexual exclusionary preferences against their racial or ethnic group.

That being said, this chapter showed that many people with immigration background *do not* identify unequivocally with Grindr's pre-selected race options. The key spokespeople in this chapter had immigration backgrounds in Iran, Turkey, Iraq, Egypt, and Pakistan. Thus it is especially the "Middle Eastern" and "South Asian" Grindr categories that seem to trouble people with immigration background in the greater Copenhagen area. This is one possible explanation for the relatively low percentage of people who identified as "South Asian" on Grindr in the greater Copenhagen area (2% of those who identified as something other than "White") despite the sizeable population of especially Pakistani immigrants and their descendants. Discomfort with labels might also explain the relatively high percentage of non-white-identified people who preferred the vague label "Mixed" (29% of that subgroup).

Rejecting the Menu Can Be a Political Practice

The "ethnicity" menu is a key reason that race permeates Grindr cultures: it encourages people to think about race and sexuality together, and implies that racial identification on Grindr is as matter-of-fact as identifying by age, height, or weight. Further, the drop-down menu affords users the possibility of filtering by race. In Chapter 5, we concluded that race-related speech is quotidian on Grindr; the menu contributes greatly to race's pervasiveness on Grindr, and imparts ideas that the human race can be neatly divided into seven-race labels, Mixed, and Other. For all of these reasons, some users reject the menu, so as to avoid contributing to race-related discourses on Grindr.

Şenol (from Turkey) and Ali (from Iraq) explicitly referred to their rejection of the menu as a "political" act: for Şenol, not utilizing the menu was a "political kind of decision," and for Ali, the menu as a whole represented "a very political power dynamic that I really don't want to support."

If rejecting Grindr's "ethnicity" menu can be political, so too can be the use of counter-hegemonic discourses about race. Thus, we considered the possibility that users who identified as "brown" were not only rejecting the menu's limited options, but were also in conversation with Spivak ("Can the Subaltern speak?"), Muñoz ("Feeling Brown, Feeling Down"), Pérez, or (*brun feminist*) Ahmed. Similarly, users who identified as "Other" brought attention to the insufficiency of Grindr's "ethnicity" menu, which omits Pacific Islander, Greenlander (Inuit), and a myriad of other labels with which a person in Copenhagen might identify their ethnic background. Finally, we considered that those who select a race label and clarify it might also do so as a "political" decision. When Yusuf identifies as black, Egyptian, and Nubian, he promotes understanding within Grindr culture about his minority group, and about the diversity of ethnic groups in both North Africa and Scandinavia.

But returning to the interviews with Şenol and Ali with a more critical eye, one can also ponder their decisions from a different angle. Both claimed that rejecting the menu benefitted Grindr culture; but how might they benefit personally from rejecting the menu in other ways? Shortly after Ali said that he did not identify with any ethnicity on Grindr, he added: "Maybe that's why I don't get these [racist] messages." Similarly, Şenol brought up that he did not identify as Turkish on Grindr during a conversation about intentionally offensive Grindr messages: he was surprised about one racist message, even though he "doesn't even say" that he is Turkish in his profile. In the last chapter, we established that the socio-political context in Denmark—in which immigrants are tied to Islam, and cultural clashes—affects the ways Scandinavian Grindr users communicate on topics related to race. Could eschewing the labels Iraqi, Turkish, or Middle Eastern be a strategy for avoiding racist messages?

Rejecting the Menu Can also Maintain the Status Quo (About Race Hierarchies in Grindr Culture)

Without having interviewed the users who identified as "brown" or "mixed" or "Other," it is impossible to determine their motivations; but critically examining the interviews with Şenol and Ali (and McGlotten), one can wager that some people of color avoid race-related labels so as to avoid attracting attention from xenophobic, Islamophobic, and racist users. But there are also users who explicitly admit to skipping the labels so as to avoid being classified as lower on the supposed race hierarchy of a Grindr culture.

Some Grindr users reject or "bend" Grindr's "ethnicity" menu so as to avoid being associated with labels that are sexually "undesirable." Saeed (from Sabaah) articulated this when he said, "You see a lot of our [Sabaah's] members... who hide specific aspects of their identity because it has less value. Hiding the fact that you're South Asian, for example." Several months later while leading a Sabaah workshop about Grindr, I heard a participant admit to doing just this: he avoided the label "South Asian" because he feared that it—in Saeed's words—"had less value" on Grindr. ("No, you shouldn't put that, because people don't like Asians," his friend told him. "You should put that you're Middle Eastern.")

People of color alone do not need to bear the burden of confronting racism (including racial-sexual stereotypes) and Islamophobia. But some people of color may uphold the status quo about racial hierarchies on Grindr when they hide their racial or ethnic identities. The young Sabaah participant learned from a friend that an "Asian" or "South Asian" identity was lower on the totem pole than a "Middle Eastern" identity. Rather than testing out this hypothesis—by identifying as South Asian and seeing how he fared—he agreed with it, and in doing so, contributed to a Grindr culture in which almost no users identify openly as South Asian.

The Technology Plays a Role in Promoting Racial Logics

Grindr's "ethnicity" drop-down menu conveys the idea that race identification on a socio-sexual platform is both imperative and natural; the menu options suggest that humans neatly fall into seven racial categories; and one major result of race reporting on Grindr is that the technology affords users the possibility of race filtering so as to "Find Your Type." Grindr as an organization and technology plays an undeniable role in promoting race-related communication—especially regarding racial-sexual preference—within Grindr cultures internationally.

But it is too easy to conclude that drop-down menus alone cause users to discuss race in tandem with sexuality. On the Danish platform Boyfriend.dk, for example, the interface has never asked users to identify racially (e.g. via drop-down menus), yet infamous lounges like "I'm not into Asians" persist in the community message boards.[72] Thus if Grindr removed the "ethnicity" drop-down menu altogether, problematic discourses such as racial-sexual exclusions might still persist in profile texts.

That being said, Grindr's menu and the option for filtering by ethnicity bring race to the foreground when encouraging users to imagine their "type." Classification systems are always sites of oppression and struggle.[73] This chapter has problematized and scrutinized Grindr's "ethnicity" drop-down menu, but it has not offered alternatives. There is no correct racial drop-down menu; even if Grindr introduced a menu with a hundred options, the labels might still echo colonial or eugenic histories, and would still inevitably omit some marginalized groups. Nevertheless, Chapter 7 presents recommendations for how Grindr and other socio-sexual platforms could update the ways they present race-related menus and their search features.

Chapter 4 established the meaning of "socio-sexual" for immigrants on Grindr, and Chapter 5 examined how white users' race-related and racist behaviors online prevented some immigrants from connecting with locals. This chapter homed in on the technology and organization of Grindr as culpable for contributing to racism on Grindr. The final chapter identifies red threads that tie these ideas together in order to highlight our main conclusions about socio-sexual networkingand race.

BIBLIOGRAPHY

Ahmed, Uzma. "About: Brown Feminists." Facebook, last accessed December 2017 via https://www.facebook.com/pg/brunefeminister/.

Albrechtslund, Anne-Mette. "Gender Values in Simulation Games: Sex and the Sims." *Proceedings of Computer Ethics Philosophical Enquiries*, 2007.

Boston, Nicholas. "Libidinal Cosmopolitanism: The Case of Digital Sexual Encounters in Post-enlargement Europe." In *Postcolonial Transitions in Europe: Contexts, Practices and Politics*, edited by Sandra Ponzanesi and Gianmaria Colpani, 291–312. London: Rowman & Littlefield, 2015.

Bovenkerk, Frank. "The Netherlands." In *International Labor Migration in Europe*, edited by Ronald E. Krane, 118–132. New York: Praeger Publishers, 1979.

[72] Sabaah, "[Debat:] Tænder ikke på asiater" [Debate: I'm Not Turned On by Asians], 19 February 2013, https://www.youtube.com/watch?v=qvSuHQPFWGw; Fahad Saeed et al., "Grindr and Sex Culture" (panel).

[73] Bowker and Star, 196.

Bowker, Geoffrey C., and Susan Leigh Star. *Sorting Things Out: Classification and Its Consequences.* Cambridge, MA: MIT Press, 1999.

Brown, Cecil, Anne Dvinge, Petter Front Fadnes, Johan Fornäs, Ole Izard Høyer, Marilyn Mazur, Michael McEachrane, and John Tchicai. "The Midnight Sun Never Sets: An Email Conversation About Jazz, Race and National Identity in Denmark, Norway and Sweden." In *Afro-Nordic Landscapes: Equality and Race in Northern Europe,* edited by Michael McEachrane, 57–86. London: Routledge, 2014.

Bureau of the Census. "Sixteenth Census of the United States: 1940—Housing." Department of Commerce, last accessed July 2016 via https://www.census.gov/prod/www/decennial.html.

Bureau of the Census. "United States Census 2010." Department of Commerce, last accessed July 2016 via https://www.census.gov/history/.

Bureau of the Census. "Untitled [1970 Census Questionnaire]." Department of Commerce, last accessed July 2016 via https://www.census.gov/prod/www/decennial.html.

Chee, Alexander. "My First (and Last) Time Dating a Rice Queen." The Strangler, 21 June 2017, https://www.thestranger.com/queer-issue-2017/2017/06/21/25227046/my-first-and-last-time-dating-a-rice-queen.

Christensen, Anne Middelboe. "Ung, brun, og søgende" [Young, Brown, and Searching]. *Information,* 28 August 2016, https://www.information.dk/kultur/anmeldelse/2016/08/ung-brun-soegende.

DaCosta, Kimberly McClain. *Making Multiracials: State, Family, and Market in the Redrawing of the Color Line.* Stanford, CA: Stanford University Press, 2007.

Drucker, Johanna. "Humanities Approaches to Interface Theory." *Culture Machine* 12 (2011): 1–20.

Duguay, Stefanie. "Three Flawed Assumptions the Daily Beast Made About Dating Apps." Social Media Collective Research Blog, 16 August 2016, https://socialmediacollective.org/2016/08/16/three-assumptions-the-daily-beast-made-about-dating-apps/.

Elliot. "Ten Money Questions: Grindr CEO Joel Simkhai." Queercents, 14 December 2010, http://queercents.com/2010/12/14/grindr-ceo-joel-simkhai-interview/.

Fanon, Franz. *Black Skin, White Masks.* Translated by Charles Lam Markmann. London: Pluto Press, 1986 [1952].

Goffman, Erving. *Frame Analysis: An Essay on the Organization of Experience.* London: Harper & Row, 1974.

Goffman, Erving. *The Presentation of Self in Everyday Life.* New York: Doubleday, 1959 [1956].

Goldhill, Olivia. "People Really Are Finding Love on Dating Apps Like Grindr and Tinder." *Business Insider,* 2 July 2013. http://www.businessinsider.com/we-found-love-on-grindr-2013-7?r=US&IR=T&IR=T.

Gonzalez-Barrera, Ana, and Mark Hugo Lopez. "Is Being Hispanic a Matter of Race, Ethnicity or Both?" Pew Research Center, 15 June 2015. http://www.pewresearch.org/fact-tank/2015/06/15/is-being-hispanic-a-matter-of-race-ethnicity-or-both/.

Gosine, Andil. "Brown to Blonde at Gay.com: Passing White in Queer Cyberspace." In *Queer Online: Media Technology and Sexuality*, edited by Kate O'Riordan and David J. Phillips, 139–154. New York: Peter Lang, 2007.

Green, Adam Isaiah. "Sexual Capital and Social Inequality: The Study of Sexual Fields." In *Introducing the New Sexuality Studies*, edited by Nancy L. Fischer and Steven Seidman. New York: Routledge, 2016.

"Grindr and Sex Culture." Panel at Copenhagen Pride with Kristian Møller, Fahad Saeed, Niels Jansen, and Andrew Shield, 16 August 2017. Archived and last accessed Autumn 2017 via http://kanal-1.dk/14-grindr-sexkultur-lystfulde-politiske-hadefulde-perspektiver/.

Hakim, Catherine. "Erotic Capital." *European Sociological Review* 26, no. 5 (2010): 499–518.

Helde, Mette Lindegren. *Du har et valg! Lærervejledning: En undervisningspakke om emnet social control* [You Have a Choice! Teacher Guidance: A Teaching Pamphlet on the Subject of Social Control]. Denmark: Danish Ministry of Immigration and Integration, April 2017.

Hoeffel, Elizabeth M., Sonya Rastogi, Myoung Ouk Kim, and Hasan Shahid. "The Asian Population: 2010." U.S. Census Bureau 2010 Census Briefs, March 2012, https://www.census.gov/2010census/data/.

Humes, Karen R., Nicholas A. Jones, and Roberto R. Ramirez. "Overview of Race and Hispanic Origin: 2010." U.S. Census Bureau: 2010 Census Briefs, March 2011, https://www.census.gov/2010census/data/.

Kaptelinin, Victor. "Affordance." In *The Encyclopedia of Human-Computer Interaction*, edited by Mads Soegaard and Rikke Friis Dam, 2nd ed. Interactive Design Foundation, 2011.

Light, Ben, Gordon Fletcher, and Alison Adam. "Gay Men, Gaydar and the Commodification of Difference." *Information Technology and People* 21, no. 3 (2008): 300–314.

Muñoz, José Esteban. "Feeling Brown, Feeling Down: Latina Affect, the Performativity of Race, and the Depressive Position." *Signs* 31, no. 3 (Spring 2006): 675–688.

Nagy, Peter, and Gina Neff. "Imagined Affordance: Reconstructing a Keyword for Communication Theory." *Social Media + Society* 1, no. 2 (2015): 1–9.

Nakamura, Lisa. *Cybertypes: Race, Ethnicity, and Identity on the Internet*. New York and London: Routledge, 2002.

Neff, Gina, Tim Jordan, and Joshua McVeigh-Schulz. "Affordances, Technical Agency, and the Politics of Technologies of Cultural Production: A Dialogue." *Culture Digitally*, 23 January 2012, http://culturedigitally.org/2012/01/

affordances-technical-agency-and-the-politics-of-technologies-of-cultural-production-2/.

Parisi, Lorenza, and Francesca Comunello. "Exploring Networked Interactions Through the Lens of Location-Based Dating Services: The Case of Italian Grindr Users." In *LGBTQs, Media, and Culture in Europe*, edited by Alexander Dhoest, Lukasz Szulc, and Bart Eeckhout, 227–243. London: Routledge, 2017.

Pérez, Hiram. *A Taste for Brown Bodies: Gay Modernity and Cosmopolitan Desire.* New York: New York University Press, 2015.

Robinson, Russell. "Structural Dimensions of Romantic Preferences." *Fordham Law Review* 76 (2008): 2786–2820.

Sabaah. "[Debat:] Tænder ikke på asiater" [Debate: I'm Not Turned On by Asians]. 19 February 2013, https://www.youtube.com/watch?v=qvSuHQPFWGw.

Said, Edward W. *Orientalism.* New York: Vintage Books and Random House, 1979.

Shield, Andrew DJ. *Immigrants in the Sexual Revolution: Perceptions and Participation in Northwest Europe.* Cham, Switzerland: Palgrave Macmillan, 2017.

Shield, Andrew DJ. "New in Town: Gay Immigrants and Geosocial Dating Apps." In *LGBTQs, Media, and Culture in Europe*, edited by Alexander Dhoest, Lukasz Szulc, and Bart Eeckhout, 244–261. London: Routledge, 2017.

Sørensen, J. W. "Der kom fremmede: Migration, Højkonjunktur, Kultursammenstød, Foreign Workers in Denmark up to 1970" [There Were Strangers Who Came: Migration, High-Conjuncture and Culture Clash]. Aarhus University, Working paper for the Center for Culture Research, 1988.

Spivak, Gayatri Chakravorty. "Can the Subaltern Speak?" In *Marxism and the Interpretation of Culture*, edited by Cary Nelson and Lawrence Grossberg. Urbana: University of Illinois Press, 1988.

Thompson, Debra Elizabeth. "Seeing Like a Racial State: The Census and the Politics of Race in the United States, Great Britain and Canada." PhD diss., University of Toronto, 2012.

CHAPTER 7

"Vi hygger os!": Challenging Socio-Sexual Online Cultures (Conclusions)

LGBTQ immigrants in Europe were once an invisible group. While they have become slightly more visible in the public sphere over the last decade, their unique problems are not always heard. Politicians and media often associate LGBTQ immigrants with oppression from their diasporic community. Indeed, at least one interviewee suggested this sentiment when he explained that he sought new housing partly to create distance from his extended family, whose proximity hindered his willingness to share photos with potential contacts on Grindr and to live openly as gay. *Immigrants on Grindr* does not deny that LGBTQ immigrants and children of immigrants face difficulties coming out to their families, but rather nuances the idea that familial intolerance is the singular or preeminent problem these groups face.

LGBTQ immigrants in Europe share many of their greatest obstacles with other immigrants, regardless of sexual orientation or gender identity; these problems include difficulties finding affordable housing, isolation, and racism. But for LGBTQ immigrants, these problems can take unique forms. While many immigrants struggle to find affordable housing in metropolitan areas, it is often LGBTQ immigrants who feel strongly about living in urban centers with LGBTQ visibility (in terms of both people and establishments) that presumably equates to safety (for LGBTQs). Urban centers, however, are more expensive than traditional "immigrant neighborhoods" on the outskirts of a city or in the suburbs. Related, the isolation felt by asylum seekers waiting on the decision of their applications

© The Author(s) 2019
A. DJ Shield, *Immigrants on Grindr*,
https://doi.org/10.1007/978-3-030-30394-5_7

takes on added stress for LGBTQs, who are often placed in remote housing and who often have little access to capital for traveling to urban centers or patronizing LGBTQ establishments or events. Finally, racism takes unique forms within LGBTQ spaces, offline and online, as immigrants confront racial-sexual stereotypes, exclusions, and fetishes, in addition to other forms of everyday and entitlement racism.

This book examined the role that online socio-sexual platforms—which are increasingly accessible at all times, from all locations—play in the lives of some gay, bi, trans and queer immigrants. Immigrants' experiences on apps like Grindr depend not only on their level of engagement, but also on their countries of origin, perceived religion, race, migration status, socio-economic backgrounds, and degree of openness about their (L)GBTQ identity, among other factors. Before turning to overall conclusions about socio-sexual online cultures and immigrants, here is a brief summary of Chapters 3 through 6.

Sexuality is still a deeply private matter for many—not least, LGBTQ people who are not open about their sexual orientation or gender identity—and scholars must question if and why they need to present material from a stranger's socio-sexual profile. Chapter 3 outlined several methodologies for collecting empirical data ethically on socio-sexual online platforms. Covert participation can ensure that researchers do not alter users' behaviors in the field, but overt participation is necessary for recruiting interviewees from these platforms. Both methods require critical self-reflection and assessment of users' conceptions of privacies in the field.

Sexual, platonic and logistical desires blur on platforms like Grindr, and this blurring can be particularly enticing for those who are new in town. But as Chapter 4 argued, not all "newcomers" are equal: tourists—presumed to be wealthy, mobile, and looking for casual connections—benefit more from the allure of newcomers than immigrants. This research found that immigrants who seek to build enduring connections via Grindr often succeed best at connecting with other immigrants. Race and (perceived) religion factor into their experiences connecting with locals, as Chapter 5 attested. Racial-sexual exclusions are some of the most discursively visible instances of racism on socio-sexual dating profiles, but they are not the only type of racism immigrants face. Chapter 6 showed that race-related discourses also proliferate from (cultural bias in) interface design: for example, Grindr's "ethnicity" menu is based in U.S. American hegemonic conceptions of racial boundaries. For some users, rejecting the menu is a "political act" that challenges racism on Grindr; for others, avoiding or bending the menu relates to a level of complacency with racial hierarchies within a Grindr culture.

Conclusions

Sex and "Hook-up" Platforms Can Be "Social Media," Especially for LGBTQs

Grindr and related platforms are indeed "hook-up apps" that facilitate sexual encounters, but they also foster much more. The concept of the "socio-sexual" online cultures established not only that Grindr and related platforms are valuable spaces for conducting ethnographic work, but also that these spaces resemble traditional social media.

Mainstream social-networking platforms like Facebook and LinkedIn encourage users to build networks based on those they know offline, while socio-sexual platforms primarily encourage interaction between strangers. Since the 1990s, online cultures for LGBTQ individuals blurred this distinction; related, conversations in chat rooms and web forums often translated to offline meet-ups, complicating notions of online/offline communication. Online communicative cultures flourished on websites—which provided LGBTQ news, content, and dating profiles, simultaneously—where users sought a variety of (platonic, sexual, and logistical) relationships, and engaged in social voyeurism by browsing a "community."[1] Socio-sexual networking and networks have since 2009 found a new home "on app." Via geo-location, these apps allow users to chat with other active users nearby, and to return to initiated conversations—or to "starred" profiles—for later communication (both asynchronous and real time). As people build informal lists of acquaintances, the platform comes to resemble a social-media "network" of GBTQ contacts, presumably with some common interests (sexual or otherwise). Eventually, members of this network might become long-term friends or lovers, and/or might serve as a node in a logistical web that connects a user to housing, jobs, or local information. Even though a user's "network" (e.g. list of starred acquaintances) is not public, users engage in network-building.

Media scholars rarely if ever consider dating platforms to be spaces for the sharing of user-generated content. Nevertheless, literature on "social

---

[1] Sharif Mowlabocus, *Gaydar Culture: Gay Men, Technology and Embodiment* (Farnham: Ashgate, 2010).

media" must include dating and other socio-sexual platforms: although users cannot readily or publicly "like," "share," or "comment" on user-generated content on Grindr, users do indeed contribute to an online culture by posting (via their profiles), and commenting on others' content (via private messages). Grindr and related platforms become communities where users share information, trends, slang, social codes, and other attributes of traditional subcultures.

Socio-sexual networking sometimes blurs the line between platonic and sexual desire, as users post for "friends and fun" among other ambiguous requests. Şenol (from Turkey) summarized this succinctly when he declared, "Sometimes the lines are not so clear." Yet many users compartmentalize their networking by separating platonic/logistical requests from cruising. Asen, Daniel, and others who sought rooms via socio-sexual platforms rejected offers from those who made sexual advances. Future research could look more at the spectrum of transactional sex that occurs online, particularly among those who do not identify as sex workers.[2]

As in other types of social media, communicative cultures flourish on socio-sexual apps like Grindr. Scholars can study both dominant discourses (e.g. about race) that appear on public profiles, as well as counterpowers: responses to problematic texts ("If ur profile includes stuff like 'no Asians, no blacks...' or any stupid sh*t... DON'T talk to me") or identity labels outside of fixed drop-down menus (e.g. "brown"). As the final section of this chapter attests, socio-sexual profiles can parallel posts on traditional social media: users broadcast personal messages to a wider audience, and ultimately allow for responses—whether through public or one-on-one communication—that contribute to a lively online communicative culture.

Socio-Sexual Cultures Are Context-Specific

Although socio-sexual cultures exist in the virtual world, they are not devoid of space. On mainstream social media, users often have the possibility of viewing the profiles/content of, and communicating with, people from all around the world; but on geo-locative platforms like Grindr, users tend to communicate with those in their immediate location, whether or not these users intend to meet up with their contacts in person.

---

[2] Joseph Brennan, "Cruising for cash: Prostitution on Grindr," *Discourse, Context & Media* 17 (2017): 1–8.

A Grindr user in the greater Copenhagen area communicates mainly with other Grindr users in the greater Copenhagen area, where Scandinavian locals make up the majority of the users. Thus, it is impossible to decouple the Grindr culture of the greater Copenhagen area from the local society more generally. It is only in Denmark that an Arabic speaker would include the phrase *"Vi hygger os!"* (roughly "Let's get cozy") as a means of ingratiating himself into the culture, establishing cultural capital, and attracting positive (sexual) attention. This performative act of integration takes place in a socio-political climate that portrays (especially Muslim) immigrants as unable and unwilling to integrate. Thus, *"Vi hygger os!"* is not just context-specific because it is written in Danish; the phrase reflects the dominant political and media frames of a specific time and place, and illustrates cultural practices of belonging.

Those working in "Grindr studies" have already acknowledged that socio-sexual cultures change across contexts: Lik Sam Chan assumed such when he embarked on his study of self-presentation via profile photos in China versus the United States, and concluded that the overarching stigma against homosexuality in China affected the culture on app (Jack'd).[3] Similarly, an interviewee observed the mercuriality of Grindr cultures when he traveled across Europe, as he concluded that the stereotype of Scandinavian "coldness" could be felt in its Grindr culture (versus in other European settings).

In the context of the so-called European refugee crisis—a period with continuous political and media attention to refugees from primarily Muslim-majority countries and their potential issues with cultural integration—some nationalist anxieties sublimated into aggressive Grindr messages. As the opening sentence of this book asserted, this context is necessary for understanding Abdul's shock (and also, lack of shock) when a fellow Grindr user accused him of having ties to ISIS; after all, news coverage and fictional programming focused on the possibility of terrorists infiltrating Europe under the guise of asylum seekers. Perhaps in 2005, an Arab immigrant in Denmark would have been confronted with (messages about)

---

[3] Lik Sam Chan, "How Sociocultural Context Matters in Self-Presentation: A Comparison of U.S. and Chinese Profiles on Jack'd, a Mobile Dating App for Men Who Have Sex with Men," *International Journal of Communication* 10 (2016): 6040–6059.

"Mohammad cartoons."[4] Other public anxieties about immigrants—fictitious marriages, public health concerns—also get projected into Grindr cultures.

Dominant conceptions about race and belonging—namely that people of color cannot *really* be European—affect online communications, prompting some European users of color to react defensively: "No, you can't ask where I'm 'originally' from."

But one discursive trope that does *not* tend to translate to the Grindr culture of the greater Copenhagen area is the idea that the queer migrant is someone in need of "saving." Stepan from Russia, who chatted with Grindr users about being an asylum seeker, was the only interviewee who mentioned receiving sympathy for the difficulties he surmounted coming to Scandinavia. Perhaps this related to public knowledge about Russia's so-called "anti-propaganda" law, a major area of protest during Copenhagen Pride 2013. By and large, however, nationalist rhetoric hinders communication between immigrants and some locals on socio-sexual platforms.

Technologies also Shape Socio-Sexual Cultures

Although socio-sexual cultures, especially on geo-locative platforms, are context-specific, there are also aspects of a socio-sexual culture that are shaped by the technology itself. There is nothing universal about Grindr cultures: GBTQs in local contexts across the world will differ tremendously in the ways they present themselves visually and textually with regard to clothing style, gender presentation, sexual kinks, and so forth. But a technology—such as its interface—can guide users to behave in a certain way.

The process of race reporting has a long history on socio-sexual platforms aimed primarily at gay men; and scholars have long documented that racial drop-down menus affect the way they communicate understandings of racial identities and boundaries. Parvin (from Iran) "learned" to identify as Middle Eastern on Grindr, despite the fact that he never used that label in Iran, where he saw his ethnicity as distinct from those in neighboring countries. In the greater Copenhagen area, nearly half of Grindr users identify as "White," despite the fact that Scandinavians almost never identify with this label in other written documents (e.g. government censuses, university applications, etc.) or day-to-day conversations, where discussions

---

[4] Jytte Klausen, *The Cartoons That Shook the World* (New Haven, CT: Yale University Press, 2009).

of cultural difference generally replace references to racial difference. In China, Chan noted that ninety-nine percent of Jack'd users identified as "Asian," despite the fact that there are huge ethnic differences across the dozens of provinces, autonomous regions, and direct-controlled municipalities from which Chan collected his data.[5]

A technology's platform shapes some of its online social codes, patterns, and behaviors. Much of this is innocuous: the ability to get someone's attention on Grindr by sending them a "tap" shows how an app can create new codes for non-textual flirtation (similar to the "poke" on Facebook); and while individual users might feel that the "tap" is useful or irritating, the general population of Grindr users can immediately understand the meaning of the technological feature. Other technology and interface decisions are more consequential: Grindr's 2018 drop-down menus "gender identity" and "pronouns" changed the communicative culture about especially trans and non-binary Grindr users. Prior to 2018, few cisgender men identified as such on Grindr; but it has since become common for cisgender men to use this label, and to provide pronouns (i.e. he/him/his) that suggest their understanding of gender variation more generally within Grindr culture.

The interface's attention to "ethnicity" similarly affects awareness of diversity within Grindr cultures, but does not necessarily promote tolerance. Rife with cultural bias, the menu simplifies racial and ethnic diversity, and does little to challenge notions about strict racial boundaries. Further, the menu allows for race-selective cruising. Overall, a technological interface guides users to behave in certain ways, and thus shapes the culture of that platform.

Race Is Both Omnipresent and Tacit Within Socio-Sexual Communication

Socio-sexual communication is never disembodied. Users seek face-to-face encounters, whether that means meeting in person, or engaging in mediated sexual conversations (e.g. on Skype). Even when users decide *not* to meet, their initial conversation often involves the exchange of photos that give some indication of skin color or general ethnic background.

---

[5] Chan, 6046.

Not all social media requires that users create profiles that disclose their race: on Twitter, for example, a user is primarily defined by her Twitter handle and (text-heavy) posts. But as André Brock argues, even the online cultures of Twitter are saturated with race, whether via hashtags, trending topics, or hate speech. This is not the case on Grindr. Few use Grindr for text-only "cybersex" conversations, which were common practice in the (gay) chat rooms of the 1990s, and which allowed for "identity tourism" (e.g. pretending to have different phenotypic attributes). The 1990s notion of "cyberutopia"—when scholars and the public idealized online communication for privileging people's ideas over their (raced or sexed) bodies—has been challenged for over two decades by critical race scholars who insist on race's omnipresence in online spaces.

Chapter 1 examined how the categories "immigrant" and "racial minority" tend to collapse in debates about multiculturalism and difference in Europe. European studies of immigration must include "race" as an analytical tool, such as for comparing similarities in the experiences of various immigrant groups with diverse migration histories.[6]

This book has viewed race as both constructed and as having real consequences worth examining. On the one hand, the boundaries between racial groups are artificial, contingent, and amorphous; on the other hand, continued attention to racial demographics (which reify racial boundaries) can benefit racial minorities. Even if a researcher believes "race" to be an uncomfortable concept—steeped in histories of slavery, eugenics, or Nazism—the researcher must seriously consider race (and not just national, cultural, or religious difference) when examining the experiences of immigrants in Europe.

Tacit racial exclusion take many forms. Race-related communications are part of a user of color's daily experience on Grindr, but racial discourses are not always overt. Some interviewees felt that race was often an unspoken shadow in their online communications. As Christina reflected, when discussing racist insults, "It's all racist—[even] if they say I'm ugly or they don't like my clothes." Others believed that they were being ignored on Grindr because of their race, and even sought to create experimental profiles to test the hypothesis. For many, the absence of flirtatious messages suggests the presence of racial stereotypes.

---

[6]Elisabeth Eide and Kaarina Nikunen, "Introduction: Change of Climate," in *Media in Motion: Cultural Complexity and Migration in the Nordic Region*, ed. Elisabeth Eide et al. (Surrey, UK: Routledge, 2011), 14–15.

Whiteness, like all racial categories, is contingent on context. Richard Dyer emphasized how white people in white-majority societies can remain oblivious to their own racial position: to them, whiteness is an unmarked norm from which other races can be contrasted.[7] Yet whiteness is also contingent: a Middle Eastern person is "White" on the U.S. census, but is excluded from the label "White" on Grindr. Ali felt similarly—that he might be "White" in his country of origin, but not in (the Grindr culture of) Scandinavia, and thus he refused to utilize the "ethnicity" label. The absence of this user's "ethnicity" selection suggests the presence of racial logics—boundaries, hierarchies—within a Grindr culture.

Race is built into the interfaces of Grindr, Scruff, PlanetRomeo, Qruiser, and numerous other (L)GBTQ platforms. It is no surprise that sexual discussions become steeped with racial assumptions, explicitly or implicitly. The narratives explored throughout this book attest that racialization and othering are part of the quotidian experiences of people of color on socio-sexual platforms.

When Race and Sexuality Intersect, so Too Do Other Subject Positions

No general conclusions can be made about "Asian immigrants on Grindr" or "Middle Eastern immigrants on Grindr"—or indeed *Immigrants on Grindr*—without an intersectional focus on other factors, including socio-economic background, transgender identities (and gender variation more broadly), (dis)ability (and notions of the "healthy" body), age, and so forth. Both Pejman to Daniel found housing through contacts on Grindr, but their situations are not readily comparable: Pejman arrived with a green card—partly because he could support himself financially in his first six months—and had a comfortable cushion when settling into the greater Copenhagen area; nevertheless, it was kismet when a fellow Iranian Grindr user connected him with the housing and employment that allowed him to remain in Europe. Daniel, by contrast, received less than 7 euros per day in governmental support while awaiting his asylum decision, and paid half of this to a local Scandinavian to share his bed, and to avoid the racism and homophobia of the refugee camp. His socio-economic (and legal) position meant that he was vulnerable to exploitation, and this proved to be the

---

[7] Richard Dyer, *White* (New York: Routledge, 1997), 4.

case when his host made unwanted sexual advances and exiled Daniel for several nights.

As a transgender woman, Christina mentioned that she commonly experienced that users of Grindr and related platforms assumed she was a sex worker. Christina attributed Grindr users' stereotypes about her foremost to her race/migration status, but one cannot untie her negative experiences on Grindr from sexist and transphobic structures. Christina's experiences suggest that Grindr users hold a constellation of stereotypes about transgender women, Asian immigrants, and sexual-economic opportunism. Related, sexist prejudice also affects cisgender male users who are perceived to be feminine; these perceptions and definitions of femininity often intersect with racial prejudice, as David Eng theorized regarding the "racial castration" of Asian men in (homo)sexual cultures.[8]

Although none of my informants identified as differently abled, one can be sure that a user's (dis)ability also saturates experiences on a socio-sexual platform like Grindr: "It's not just racism flourishing on Grindr," a white Danish user wrote me one afternoon. "There is also audism and ableism." The Dane was "very open" about being deaf, even though it turned some people off, but he had deaf friends who avoided identifying as deaf in their profiles for fear of exclusion. Body-related prejudice also affects people, whether related to size (e.g. body fat) or sero-status. Scholarship on Grindr cultures must always strive for an intersectional analysis that acknowledges the power and privileges attributed to various subject positions.

IS A GRINDR PROFILE A TWEET? TOWARD A MORE INCLUSIVE GRINDR CULTURE

As an immigrant in Copenhagen, as a user of socio-sexual platforms, and as an LGBTQ spokesperson, I close this book by sharing some of my ideas for building a more inclusive Grindr culture. When I embarked upon this research—and it's hard to believe that the first proposal was submitted in 2012—I hypothesized that the online culture of Grindr and related platforms influenced many people's feelings of inclusion within a (so-called) LGBTQ community. Since then, I have only seen this hypothesis

---

[8] David Eng, *Racial Castration: Managing Masculinity in Asian America* (Durham: Duke University Press, 2001).

confirmed, no less in Scandinavia, where panelists at Copenhagen Pride,[9] journalists at major mainstream newspapers,[10] and fictional characters on popular television have attested to Grindr's significance in their coming-out narratives, sexual identities, understandings of queer culture (e.g. slang), and more generally, their feelings of belonging to an (L)GBTQ community. I also hypothesized that foreigners, such as myself, would be particularly attuned to how Copenhagen's Grindr culture compared and contrasted with offline cultures in Scandinavia. Many narratives in this book confirm that feelings of exclusion on Grindr—often the result of racialization and othering—translate to feelings of exclusion in offline cultures as well.

Ameliorating the problems of Grindr culture could cement more individuals' feelings of belonging to a greater LGBTQ community, which in turn could diversify that community lastingly. But there is no easy way to prevent problematic or exclusionary discourses about race. Discourses about race saturate online socio-sexual environments, partly because these environments mirror the socio-political contexts in which their users are based, and partly because some platforms' interfaces draw explicit attention to race.

Beginning with what the platform itself can do: Grindr and other socio-sexual platforms that have "ethnicity" menus could more seriously reflect on the terms used in the menu, and the ways the menu can be used. Grindr advertises itself as an international app, with users in almost every country in the world. Yet the "ethnicity" menu only includes nine options, options that reflect the racialized division of people in especially the United States historically. Interestingly, Grindr's "Gender" menu *also* contains nine options, options that are quite progressive with regard to normative assumptions about gender binary; furthermore, Grindr allows users to customize their gender (and pronouns) and thus Grindr users have infinite possibilities when choosing a gender label. Grindr could consider doing the same with "ethnicity."

---

[9] In addition to the 2017 "Grindr and sex culture" panel cited in Chapters 1 and 6, see for example, Copenhagen Pride 2018 panel, "Femme-Shaming: Gender and Masculinity" with Anders Larsen, Bjørn Dotzauer, Mikkel Radicke, Lai Christian Balsig, and Andrew Shield.

[10] Rasmus Helmann, "'Er du den sutteglade fyr, jeg søger?': Efter ti år er appen Grindr mere end bare et kødkatalog" [After Ten Years: Grindr Is More Than Just a Meat Catalog], *Politiken*, 7 January 2019, https://politiken.dk/kultur/art6937614/Efter-ti-%C3%A5r-er-appen-Grindr-mere-end-bare-et-k%C3%B8dkatalog.

Allowing users to customize their race or ethnic background could bring attention to the social constructions and cultural contingencies of race. Even if Grindr did not allow for customization of race labels, the interface could easily adapt to allow users to select all options that apply.

Grindr and related socio-sexual platforms could also remove their "ethnicity" menus altogether. Doing so would prevent race-selective filtering, and could overall decouple some users' linkages between sexual preferences and race. For the sake of argument, however, there are two reasons that removing the menu entirely might not be the best solution. First, some users of color defend the menu and race-selective filtering. One Grindr user conveyed to me that he was pleased with the attention he got—sometimes from men as far as Germany—from those who used the advanced search to find their "type," namely people with his particular racial identity. For this Grindr user, this affordance was an advantage on Grindr, as he could connect more easily with interested men who lived outside of the small (unfiltered) radius of his metropolitan area. Second, users' attention to race is not entirely the fault of the "ethnicity" menu, but also the result of user-generated content. The platform Boyfriend.dk does not ask users to identify by race or ethnicity, yet users create and propagate forums about racial-sexual preferences. Even in the absence of a race-related menu, users still circulate problematic discourses about racial difference.

Online trends like "Douchebags of Grindr" have served to change the culture of socio-sexual platforms in the past decade by empowering people to call out problematic discourses, and to think intersectionally about race, gender presentation, and bodies, among other areas. But there are ethical concerns with posting profiles with personally identifiable information to a general public, even if the activist-user feels doing so is politically justifiable. Similar to "doxing"—the practice of posting the name, address, or other personal information of a public personality—the act of screen-capturing and posting Grindr profiles risks inviting harassment or violence to the person being exposed. Many aspects of sexuality—including one's openness about one's sexual orientation, gender identity, specific sexual desires, or sero-status—can be intensely private, and the risk of exposing these details to an unwanted (and possibly hateful) audience might not outweigh the benefit of calling out the user for problematic speech. Further, Jesus Smith has posited that trends like "Douchebags of Grindr" might serve to push racism and discrimination "back stage," but not to remove it from socio-sexual cultures.[11]

Changing the culture of a socio-sexual platform requires changing the socio-political culture of the geography or context in which the platform is used. LGBTQ people of color continue to attest to the ways that race-related discourses in LGBTQ environments affect their feelings of belonging; in doing so, they do not frame themselves as "victims" in need of pity, but as expert witnesses. The labor of calling out racism in LGBTQ environments, or explaining when and why attention to race can be problematic, does not need to be the burden of people of color alone. Larger swaths of the LGBTQ community must address the ways that race and racism circulate offline and online.

I am optimistic that cultural change can occur via on-app activism. People of color already confront racist speech via one-on-one chats and their profile texts, just as others call out sexism, body shaming, and other problematic speech. In doing so, these participants have contributed to their region's Grindr culture by making inclusive discourses about race and other minoritized positions more visible.

Grindr and other dating and hook-up apps share much in common with mainstream social media, such as Twitter. A Tweet can be 280 characters; a Grindr profile can be 250. A tweet can be readily shared, liked, or direct-replied; a Grindr profile, however, cannot. That being said, a Grindr profile is still broadcast to a networked platform. Grindr users should expect that dozens, hundreds, even thousands of people will read their profile texts. Regardless of whether these readers engage with a profile's text, each text contributes to the overall culture of the platform. So why not use this platform as one might use Twitter, and say something political? An individual's socio-sexual networking profile can be deeply personal; but as second-wave feminists rallied, and as the history of race-based and LGBTQ activism has confirmed, the personal is damn well political.

---

[11] Jesus G. Smith, "Two-Faced Racism in Gay Online Sex: Preference in the Frontstage or Racism in the Backstage?" in *Sex in the Digital Age*, ed. Paul Nixon and Isabel Düsterhöft (New York: Routledge, 2018), 134–145.

BIBLIOGRAPHY

Brennan, Joseph. "Cruising for Cash: Prostitution on Grindr." *Discourse, Context & Media* 17 (2017): 1–8.

Chan, Lik Sam. "How Sociocultural Context Matters in Self-Presentation: A Comparison of U.S. and Chinese Profiles on Jack'd, a Mobile Dating App for Men Who Have Sex with Men." *International Journal of Communication* 10 (2016): 6040–6059.

Dyer, Richard. *White.* New York: Routledge, 1997.

Eide, Elisabeth, and Kaarina Nikunen. "Introduction: Change of Climate." In *Media in Motion: Cultural Complexity and Migration in the Nordic Region,* edited by Elisabeth Eide and Kaarina Nikunen, 1–18. Surrey, UK: Routledge, 2011.

Eng, David. *Racial Castration: Managing Masculinity in Asian America.* Durham: Duke University Press, 2001.

"Femme-Shaming: Gender and Masculinity." Panel at Copenhagen Pride with Anders Larsen, Bjørn Dotzauer, Mikkel Radicke, Lai Christian Balsig, and Andrew Shield, 15 August 2018.

Helmann, Rasmus. "'Er du den sutteglade fyr, jeg søger?': Efter ti år er appen Grindr mere end bare et kødkatalog" [After Ten Years, Grindr Is More Than Just a Meat Catalog]. *Politiken,* 7 January 2019. https://politiken.dk/kultur/art6937614/Efter-ti-%C3%A5r-er-appen-Grindr-mere-end-bare-et-k%C3%B8dkatalog.

Humes, Karen R., Nicholas A. Jones, and Roberto R. Ramirez. "Overview of Race and Hispanic Origin: 2010." U.S. Census Bureau: 2010 Census Briefs, March 2011. https://www.census.gov/2010census/data/.

Klausen, Jytte. *The Cartoons That Shook the World.* New Haven, CT: Yale University Press, 2009.

Mowlabocus, Sharif. *Gaydar Culture: Gay Men, Technology and Embodiment.* Burlington, VT: Ashgate, 2010.

Smith, Jesus G. "Two-Faced Racism in Gay Online Sex: Preference in the Frontstage or Racism in the Backstage?" In *Sex in the Digital Age,* edited by Paul Nixon and Isabel Düsterhöft, 134–145. New York: Routledge, 2018.

INDEX

pre-exposure prophylaxis (PrEP), 158
Privacy, 41, 54, 84–86, 103, 105

Q
Qruiser, 15, 204, 205, 235
quantitative methods, 104
queer, 3, 7, 12, 14, 19, 21, 27, 39, 44,
    48, 49, 51, 56, 58, 61, 62, 91, 96,
    99, 111–113, 115, 125, 138, 143,
    145, 147, 174, 177, 179, 195,
    196, 211, 228, 232, 237

R
race (meanings of), 47, 100, 209
race filtering, 190–192
racial-sexual preferences, 9, 86,
    143–146, 148, 158, 162, 163,
    165, 166, 168, 179, 181, 185,
    221, 238
refugee camps, 129, 136, 235
Rita (TV series), 30
roommates, 15, 129, 132, 133, 136

S
"South Asian" identity, 201–203, 216,
    217, 219, 221
"situationally gay", 12
"socio-sexual", 8, 14, 15, 222, 229
Sabaah, 4–7, 145, 167, 178, 216, 217,
    222
Sami (from Israel), 11, 130
scams, 139
semi-structured interviews, 7, 13, 94,
    101, 102
Şenol (from Turkey), 129, 138, 175,
    230
sex tourism, 85, 116
sex work (transactional sex), 118, 121,
    122, 230
    sugardating, 121, 122

sexual racism, 6, 36, 56, 102, 143–148,
    152, 156, 158, 161, 162, 164,
    166, 168, 173, 175, 179, 208
Skam (TV series), 30
skeleton profile, 86, 88–90, 105
Smith, Jesus G., 6, 36, 144, 147, 148,
    156, 161, 162, 164, 179, 238,
    239
social desirability bias, 162–164, 177
social voyeurism, 48, 53, 229
    lurking, 48, 79
Spanish Grindr, 116, 203
Stepan (from Russia), 11, 116, 135,
    137, 232
strategic essentialism, 199
Swedish Democrats, 3, 21

T
"tribe" menu, 189
"type" (as in, Find Your Type), 191,
    192, 221
terms of service, 84, 118
Tinder, 15, 27, 128, 129
tour guides, 15, 123, 125, 126, 176
tourism, 114
transgender, 7, 10, 14, 189, 235, 236
Twitter, 29, 57, 87, 89, 234, 239

U
U.S. Census, 199–204, 215, 235

V
virtual communities, 43, 44, 46, 53

W
"White" identity, 9, 12, 17, 34, 47, 50,
    51, 61, 115, 116, 135, 174, 178,
    185, 196, 200, 201, 203, 211,
    213, 217–219, 232, 236

CPSIA information can be obtained
at www.ICGtesting.com
Printed in the USA
LVHW081951111119
637000LV00012B/398/P